IMAGES
of America

HISTORIC WEST SALEM

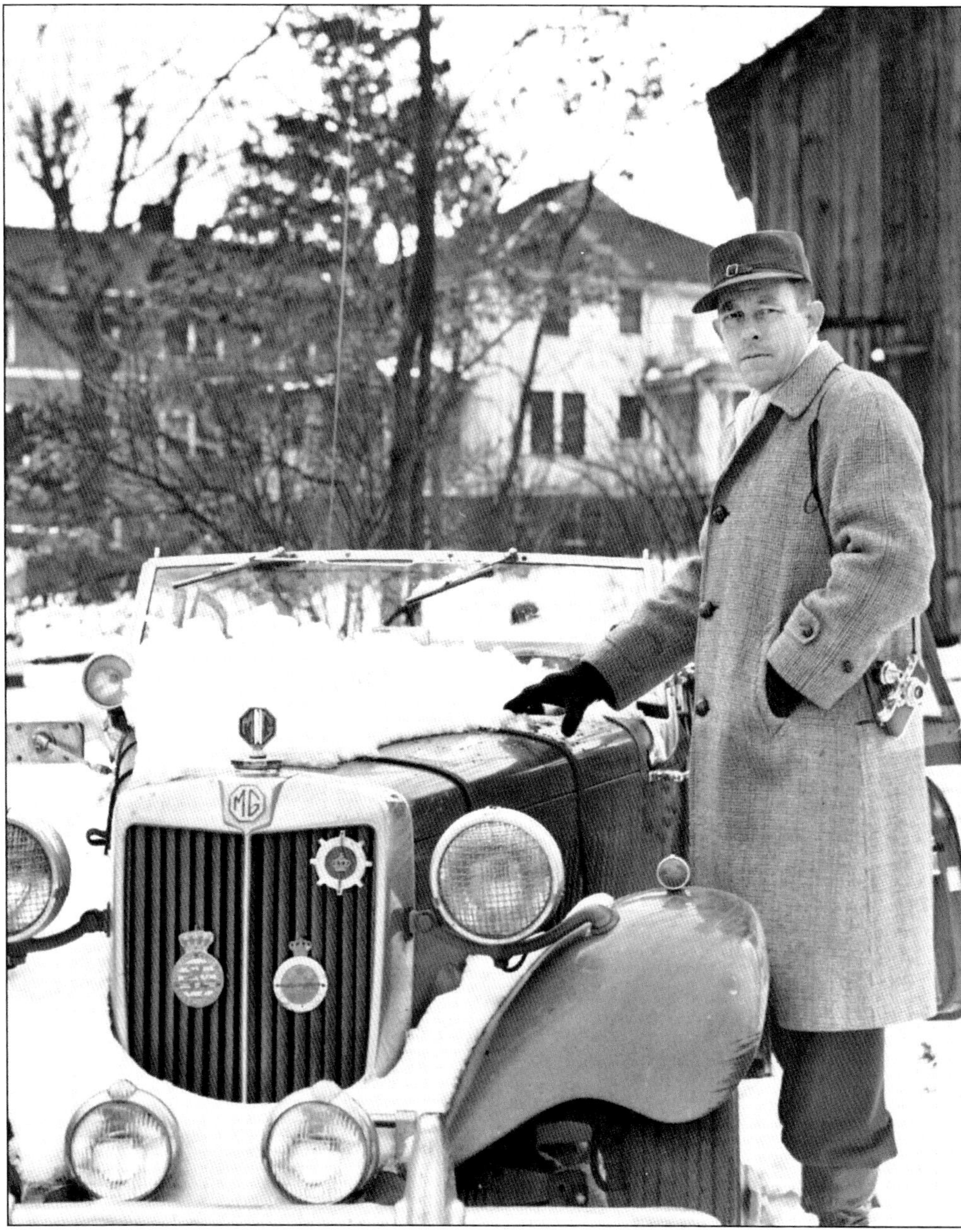

As in all beginnings of pictorial histories, the first picture shown will set the stage for the rest of the story. This story is no exception to that rule. Mr. Frank Jones, camera and prized vintage MG automobile by his side, gave this story's author a glimpse of life in early West Salem. The large, *c.* 1919 home, 119 South Broad Street, to the left of the white house was the author's home at a young age. Jones sparked the fire in a young boy's interest in local history. That spark gave rise to rediscovering a 200-plus-year-old historic neighborhood in the heart of Winston-Salem. Thank you, Mr. Jones.

ON THE COVER: Christ Moravian congregation on Academy Street was West Salem's first organized church. It was established in the late 19th century. This photograph was taken *c.* 1920s.

IMAGES
of America

HISTORIC WEST SALEM

Michael L. Bricker

ARCADIA
PUBLISHING

ISBN 978-0-7385-4322-2

Published by Arcadia Publishing
Charleston, South Carolina

Printed in the United States of America

Library of Congress Catalog Card Number: 2006926513

For all general information contact Arcadia Publishing at:
Telephone 843-853-2070
Fax 843-853-0044
E-mail sales@arcadiapublishing.com
For customer service and orders:
Toll-Free 1-888-313-2665

Visit us on the Internet at www.arcadiapublishing.com

To my wife, Tommie, my guiding light.

Contents

ACKNOWLEDGMENTS

West Salem's story covers 200-plus years of United States history. To acknowledge all that is involved is impossible. This book attempts to showcase photographs and details of those people. I thank you all!

The providers of those photographs and stories are presented below. Thanks to the neighborhood churches and their archivists: Ms. Sabrina Maksi, archivist, Christ Moravian Church on Academy Street; Mrs. Joann Hughes, archivist, Salem Baptist Church on Broad Street; Rev. Tim Wolf, pastor, Pentecostal Holiness Church on Hutton Street; and Rev. Kelly Carpenter, pastor, Green Street United Methodist Church on Green Street.

Individual West Salem families have contributed their photographs and histories. Thanks go to the Martin-Howell family, Mrs. Shelby Martin Howell, Sgt. Thomas Howell, the Ruff family, Mrs. Marilyn Ruff-Clemmons, Ms. Bobbie Ruff, Ms. Judith Ruff, the Chambers family, Mrs. Mildred Goff, and Mr. Thomas A. Holcomb.

A special thanks goes to Rev. William Cranford, retired pastor, Christ Moravian Church, who was the first historian of West Salem. His research of the Moravian Church and his pioneering family, the Pfaffs, gave a base for this publication.

Research was used from the Moravian archives from the Forsyth County Public Library and Mr. Frank Jones. This book owes much to these organizations and the West Salem Historical Society. The West Salem Historical Society has collected many photographs and histories, too many to list. The Library of Congress and Mr. Jim Jurney's genealogy research of the Brietz family contributed greatly.

A heartfelt thank-you goes to Mrs. Mary Young Bricker, the author's grandmother. Her inspiration of love for her family and friends along with the stories she conveyed nurtured a love of history in me. Also, to my wife Tommie, and daughters, Alexandria, Sophia, and Vivian, this wouldn't be a book without them. Their assistance has been priceless.

FOREWORD

The neighborhood of West Salem lies in the "New South." That's not only a geographic designation but also a historic one.

Historians agree that undergirding this New South was an industrial revolution in its Piedmont section. Too often, though, it is imagined as an overnight event.

In the 20 years leading up to 1900, visitors from outside the region sent back dazzling reports: huge brick cotton mills with majestic towers popping up like mushrooms, dotting the river banks, country hamlets, and country crossroads. They had no doubt that a war-ravaged Carolina countryside was in the midst of something very revolutionary.

But like most stories, this risen-from-the-ashes story is more complex and far more interesting. Michael Bricker's book about West Salem will allow you to peer through time back to its fascinating and honorable roots.

The birth of this proud neighborhood is intertwined with textiles, and this Southern industry proves to have its solid roots back to a time Michael's beloved West Salem was part of America's frontier. This story is about how ordinary working folk made extraordinary contributions to the Piedmont's cultural heritage—a way of life from which springs its economic ways, its architecture, its often-time political stubbornness, its food, and its music.

Whether they were Scots-Irish from Northern Ireland or Germans (Lutheran, Reformed, Moravian, and others), the bulk of Carolina backcountry settlers did not move inland from existing British Colonial settlements. Rather, by the time of the American Revolution, this section of North Carolina was being filled by sturdy pioneers who had entered the "New World" in Pennsylvania. Traveling southward along a narrow Native American path, now called "the Great Wagon Road," they settled the Carolina Piedmont. With little more than sheer character, ingenuity, hard work, and dreams, these ancestors of West Salem transformed a wilderness.

Every backcountry neighborhood had some outpost to connect it with the outside world, including tiny towns like Salem. God's bounty provided the basics of the settler's needs. The rest was done by the pioneers' own hands. By necessity and commandment, neighbors helped each other. To advance their settlement, most rural communities sought to create two other key items: a meeting house—for church and school—and a mill to grind its grain for bread.

Conjure, for a moment, the image of a farm field next to a flowing stream. For miles in most directions is forest, dotted by other small clearings and farmsteads. This was the landscape setting for a much earlier Southern industrial revolution. Picture rough-hewn or wood-boarded gristmills with their water wheels and grinding stones. These were the birthplaces for the South's textile industry—gristmill sites that evolved into rural industrial complexes.

North Carolina has several such textile industry "cradles"—Cross Creek (now Fayetteville), Lincoln County, and Alamance County. West Salem must also be counted among them. With the advent of the Salem Cotton Mill founded by the Fries family in 1836, the neighborhood that became West Salem grew to house its mill workers, later to include those who operated F&H Woolen, which eventually provided uniforms for Confederate soldiers.

Today people toss around the terms "community" and "neighborhood" lightly. But in the South's backcountry, "neighborhood" meant a set of intertwined homesteads engaged in a moral economy with face-to-face transactions. It survived because both individual as well as community needs and traditions were recognized. These clusters composed the backbone of early republican America.

As you take this book's pictorial walk through old West Salem, as you eye historic photographs of Wachovia, Marshall, Green, Apple, Albert, and Cotton Streets, please remember the people who later established the New South mills called Arista, Indera, and Maline.

I hate it when some historian refer to mill people as "unskilled textile operatives" because, in addition to textile skills dating back to Ulster and the Rhineland, these men and women were skilled in all manner of things. Passed to them by their pioneer ancestors was the practice of "making do" and its consequent technical ingenuity. Most men could fix about anything, and the women were experts at running what can only be imagined as a "home factory"—preserving and cooking food as well as sewing garments. I should also mention ancestral blueprints that got passed along for how to forge a real neighborhood, how to plant a church, and how to be parents who educated their children for life.

Many from this pool of experienced, skilled people would later operate the Hanes mills. Not only did they know how to card, spin, doff, draw-in, and weave—they knew how to make the most of life.

This book honors forebears of West Salem. On its pages, you will see mostly the structures they built—some that still stand and some that are long gone. As you turn the pages, remember those people. Use this as a beginning to learn of their wisdom, traditions, and values—items we will all need to face a future with so many unknowns and new frontiers.

—Lynn Rumley
Executive Director
Textile Heritage Center
Cooleemee, North Carolina

The Textile Heritage Center coordinates a growing movement to preserve the stories of the South's cotton mill people and the places where those stories unfolded. Working with groups such as the West Salem Historical Society, they are planning a Southern Textile Heritage Corridor from Montgomery, Alabama, to Richmond, Virginia. This corridor will showcase textile heritage in a 700-mile expanse across five states.

INTRODUCTION

West Salem began with the expansion of the town of Salem to the west in 1770. Unlike most of the older neighborhoods of Winston-Salem, West Salem's existence parallels the beginning of Salem. The development of the neighborhood is complex, beginning with 18th- and early-19th-century farmsteads on Salem outlots. In the architectural makeup of our housing stock lies the historical proof. The earliest resource in the district is a *c.* 1782 Stockburger farmhouse with current appearances reflecting significant *c.* 1900 alterations. The Stockburger home's alteration is reflected in other old homes in our district with similar early-1900s changes. This shows a true evolution feature only found in the oldest of neighborhoods and towns across America.

The second oldest resource is the *c.* 1843 Ackerman-Reich-Ruff house. After 1843, development was primarily on Poplar Street until the main wave of construction after the War Between the States, *c.* 1865, with the significant additions made to the *c.* 1854 Tesh-Butner-Bryant house. The popularity of the cotton mill concept arrived in Salem in 1837 with the founding of the Salem Cotton Mill. Our West Salem housing stock grew considerably with this mill and the others that followed. Beginning with the Salem Cotton Mill, important West Salem streets were begun to accommodate the many mill workers here. For example, Wachovia Street expanded from Marshall Street westward to the heart of West Salem land. The mill workers built along Wachovia, Green, Apple, Albert, and Cotton Streets throughout the mill time period of West Salem. West Salem is unique not only in Winston-Salem, but among many other North Carolina towns. The reason is in its older age (more than 200 years) and examples of its older housing stock. With the recent historical designation of our neighborhood by the National Register of Historic Places, West Salem became the second oldest neighborhood historic district in the original boundaries of Winston-Salem, second only to the Old Salem historic district, *c.* 1766. An overview of West Salem's historic district excerpted from the West Salem Historical Society's archives reads:

> "The West Salem Historic District *c.* 1782 had its earliest beginnings as the farms and industry of the Moravian church in the town of Salem. The Stockburger farm *c.* 1782; the Kreuser-Brietz farm *c.* 1819; the paper mill settlement *c.* 1790; Salem flour mill *c.* 1820 are some examples of these early farms and industrial outlots. The first textile mill arrived in West Salem in 1837. Many mills followed before the Civil War and after. The first residential housing block was the 600 block of Poplar Street, consisting of Ackerman-Reich-Ruff house *c.* 1843; Tesh-Butner-Bryant house *c.* 1854 as examples."

West Salem education from 1847 to the present produced five different periods of schools. Religion saw diversity in Moravian, Methodist, Quaker, Baptist, and Pentecostal services here. The 1880s–1920s saw residential expansion in every form of building architecture. The Granville Park division *c.* 1914 was our newest and last residential development. Even though West Salem is known today only as one neighborhood, its history reads like a much-older town. The following is a quote from the official National Register Historic Places Report as proof:

> "The predominance of the resources in West Salem represents the architecture of 18th and mid-19th century Salem with later Winston-Salem's 19th and early 20th century moderate income citizens.
>
> "A mix of industrial workers' housing and suburban bungalows marks West Salem as having an unusually diverse architectural collection, much like a small Southern town. The neighborhood has excellent church design and the continued presence of a large number of historic neighborhood store buildings makes West Salem especially noteworthy among Winston-Salem's historic neighborhoods."

The West Salem historic district, *c.* 1782, has approximately five percent of its housing stock before the Civil War period, while roughly 30 percent of its housing stock dates between 1880 and 1915. The West Salem neighborhood has more 19th-century structures than any other neighborhood in Forsyth County.

The number of 19th-century structures rivals the numbers of those in most smaller, older towns of North Carolina. Also 40 percent of our houses and businesses were constructed between 1915 and 1935. The remaining 25 percent of structures encompass the time period after 1935–1957. The West Salem Historic District will complete much of the puzzle of our city's historic past with the hopes of securing a place in American history for our West Salem ancestors and the history they produced. The pictorial journey presented in this publication will be the public's first glimpse into the other side of Salem—West Salem.

One

The Other Side of Salem Begins

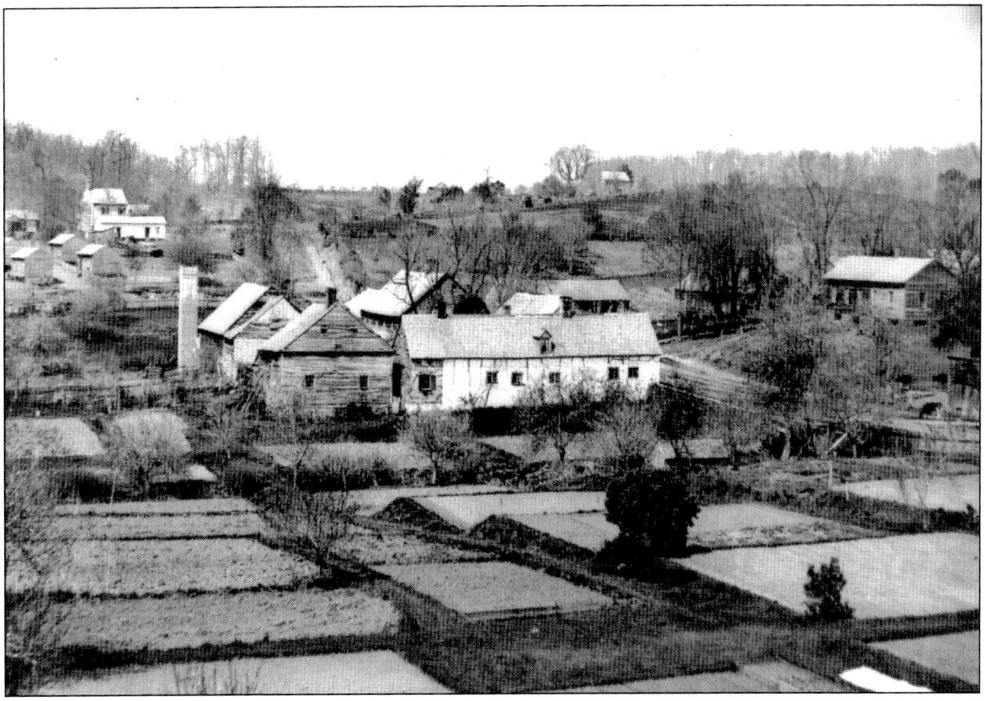

The first industrial area of Salem, established in 1770, along with the farm outlots gave rise to the townspeople's expressions: "West of Salem and our western neighborhood." The photograph from the late 1860s illustrates vividly the Civil War–period landscape. The buildings in the foreground are the Salem Slaughter House, Salem Brewery, and Tannery. The structure standing alone to the right of this complex is the earliest church and second school of West Salem, the Elm Street Chapel, *c.* 1867. The two-story brick house in the center and farthest west is the Kreuser-Brietz farmhouse, *c.* 1818. The building to the left of background is the two-story white Ackerman farmhouse, and left of that structure is the Tesh-Butner-Bryant house, *c.* 1854.

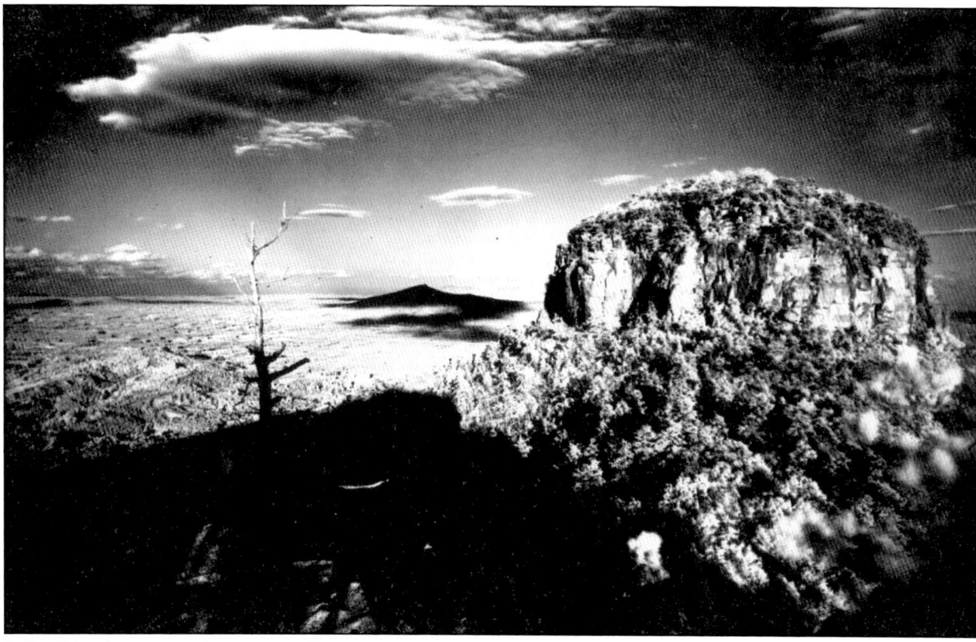

Pilot Knob is a prehistoric reference point and the first recorded citing by Native Americans of the early Piedmont, *c.* 8000 BC. Pilot Knob and the Sauratown Mountain Range were used as a point of reference in traveling and hunting. The first Moravians on their way to settle the Granville tract of the Piedmont had their first vision of North Carolina. The knob was visible while the Moravians were still within the Virginia border.

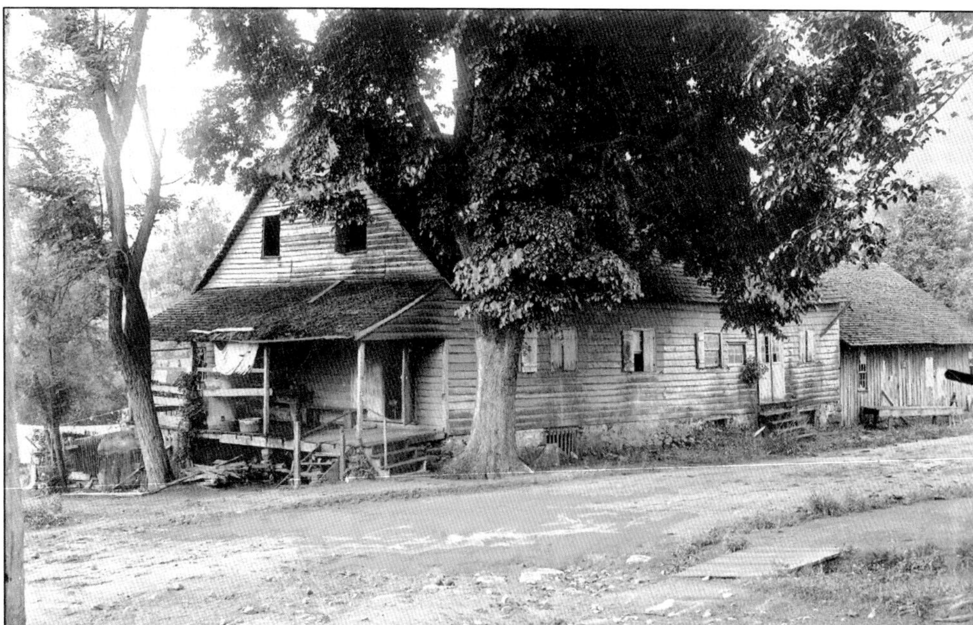

The Salem Brewery was an important addition to the first industrial area of Salem. The brewery, tannery, and slaughterhouse were very important business operations in early Salem. The industrial venture of these businesses was as important as the town's intricate water system. The water system captivated the attention of Pres. George Washington with his visit to Salem in 1791.

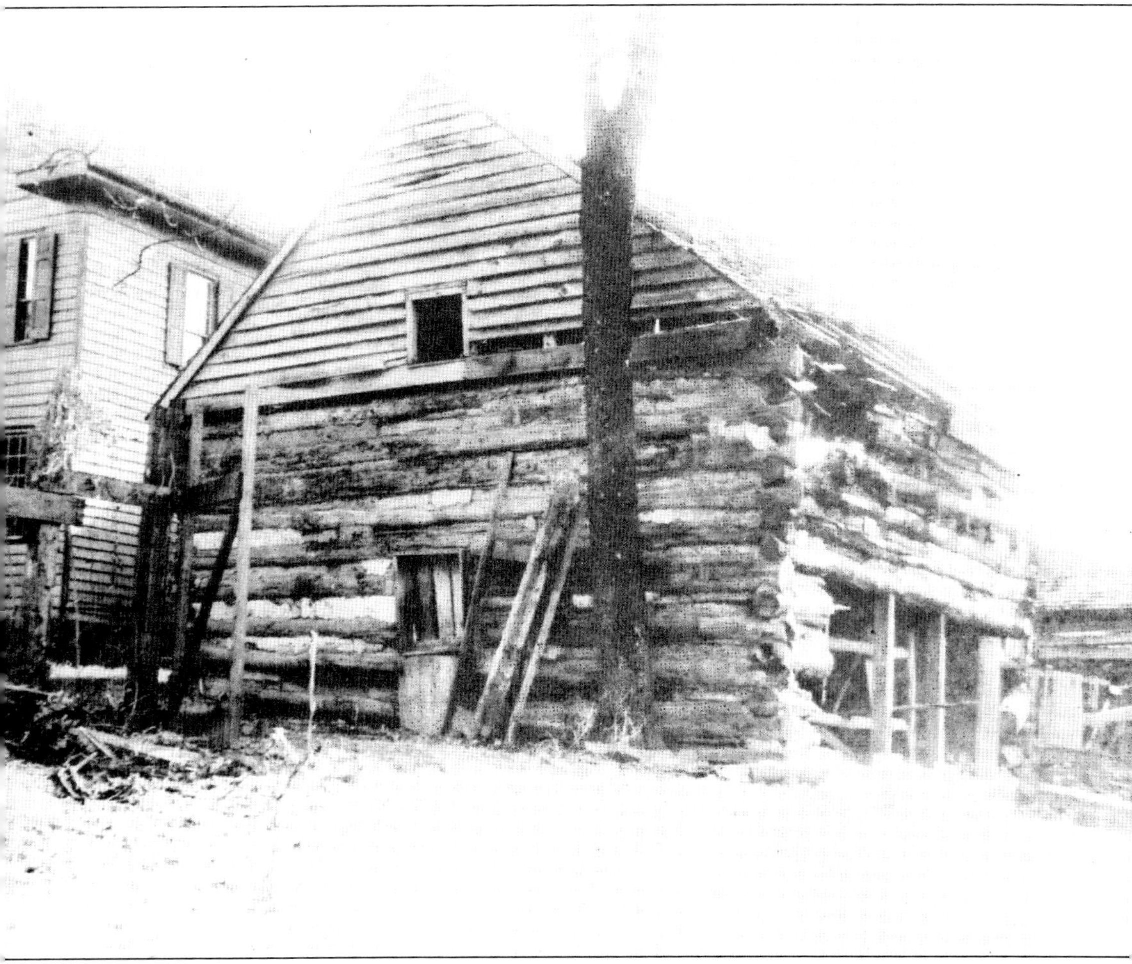

This is the first home constructed in Salem. The house was built for the workers who began the construction of Salem in 1766. This log structure was located near the present intersection of Liberty Street and Brookstown Avenue in what was then called West of Salem. The town of Salem owes its early existence to the blue-collar residents, who resided in this log structure. While building the first houses of Salem, the building served many functions over its long life. One important usage was as a pottery shop. The log structure stood for 140 years before falling down on its own accord in 1907.

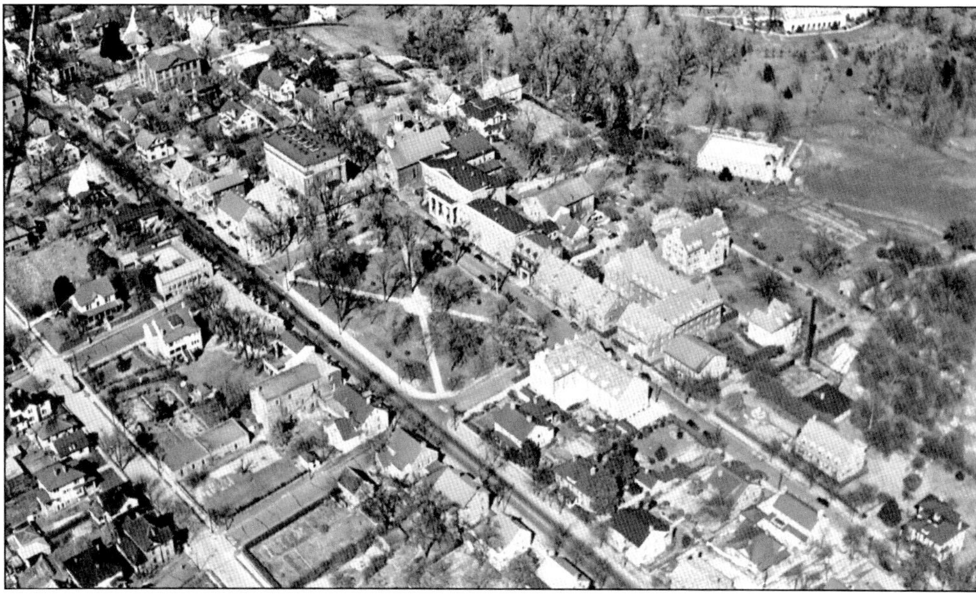

The central district of Salem is shown before 18th-century reconstruction for Old Salem. The Salem square in the center of the photograph gives a reference point for the large, white Salem College Library building to the right. This building was moved South on Church Street to make way for the reconstruction of Brother Gottlieb Schober's residence, which currently houses the Salem College Admissions. West Salem's first patriarch was Brother Schober, whose paper mill brought industrial growth farther into West Salem land. He was also Salem's first postmaster.

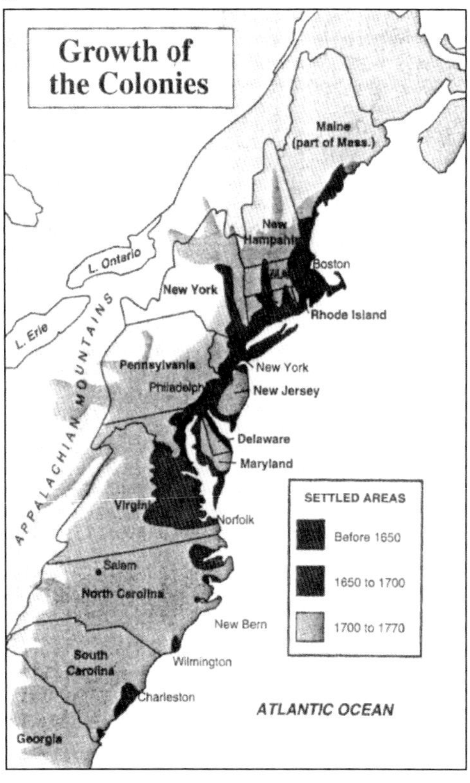

The map depicts the 13 original colonies before the American Revolution. This map shows the town of Salem as the farthest inland town of importance in the complete future United States of America. Salem's importance gave rise to many settlers in the early 19th century, who colonized the early United States to the Mississippi River. The settlers' last stop for supplies and a last glimpse of civilization was the Salem town limits. Upon exiting the town to continue their journey, they passed through the second industrial area, known as the paper mill settlement, c. 1791. The paper mill settlement was located in the area of Peters Creek, Academy Street, and Bank Street in today's West Salem landscape.

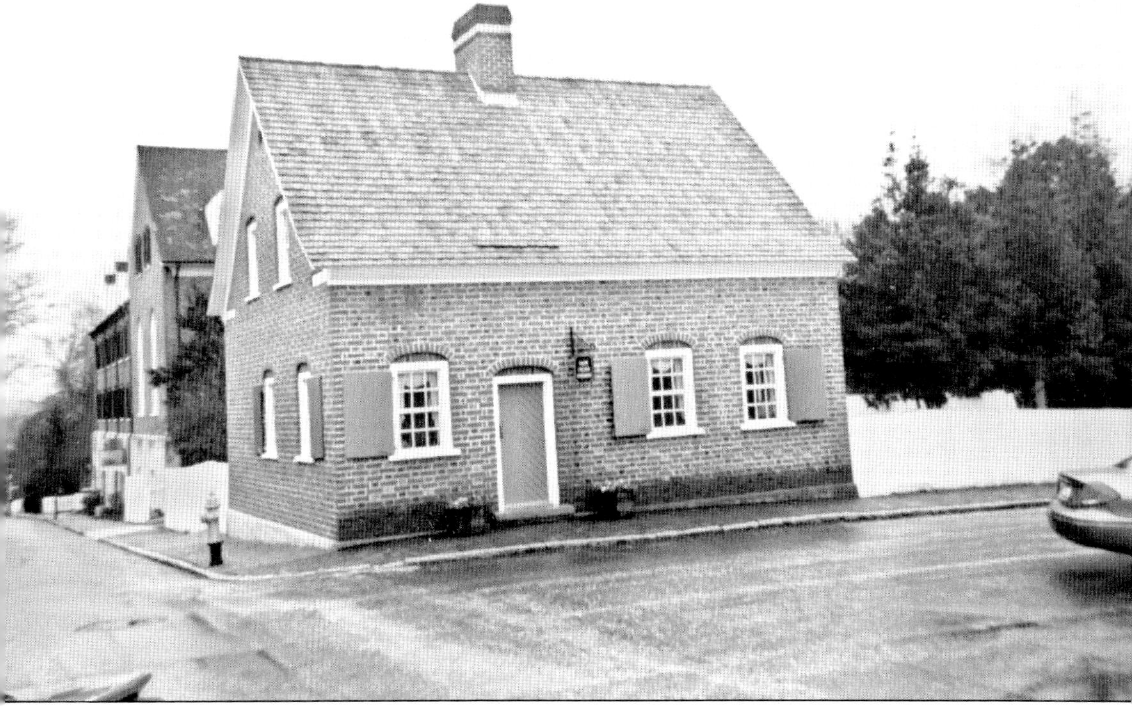

Brother Gottlieb Schober was the first patriarch of West Salem. His life reads like a who's who in his accomplishments. In 1782, Brother Schober worked as an apprentice in the Traugott Bagge mercantile store. The store, reconstructed by Old Salem Inc., resides at the corner of Main Street and West Street presently. The Aufseher Collegian controlled the business interest of the congregational town. They constantly called Brother Schober on the carpet to reprimand his mercantile business, since he was chosen as a tinsmith and britches maker. Brother Schober found his true calling in 1790 with his construction of the first Salem paper mill, west of Salem. The mill began production in the spring of 1791 and was the first modern paper mill in the South. Schober's progressive nature constantly tested the Moravians' patience. He championed early schools for all citizens and believed in equality for all children of God. The second industrial area of Salem, c. 1790, is illustrated in the 1870s Vogler map, located in the Old Salem Archives. This thriving part of West Salem was a town within the town of Salem and included a paper mill, paper mill pond, sawmill, and granite quarry. Settlers on their way to colonize much of the western United States during the 18th and 19th centuries gathered and replenished their supplies before continuing their journey westward.

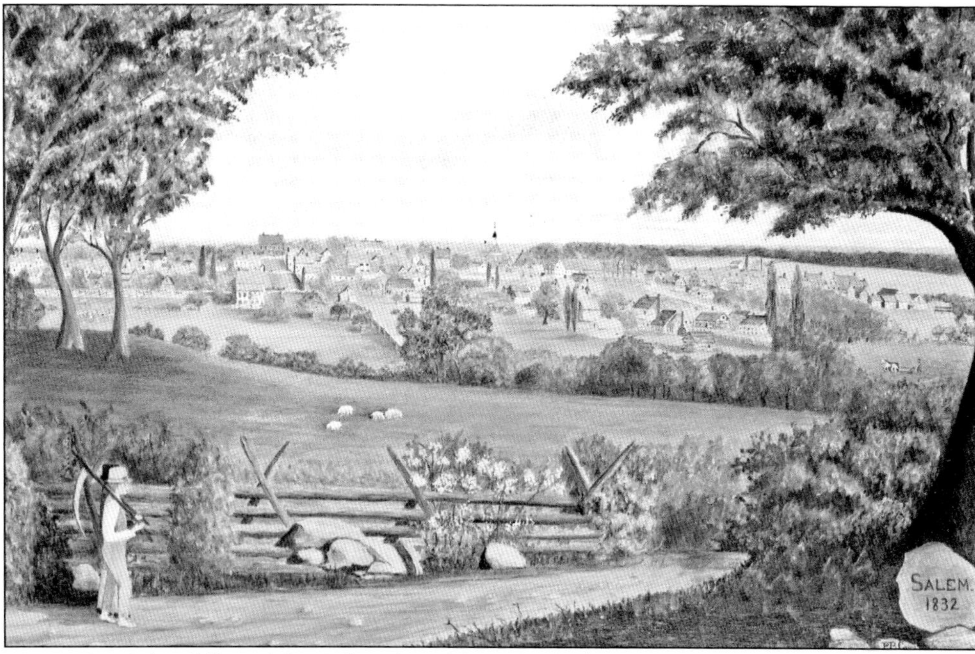

The road to Salem followed the Colonial road from the shallow crossing of the Yadkin River through the town of Bethabara and ending in Salem. The young gentleman in the foreground strolls on the Old Shallowford Road of West Salem directly in front of the Brietz farm, with the congregational town on the horizon. The Old Shallowford Road was the main road into Salem.

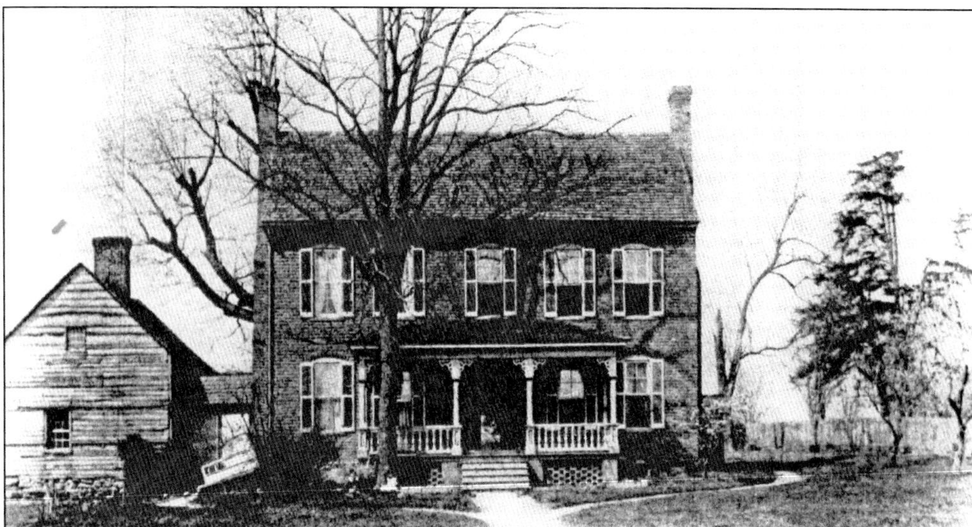

Over 200 years ago, the new United States of America had a population of less than four million people. More than 90 out of 100 of these people lived and worked on farms. Salem outlots and farms were the lifeblood of the congregational town. The Kreuser-Brietz farm provided many essential food products. Mr. Kreuser had planned the 30-plus acres of farmland to be his retirement homestead from the Salem store, a store located in the heart of the congregational town. The photograph above, *c.* 1890s, shows the Brietz's homestead. The homestead encompassed the 400 block of Broad Street in today's landscape.

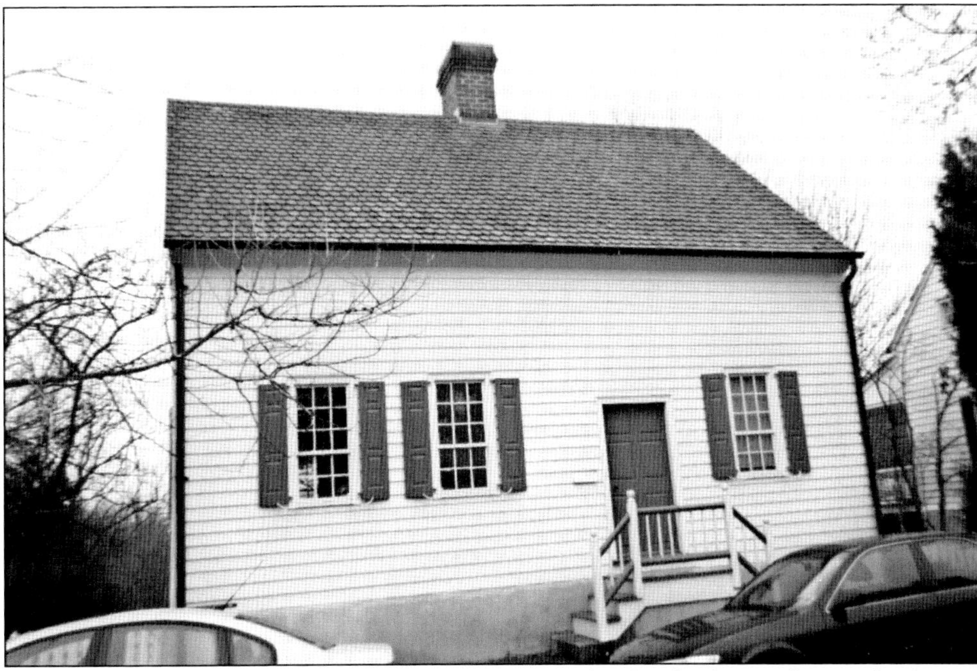

Kreuser handled his farm for nine years. The Levering family of Salem took over the farm in 1825, exchanging their house on Main Street for Kreuser's farm and outlot. The Levering house is still in existence after being rebuilt by Old Salem Inc. on Main Street.

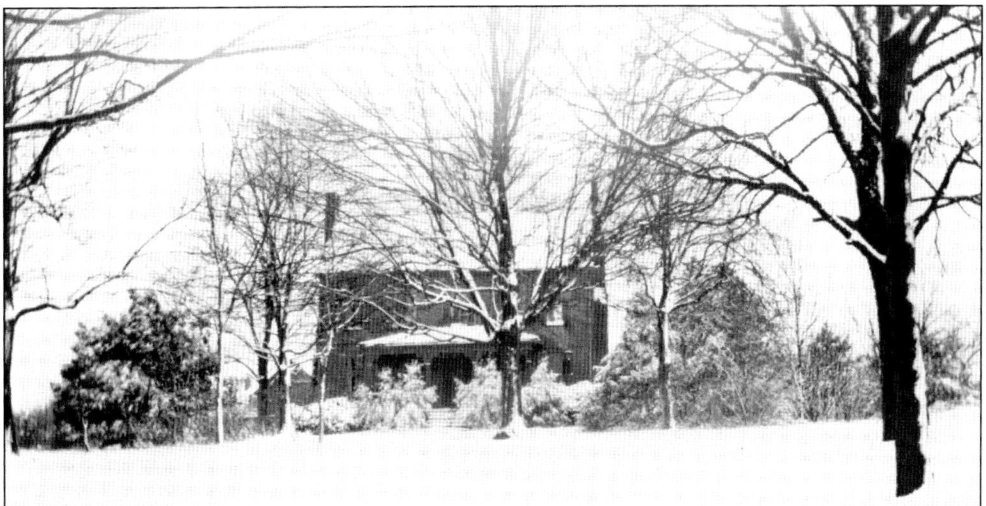

In the mid- to late 19th century, Levin Brietz began a large commercial hog trade on his farm. He sold his wares throughout the town and beyond. His farm success was due to an ingenious industrial invention involving a refrigeration process. In the 18th and 19th centuries, the winter climate of the area was much colder than it is today. The story goes that Brietz ventured down to Peters Creek at the paper mill pond. There he cut the newly frozen ice from the pond by hand. He hauled the ice by wagon up Paper Mill Road, Bank Street today, to his farm. He had a pit dug close to his barn and filled the pit with ice and straw. Then his wares were stored safely in the ice. The process kept the product until the summer. Brietz was by all accounts one of the state's first commercial meat packers.

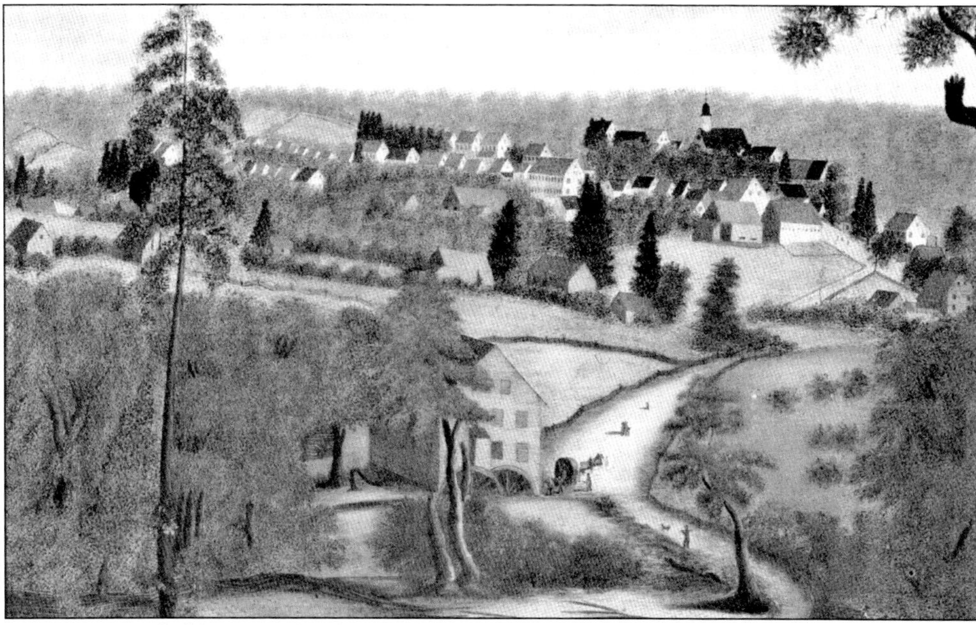

A meeting was held in 1819 that began the discussion of constructing a large flour mill for Salem. The Salem Flour Mill became the mill that changed Salem. When the Salem Mill was constructed in 1820, it was the showplace of the town. Its difference from previous mills was in its construction as a merchant mill. A merchant mill bought the grain and manufactured flour for public sale. It took in a great deal of money, and the construction was built to last the test of time.

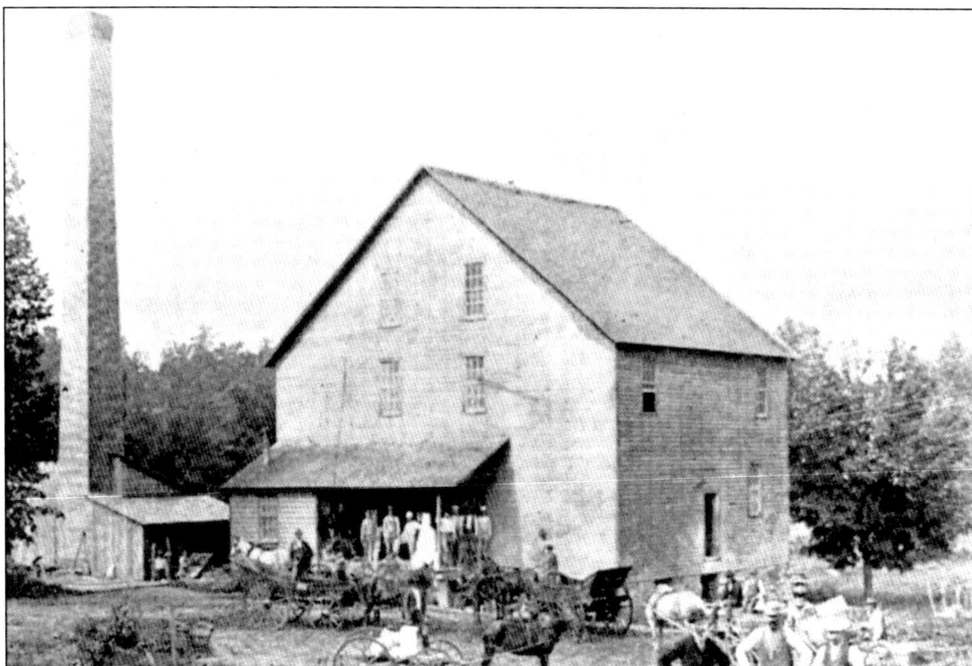

The mill company prospered during the 1830s and 1840s. With the death of Jacob Blum in 1847, the mill company dissolved. In November 1847, Jacob's son, Nathaniel, and Jacob's son-in-law, Renatus Levin Brietz, consolidated ownership. Brietz was associated with the Brietz farm.

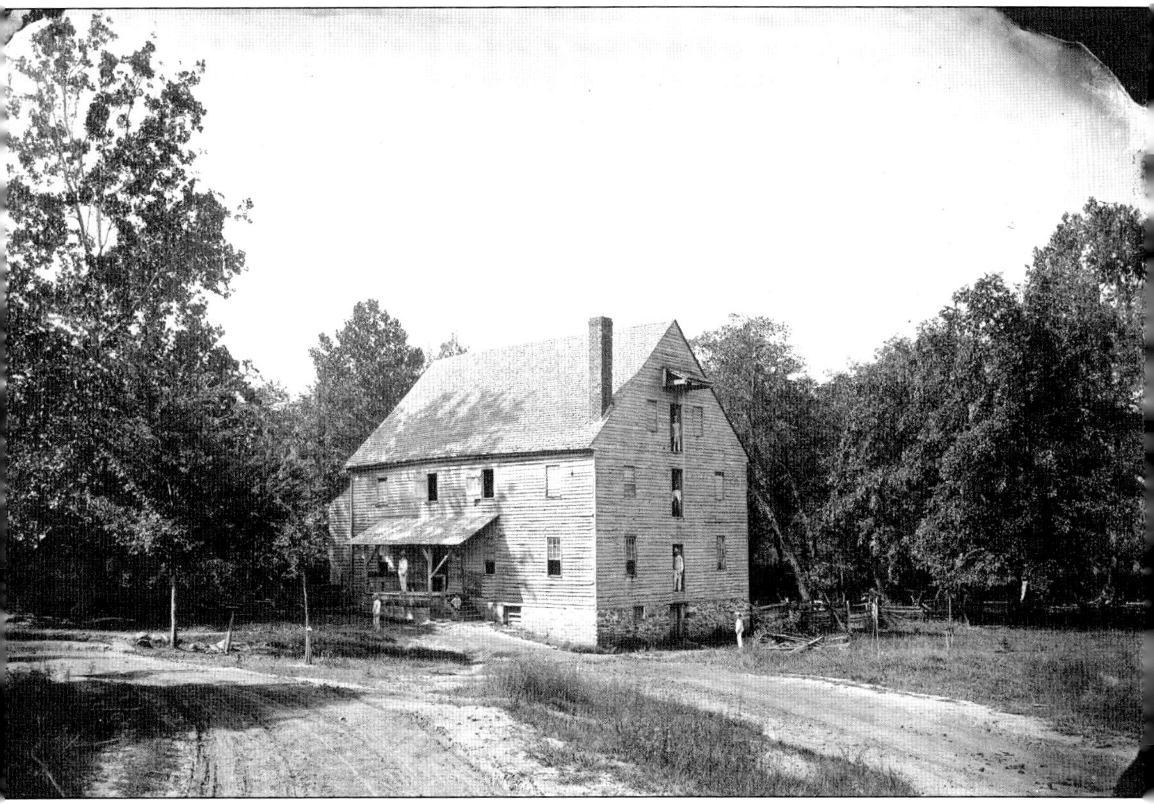

By 1850, the Salem Mill was the largest gristmill in Forsyth County. The mill was not altered during the tenure of Blum and Brietz, and as in many industrial interests of Salem, this mill managed to survive the Civil War intact. Around 1871, Brietz decided to leave his interest and rented it to Lee Hendricks. With the death of Nathaniel Blum in 1875, the ownership entered a partnership with Hendricks and Blum's son-in-law, William J. Cooper. The deed showed that the tract contained a mill, a mill house, a race, and meadowlands for a total of 32 acres. The mill survived into the 20th century. It burned in 1902, and its land was developed. To the right of the building, a road was cut and extended over Salem Creek beyond the trees. The intersection today is Broad Street and Salem Avenue.

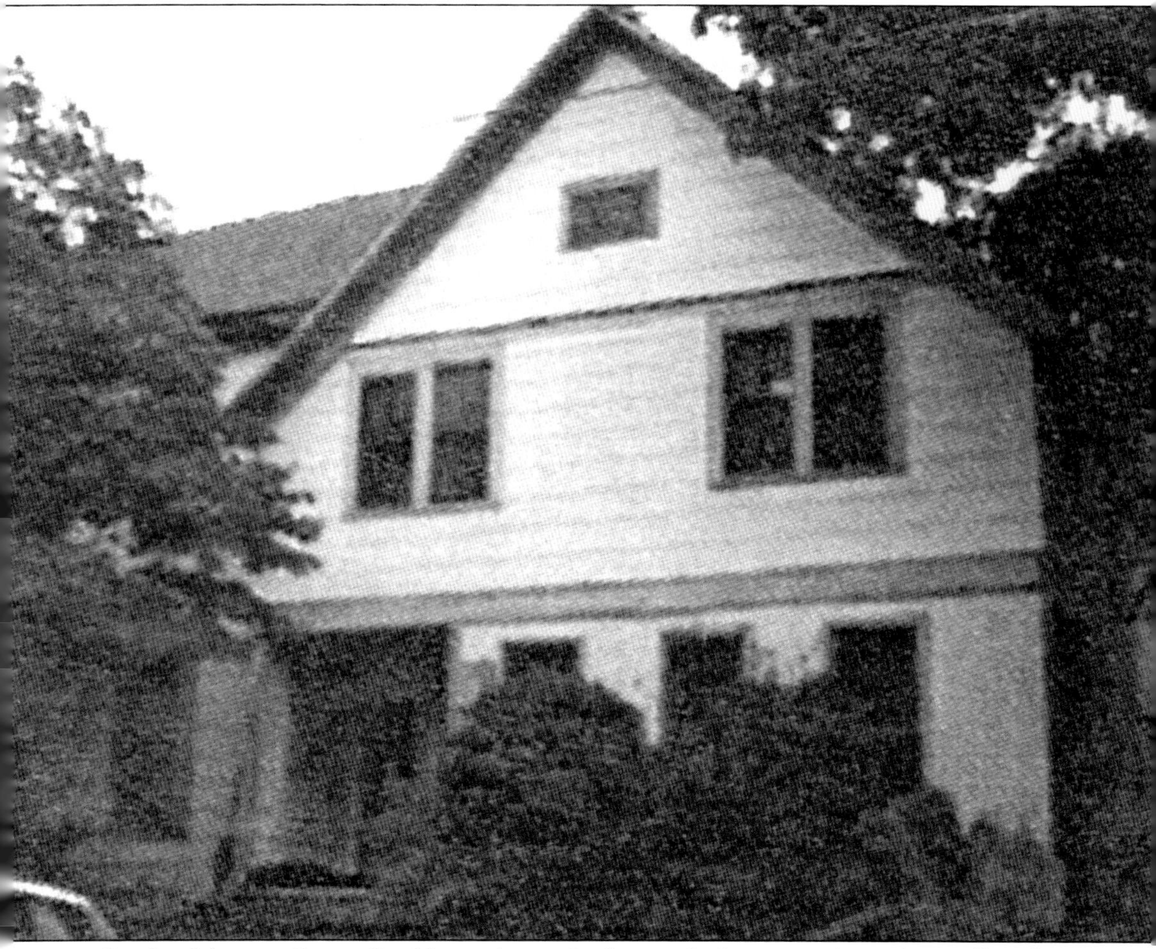

Brother Johannes George Stockburger began the farm with the intent of providing milk and meat for the congregational town. The farmhouse was built in 1782, when the evolutionary use of its land began. The 68-acre farm was intended to provide these essentials; however, Stockburger departed in 1789 and the succession of other farmers only encountered failure. By 1819, the land was leased to the Salem Flour Mill. The Stockburger farmhouse and its story is a perfect example of the evolution of West Salem's landscape. The Stockburger farmhouse solidified the West Salem Historic District. The Salem Flour Mill, c. 1820, and the use of the Stockburger house as its mill house continued throughout the 19th century. The Stockburger house enters the 21st century as West Salem's oldest structure to date.

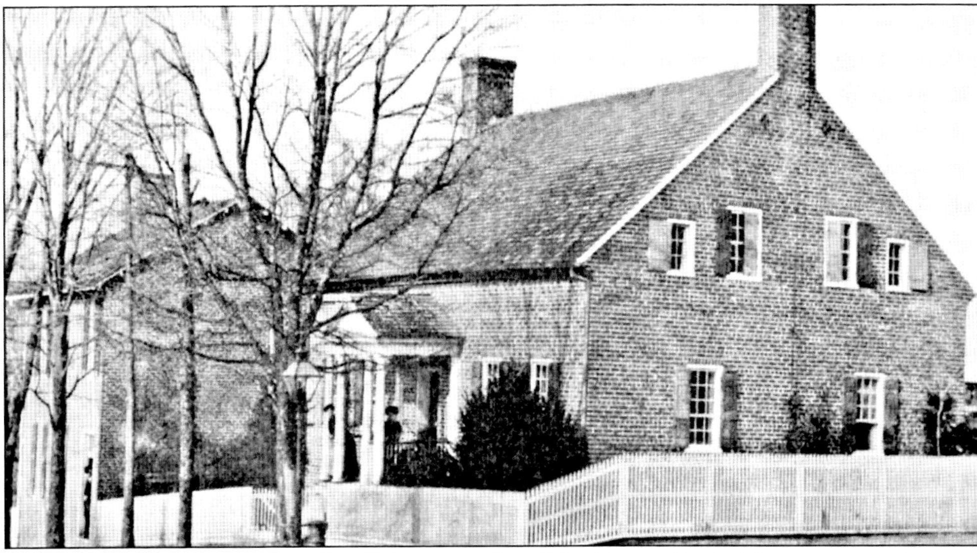

The first venture for a textile mill in Salem arrived in 1836. Originally the Moravians were hesitant to allow such an establishment. The Moravians believed their way of life would be compromised with such a business. Unfortunately, the town's crafts and trade operations were not doing well financially, and the 15–20 percent profit that other textile mills experienced was enticing. The Moravian hierarchy agreed to the venture but only after strict control by Moravian elders over the mills' operation. The Fries homestead on New Shallowford Road (Brookstown Avenue) is shown.

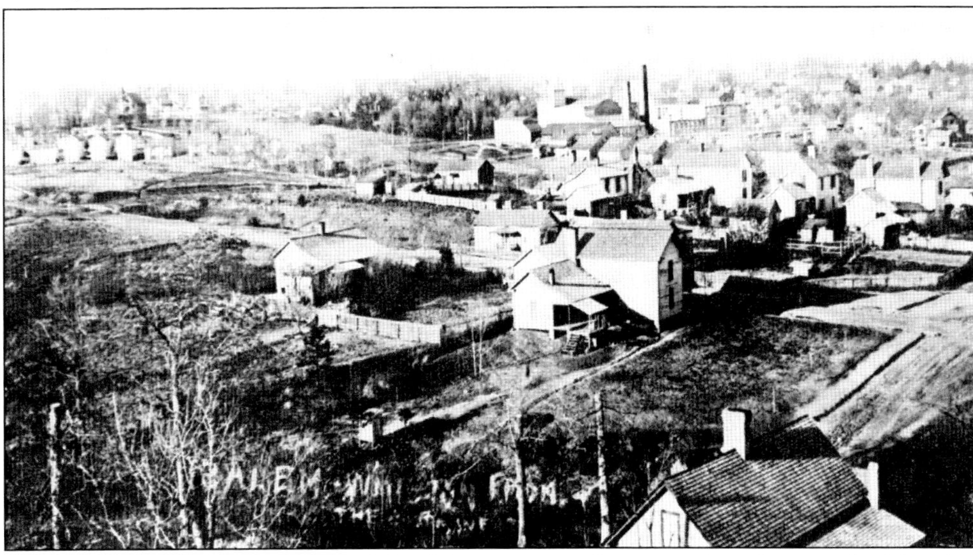

Life in Salem's first textile mill, the Salem Manufacturing Company, brought a new livelihood to West Salem. Of historical significance, the first steam-powered wool carting business in North Carolina had arrived. Located in the top portion of this photograph is the 1880 mill complex on Brookstown Avenue below Cherry Street. Historians have pointed out in the past that West Salem was never a mill town. However, when one draws together West Salem's long history, a mill time was present. Also the growth of the West Salem neighborhood is apparent in the many houses present here. The two houses at the bottom of the photograph are 516 Spring Street and 518 Spring Street, both c. 1880. The 516 Spring Street home is the Cooke house and 518 Spring Street is the Mosley house, both still standing today.

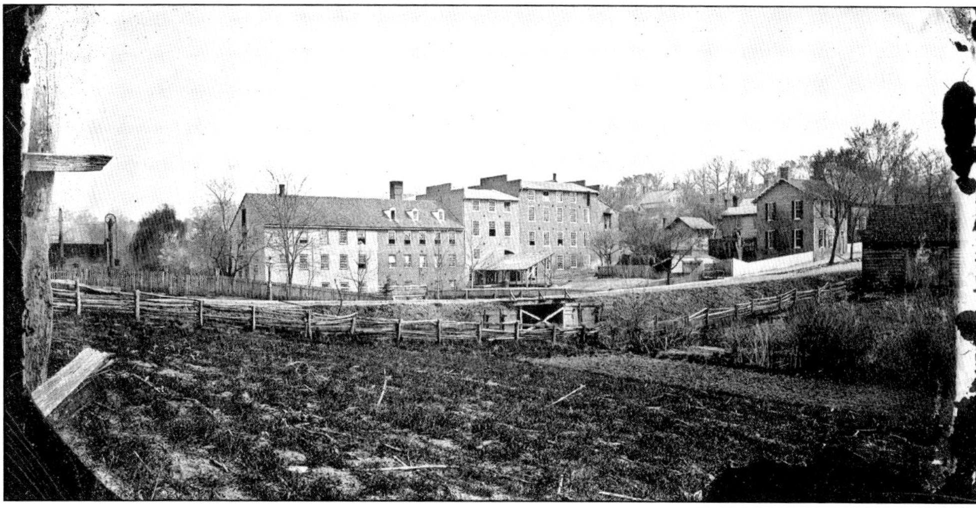

The Salem Textile Mill brought to Salem a large problem: more outsiders. The industrial revolution had arrived in Salem. In the 1830s, farms in the Piedmont of North Carolina were devastated by drought, depression, and failing crops. Many people from Stokes, Guilford, and Davidson Counties came to the mill looking for steady pay and steady work. The Fries Woolen Mill was begun by Francis Fries. The textile mill that he built in 1840 survived well into the 20th century and was a forerunner of the factories, which made the city a manufacturing giant. He was previously an agent for the Salem Manufacturing Factory of the first textile mill in 1836. His mill education took him to New England to study machinery and its functions. As an indication of how times have changed, during the early 20th century, one of the mills' most prominent customers was China.

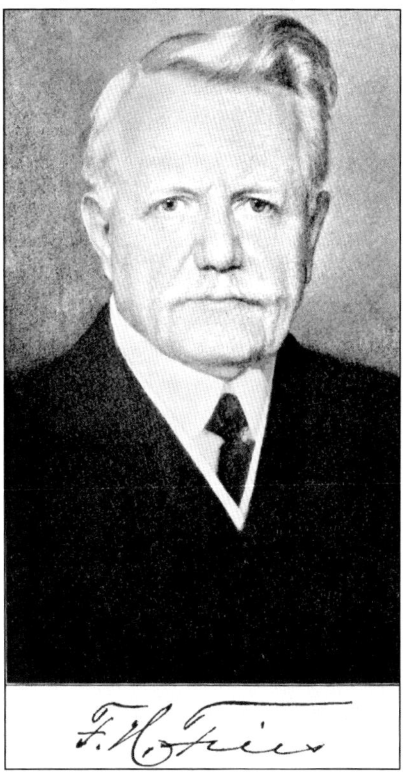

The Fries family contributed heavily to the mills of Salem and the surrounding area. Francis, his brother, Henry, and a few workers literally built the factory with their own hands brick by brick. The mill supplied the wool for the Confederate soldiers' uniforms and survived Reconstruction after the Civil War. By 1870, the Fries family operation was manufacturing products valued at over $70,000 annually. The next 10 years witnessed even greater profits, and in 1880, cotton goods totaled $23,000 and woolens an all-time high of $150,000.

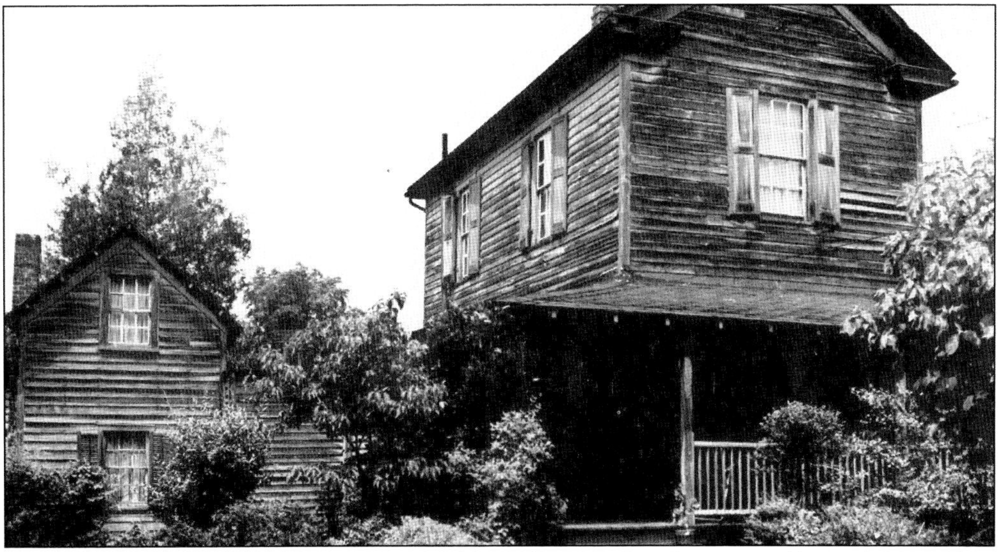

The Samuel Edward Butner house, *c.* 1854, is shown above. Butner, foreman and later superintendent and general manager of the Francis and Henry Fries Mills, bought a lot on Poplar Street in 1865 and shortly thereafter constructed a two-room house on its site. The house was one of the earliest residences in what is now known as West Salem's first neighborhood. The Butner house was originally built by Samuel Tesch. Phillip Edward and his wife, Dora Emma Bryant, purchased this property in 1920. The house has joined the Ruff family, with current owners Jack Clemmons and his wife, Marilyn Ruff-Clemmons, residing.

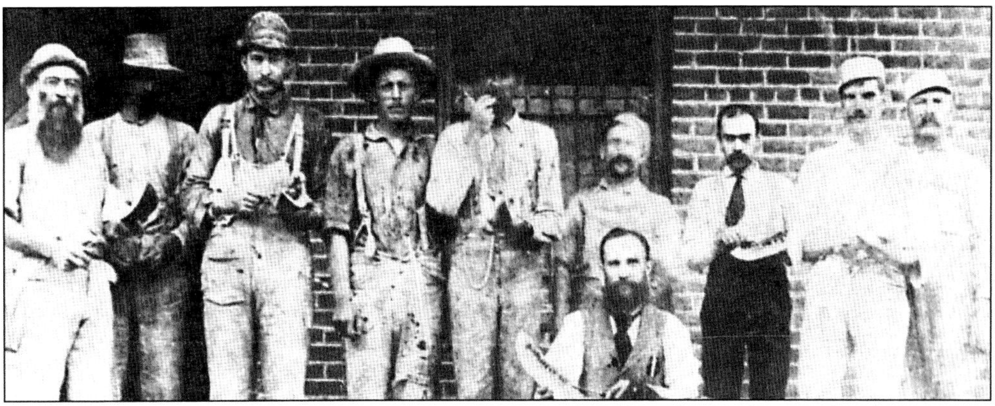

The employees of Francis and Henry Fries Flour and Grist Mill are shown during a break from work indulging in a watermelon feast, *c.* 1880. Many small mill houses were located on the east side of Elm Street (Factory Row). In 1905, the Southbound Railway train line changed the landscape, and many structures were razed. Shown from left to right are (first row) overseer Frank Hege, 607 Mulberry Street; (second row) mill hand Daniel Barton, who lived at Elm Street (Factory Row) and Bank Street (house razed); mill hand Lee Hanes, 603 West Street (historic house); mill hand William H. Turner, who lived on South Spruce Street near First Street (today the house is located in the Holly Avenue Historic District); mill hand John Spainhour, who lived on Elm Street near Bank Street (house razed); mill hand, fireman, and carpenter Andy Peddicord, 618 Mulberry Street; driver Jim Spach lived on Elm Street near Bank Street (razed) and would join his family's company, Spach Wagon Company, in Waughton and move there; bookkeeper William Boyd, 211 West Street (razed); miller Curd Disher, 715 Broad Street (home rebuilt); and miller Samuel Shore, 521 S. Poplar Street, later bought Salem Flour Mill around 1890.

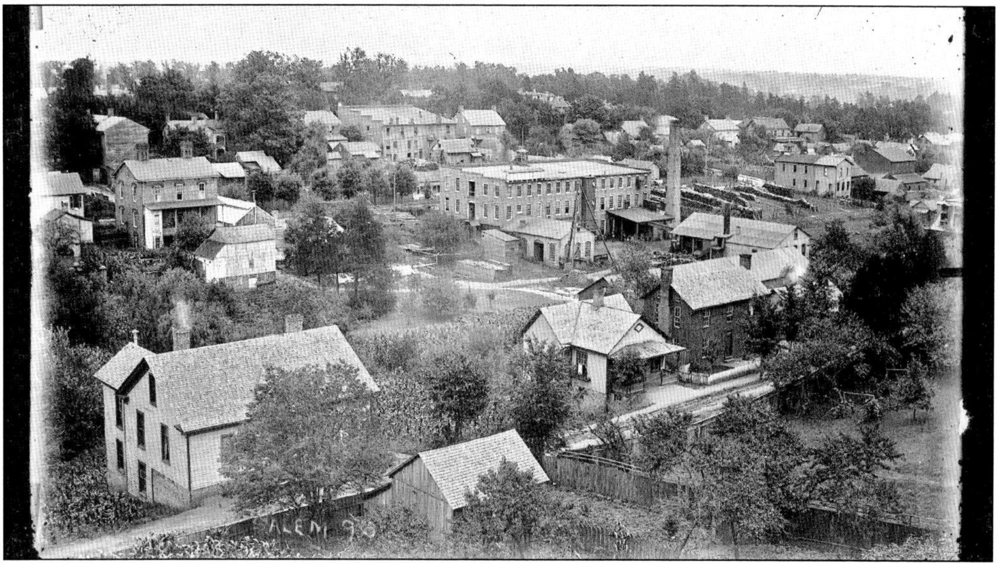

After the Civil War, the industrial revolution saw industry abound in the West Salem neighborhood. The Salem Iron Works, *c.* 1873, is depicted in this photograph from 1893, which shows the area between Liberty Street and Marshall Street. The expanding iron works in the middle of the photograph was responsible for producing woodworking machinery and other mechanical devices. The long, low building behind the two-story frame house at right is the Hosiery Manufactory of A. G. Hough. The double-chimney, three-story house to the left is that of the iron works' owner, Christian A. Hege. The Salem Iron Works building still exists as the oldest part of the present Downtown Middle School.

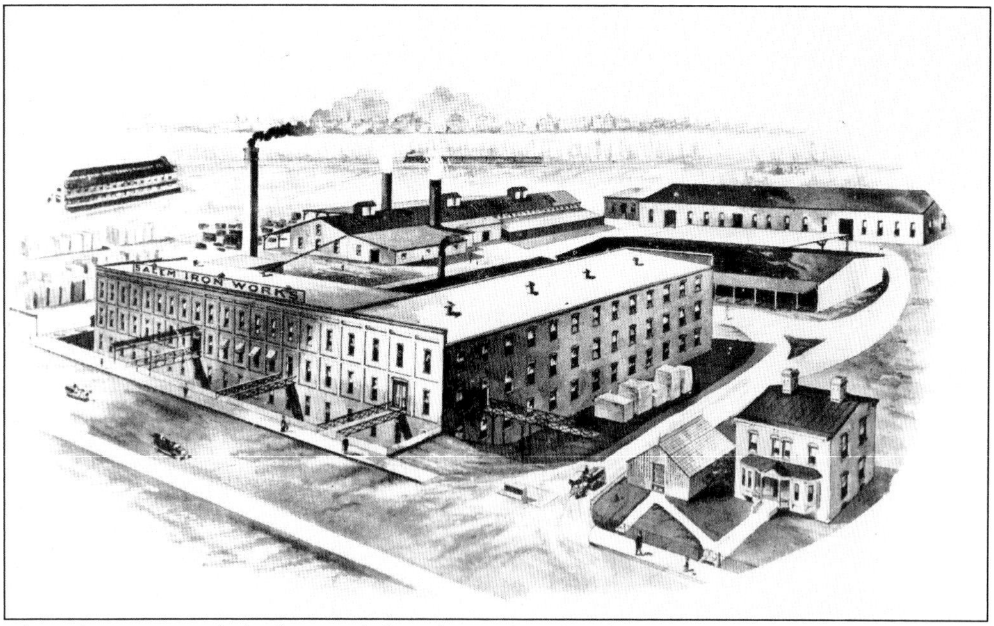

The Salem Iron Works had expanded, as depicted in this drawing. The business of the Salem Iron Works was incorporated with W. T. Spaugh as president, treasurer, and general manager, who kept the plant up to the minute in its equipment. Each and every machine was inspected to the minutest detail before being shipped.

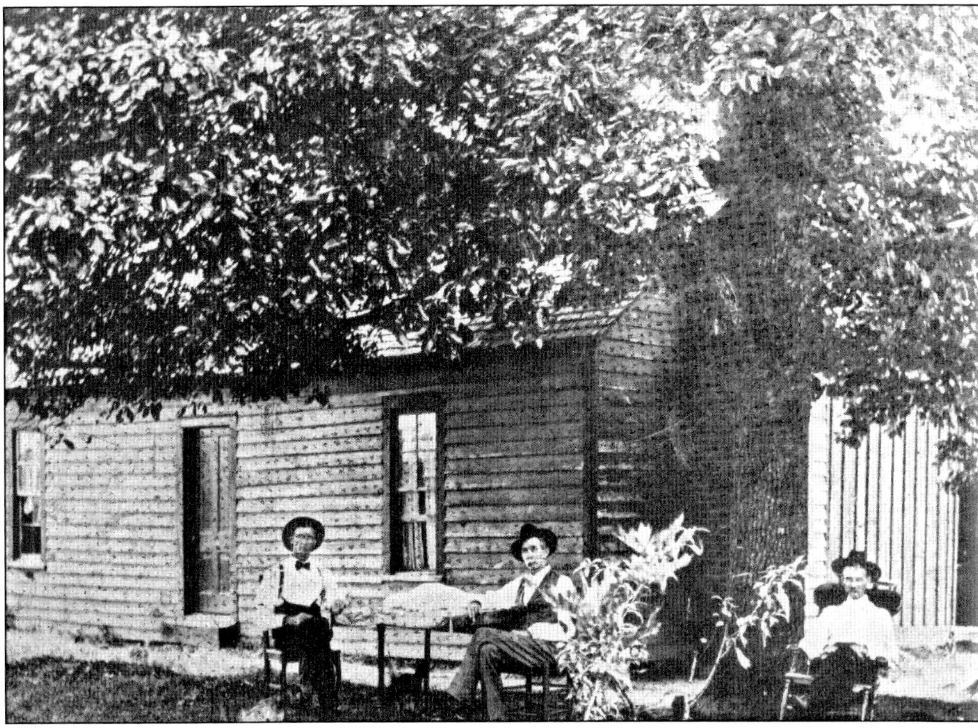

The land to the west, which included the western rise of Petersbach, Peters Creek, was overseen by Brother Gottlieb Schober, patriarch of West Salem. He and his heirs—including his daughter, Sophia, and son-in-law, Brother Van Zeverly, tested the strict rules of the early Moravian Church in Salem. The land they owned was sold to the Fansler family. The Fansler family took ownership of the property after the Civil War, acquiring it from the Van Zeverly heirs in the 1870s. Reynolds High School auditorium was built on the land of the Fanslers' apple orchards, and Society Hill was born. The Fansler family is shown above with Brother Gottlieb Schober to the right, copied from an 18th-century painting.

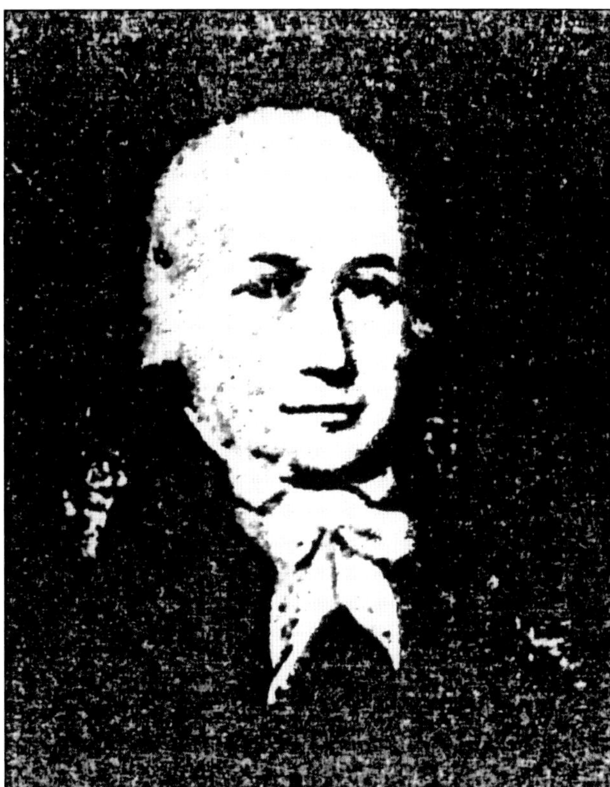

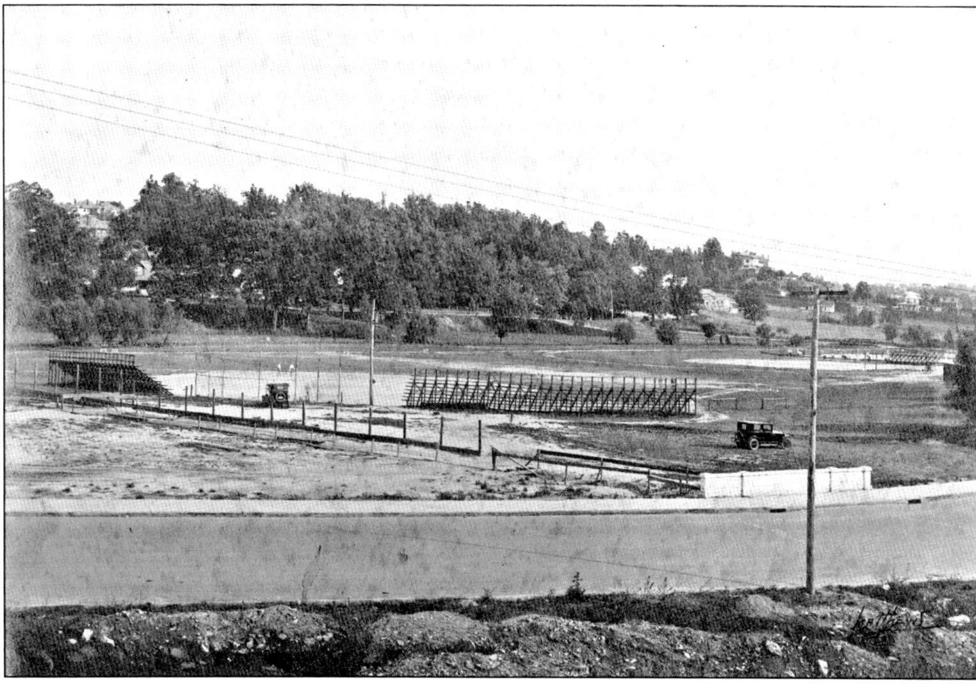

This park became the school grounds for Reynolds High School. Hanes Park is shown in its early stages of development. The former land of the Schobers and Van Zeverlys is developed for education and recreation.

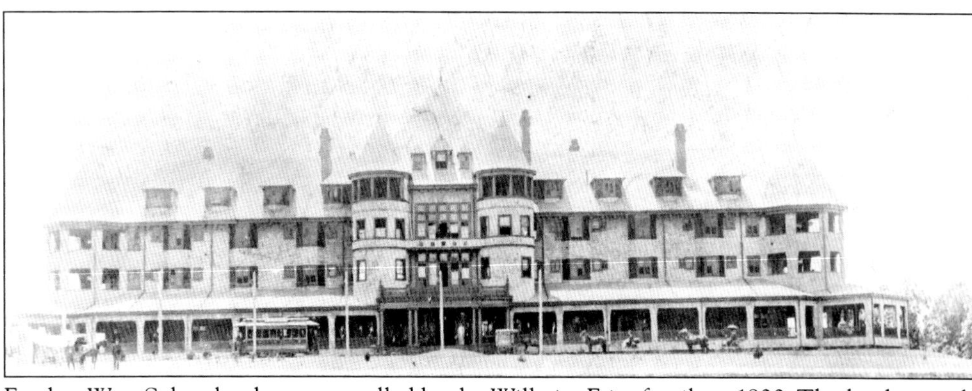

Further West Salem land was controlled by the Wilheim Fries family *c.* 1800. The land was sold after the Civil War as an extension of the town of Winston. The photograph shows the Zinzendorf Resort Hotel in the area of the original Fries plantation. The resort hotel burned not long after its construction in the 1890s. With the abandonment of the resort theme for the land, the West End neighborhood was born. Other neighborhoods were cut and developed from original West of Salem land, examples being Ardmore, Southside, and Washington Park.

Two

THE BUILDERS

Religion and Education

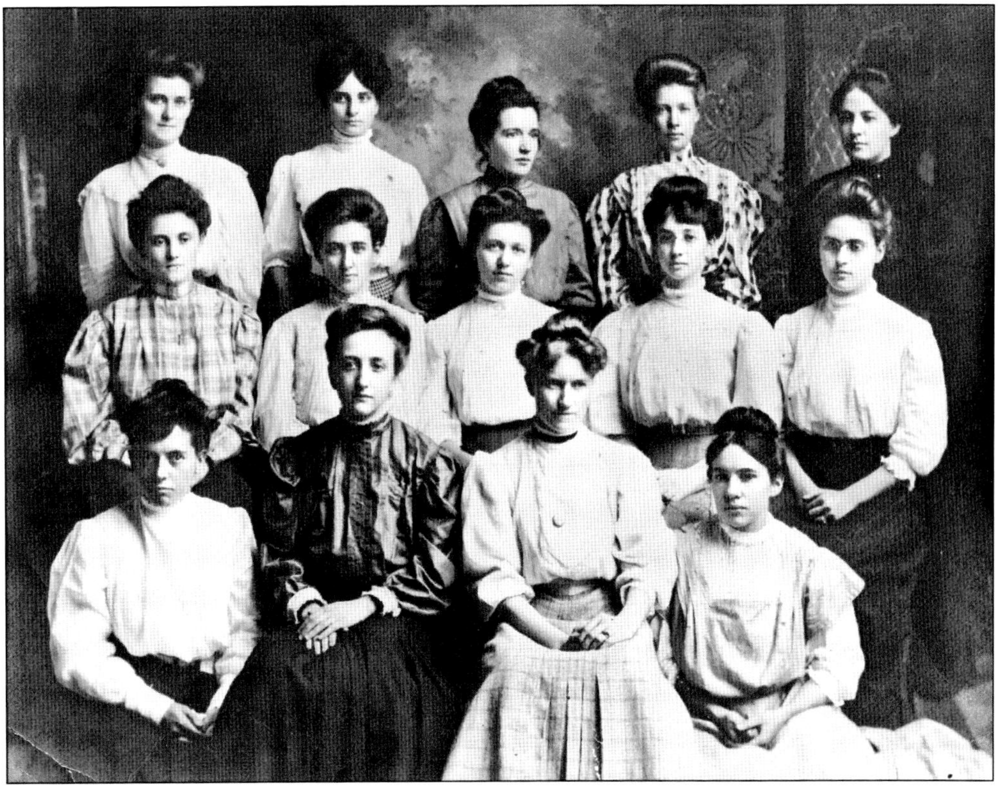

The ladies who were the force behind their husbands in creating the neighborhood, which included Christ Moravian Chapel and Church, are shown. The West Salem neighborhood had extended westward from Poplar Street and the area around the West Salem Graded School, *c.* 1890, on Mulberry Street. Green Street and Academy Street were pioneered by these women and their husbands by convincing the governing body of Home Moravian Church that an outlot church congregation could be formed in West Salem. Home Church elders agreed to this proposition only as an experimental chapel. Research has shown the elders never believed the chapel, much less an organized full church, could be successful. These ladies assisted in proving them wrong.

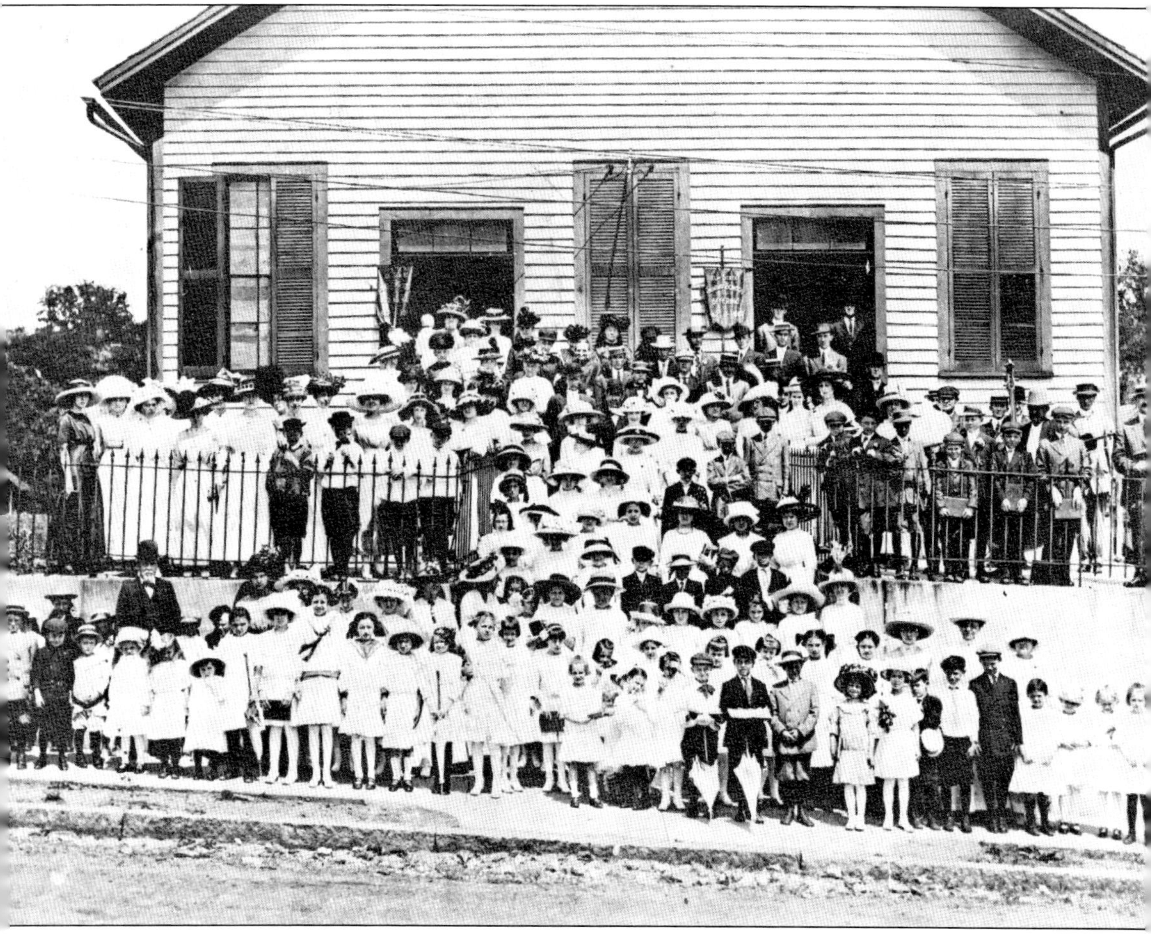

The Elm Street Chapel, *c.* 1867, was the first organized church in West Salem. It served as the second school of West Salem after the close of the Civil War. Throughout the Reconstruction period, the 1870s and 1880s were a rebuilding period of the economy as well as the rebuilding of the churches and schools in Winston and Salem. Elm Street Chapel served the area as a school until the large, state-supported public school system led by West Salem's own Calvin Wiley began in the 1880s. The West Salem Graded School opened in 1890 as the third neighborhood school. The Elm Chapel continued until 1911, when it was disbanded by the congregation and merged with Home Moravian Church. The Southbound Railroad was routed through this area, and the second decade of the 1900s began a movement to reconnect East Salem and West Salem.

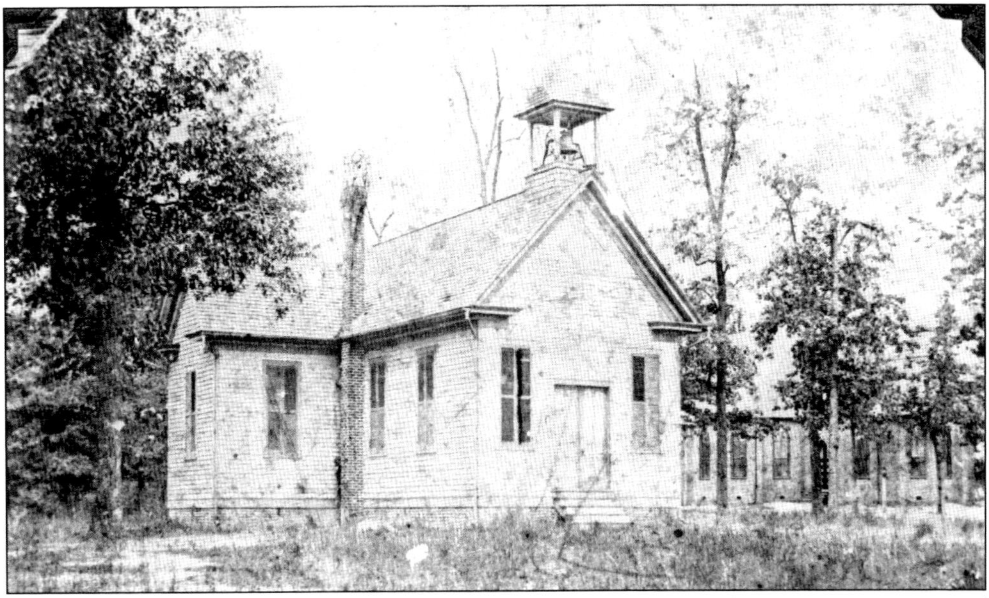

The Brietz family and the Vogler family were early West Salem residents. George Brietz and Mrs. Maria Vogler surveyed the community and discovered more than 30 children interested in attending a Sunday school. The Southern providence of the Moravians organized many new congregations in the 1890s. The Christ Chapel was born. The 20-by-50-foot building consisted of two rooms and seated around 150 people. The small structure was located across from the present church at Academy and Green Streets. The building was moved around 1900 and exists today as 618 South Green Street.

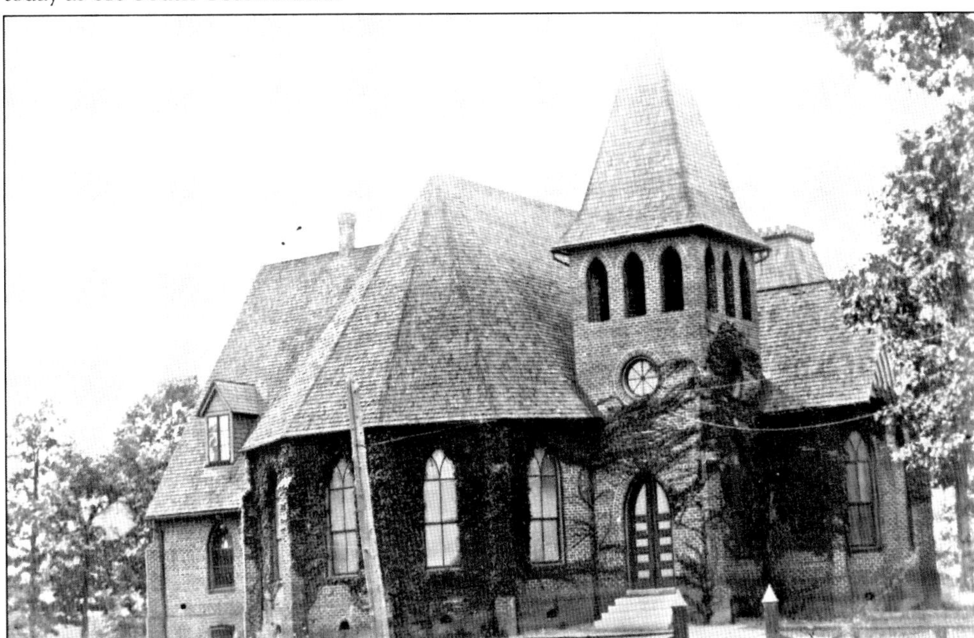

The experiment of Christ Church grew larger than anyone ever imagined. The chapel and extra tents gave way when the cornerstone was laid on July 21, 1895, for a new chapel. The consecration of Christ Moravian Church occurred nearly one year later, July 18, 1896.

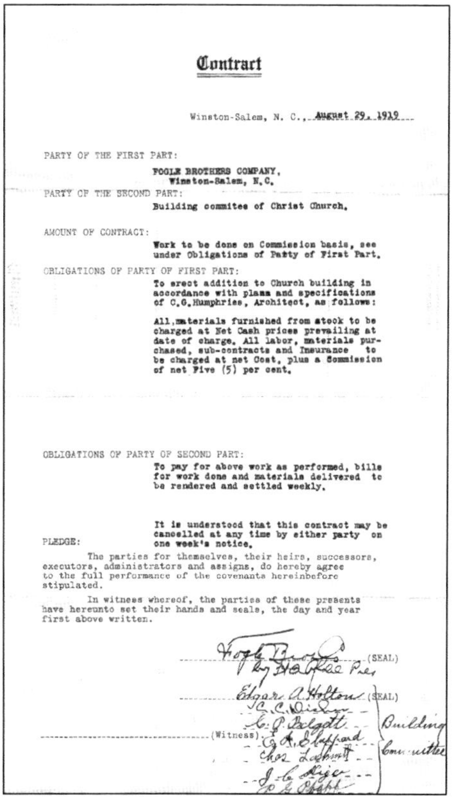

Contract

Winston-Salem, N. C., August 29, 1919

PARTY OF THE FIRST PART:
FOGLE BROTHERS COMPANY,
Winston-Salem, N.C.

PARTY OF THE SECOND PART:
Building commitee of Christ Church.

AMOUNT OF CONTRACT:
Work to be done on Commission basis, see under Obligations of Patty of First Part.

OBLIGATIONS OF PARTY OF FIRST PART:
To erect addition to Church building in accordance with plams and specifications of C.G.Humphries, Architect, as follows:

All materials furnished from stock to be charged at Net Cash prices prevailing at date of charge. All labor, materials purchased, sub-contracts and Insurance to be charged at net Cost, plus a Commission of net Five (5) per cent.

OBLIGATIONS OF PARTY OF SECOND PART:
To pay for above work as performed, bills for work done and materials delivered to be rendered and settled weekly.

PLEDGE:
It is understood that this contract may be cancelled at any time by either party on one week's notice.

The parties for themselves, their heirs, successors, executors, administrators and assigns, do hereby agree to the full performance of the covenants hereinbefore stipulated.

In witness whereof, the parties of these presents have hereunto set their hands and seals, the day and year first above written.

(SEAL)

Edgar A. Holton (SEAL)

(Witness).

Building Committee

This contract was drawn between Christ Moravian Church and Fogle Brothers Lumber Company in order to construct an addition in 1919.

Fogle Brothers Lumber Company constructed the 300-seat Christ Moravian Church in 1895. Fogle Brothers was a long-established company tracing its roots to founder brothers Charles A. and Christian H. Fogle in 1871. During the house and business boom of 1880–1920, Fogle Brothers Lumber Company led the way. They were responsible for building most of the structures in Winston. Winston-Salem city records show that "The Fogle Furniture Company was organized as a corporation in January 1923 with F. A. Fogle as president. It originally produced hand-woven fiber furniture but began making matched living-room furniture in 1928 and abandoned the fiber line in 1936."

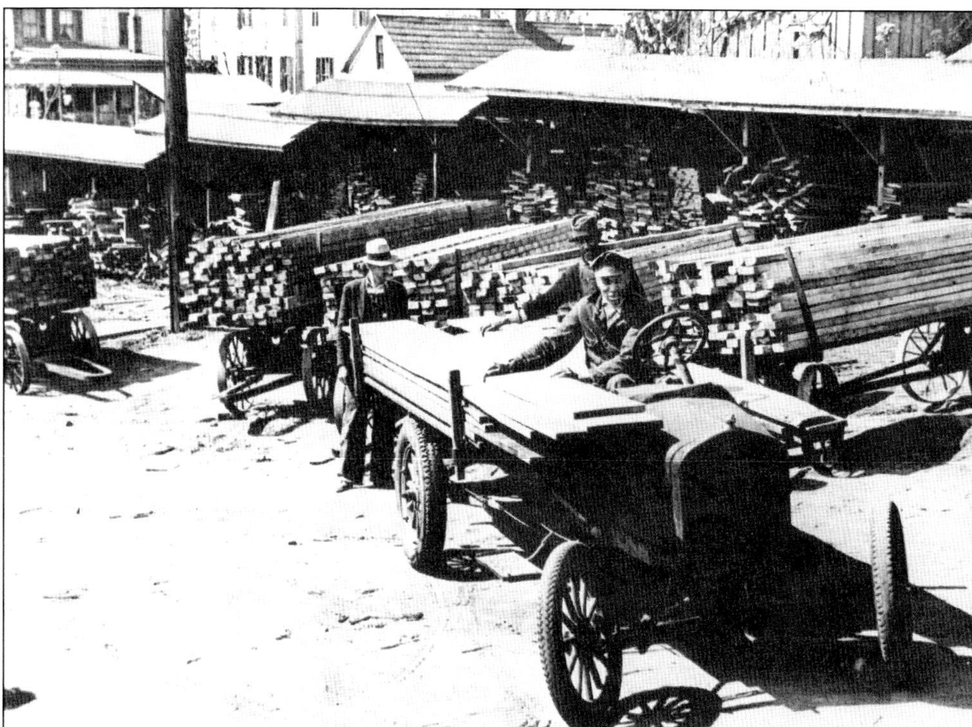

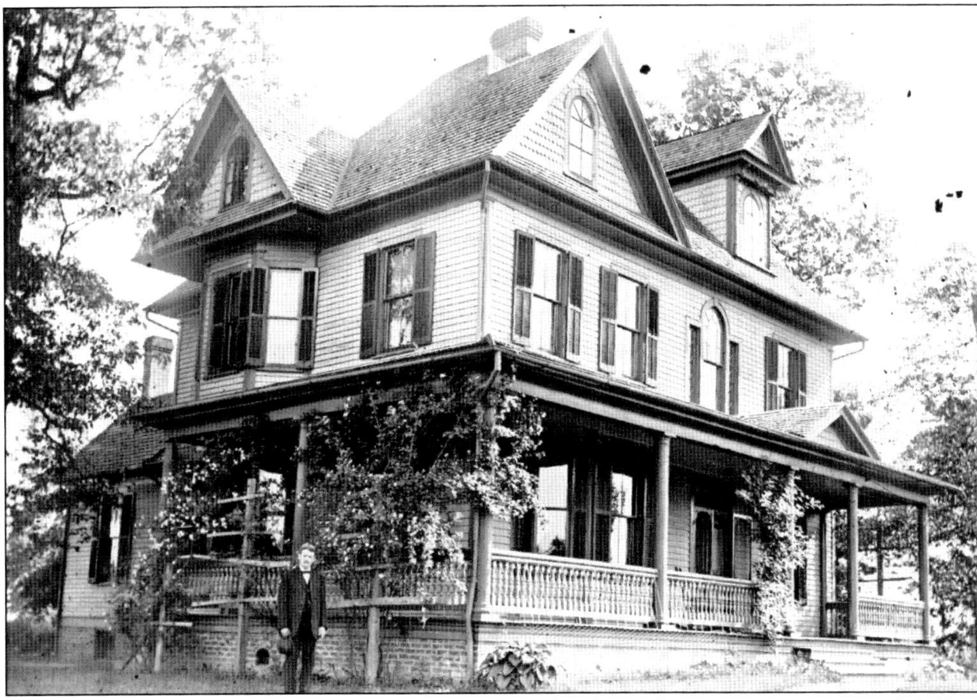

In April 1899, the congregation rose to 200 members thanks to the strong organizational skills of its early Moravian teachers. A parsonage was needed. The two-story parsonage was built on the knoll where the first Christ Moravian Church had been located before being moved to Green Street. Rev. John F. McCuiston is shown in the top photograph, and a later, remodeled parsonage is shown below.

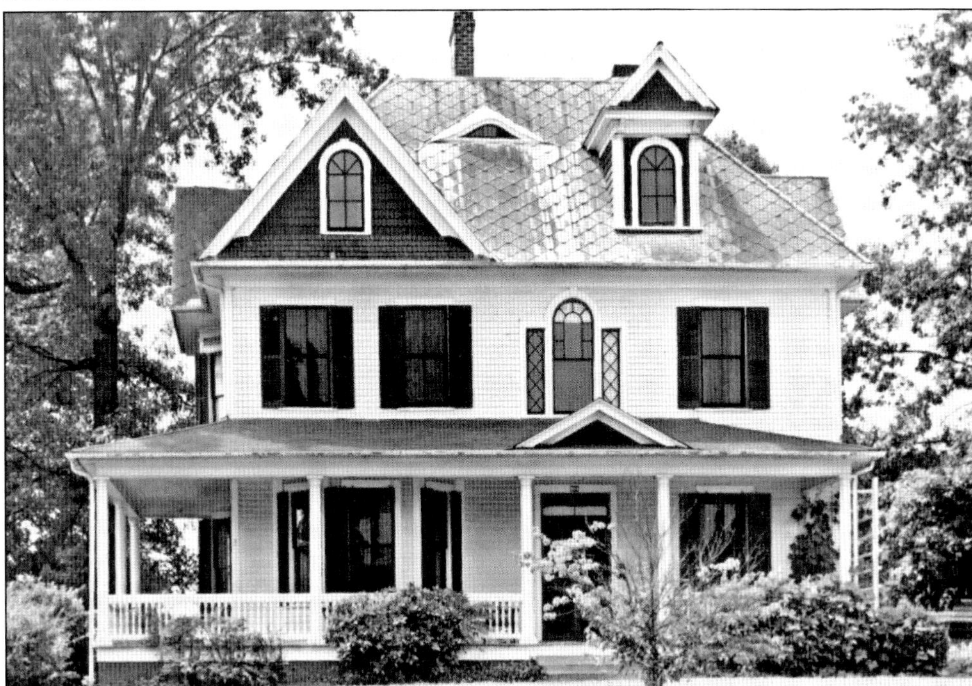

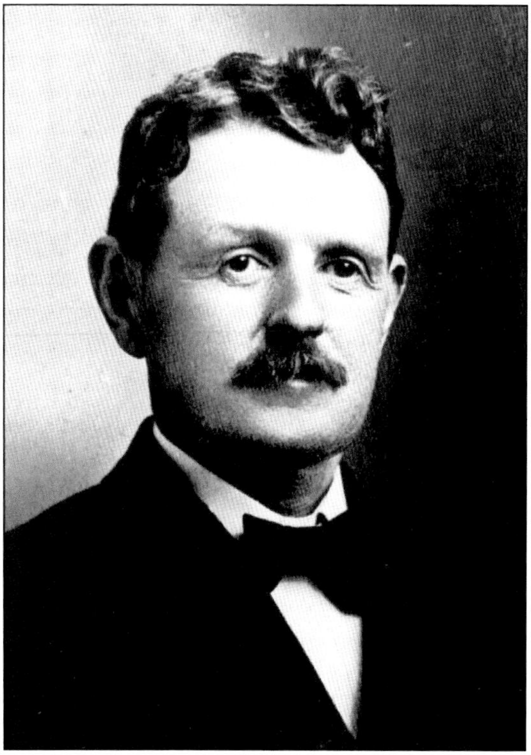

One of the first pastors of Christ Moravian was Rev. John F. McCuiston. In the beginning, Brother McCuiston led the prayer services at the first Christ Chapel in 1892. These services were held on Saturday evenings with the Sunday school meetings the next day. At the close of the Saturday prayer meetings, a 15-minute church service was held. Reverend McCuiston served as an assistant missionary pastor from 1893 to 1896 until receiving his full pastorate duties from 1908 to 1911.

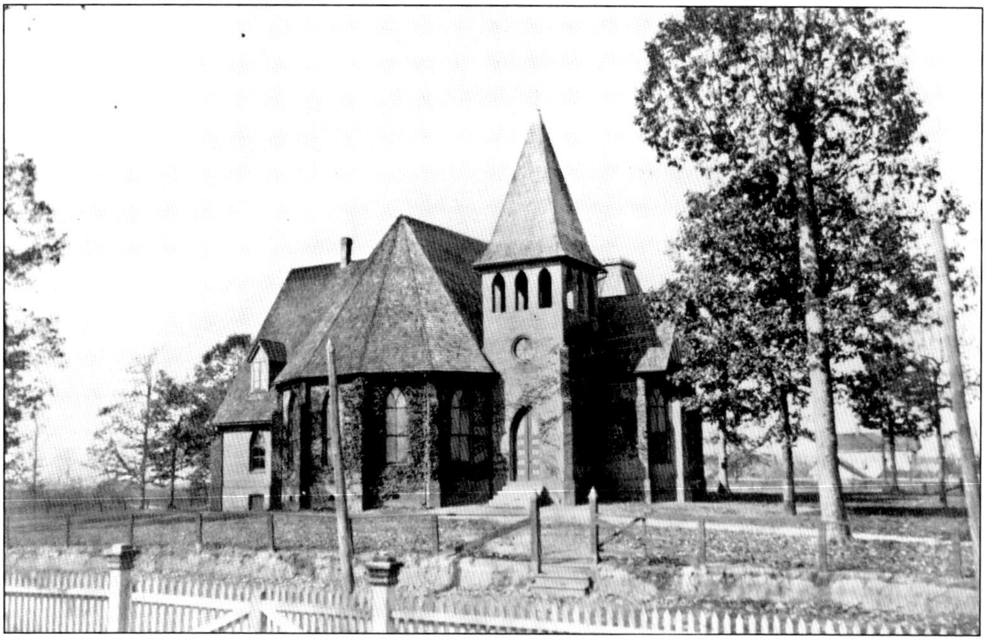

The photograph shows Christ Moravian Church in its earliest stage. Rev. Howard E. Rondthaler was pastor from 1896 to 1903. He also served Fairview, Mayodan, and Moravian congregations. His busy schedule was not enough to keep him and his strong Sunday school members from improving on this structure. A coal bin was built by several members working at night. The ladies raised the money for carpet. This is another example of West Salem's strong work ethic.

First pastor Howard E. Rondthaler and his wife and son, Theodore, are shown c. 1915. Rondthaler's father, Edward, arrived in Salem at the end of the Civil War during Reconstruction. All Reverend Rondthaler found when he rode into the train station were flatbed cars loaded with dried fruit. Dried fruit was the number-one commodity in the area. Winston and Salem were totally broke from the Civil War. In 1909, Dr. Howard E. Rondthaler began a 40-year career as president of Salem College and Academy. His administration saw the greatest growth in the college by a single president. The campus expanded from 3.5 acres at his arrival to 56.5 acres at his retirement.

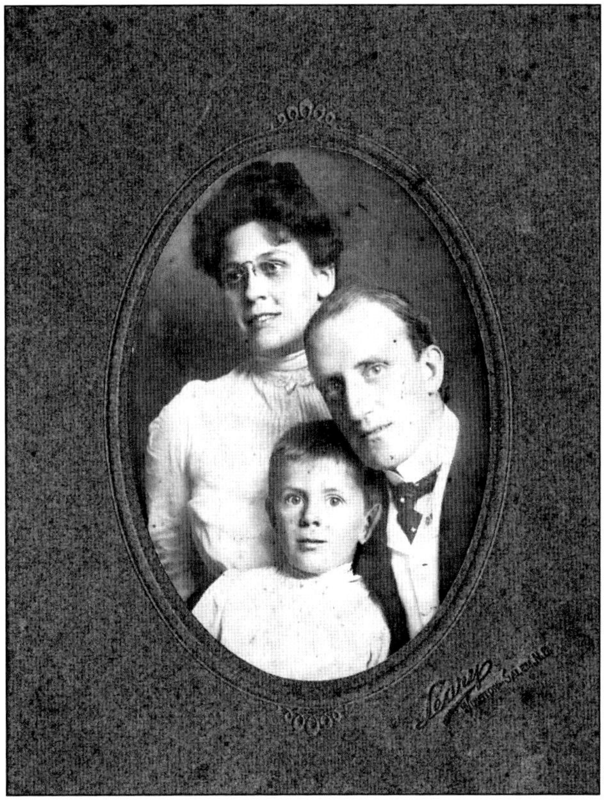

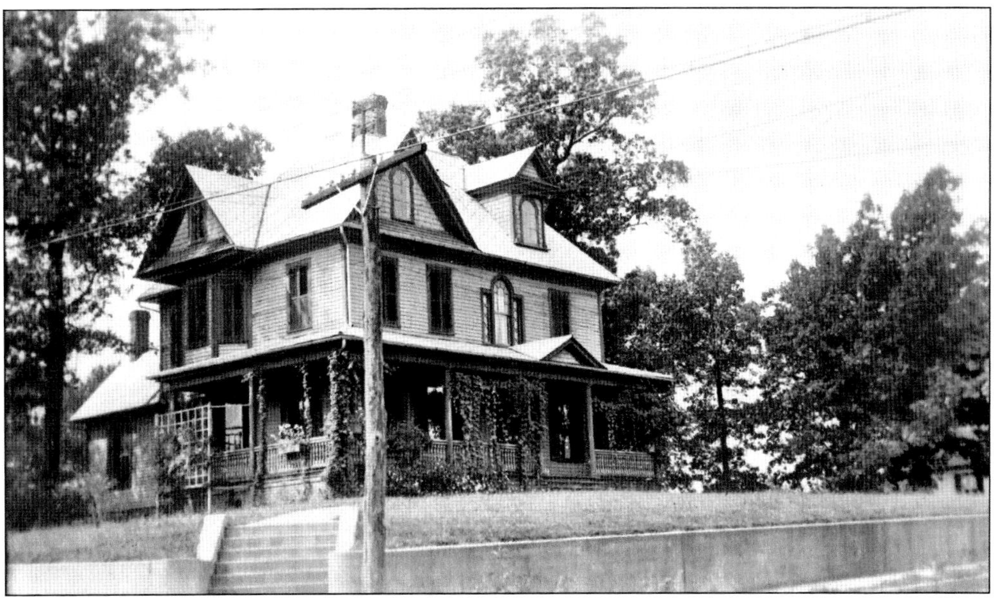

At the time this photograph was taken, it was the height of the postcard era. This made it possible for photographs to be exchanged across America. Regular photographs were much too expensive for the regular Americans, so professional postcards were in great demand. This is an early postcard of the parsonage of Christ Moravian.

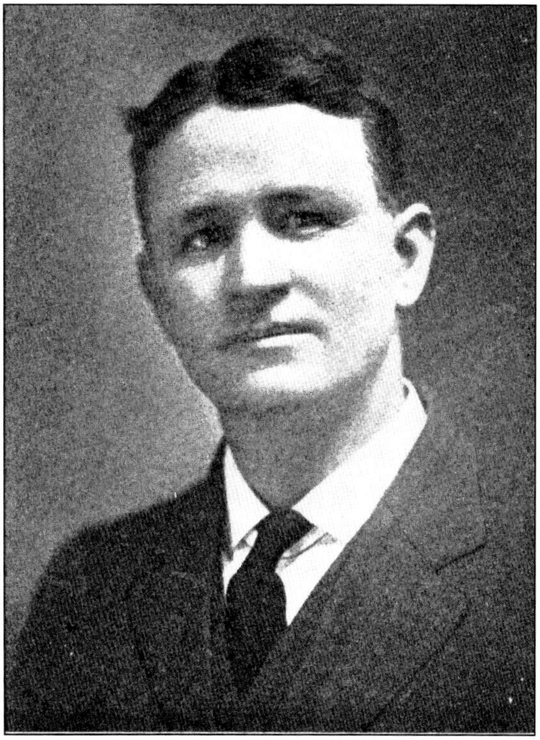

Rev. Edgar A. Holton served the church from 1916 to 1924. Reverend Holton oversaw the 1919 additions performed by Fogle Brothers Lumber Company. The new wing that was added showed a unique situation to overcome. The roof needed to be higher than the original sanctuary. Instead of raising the roof, a new room was built over the old one.

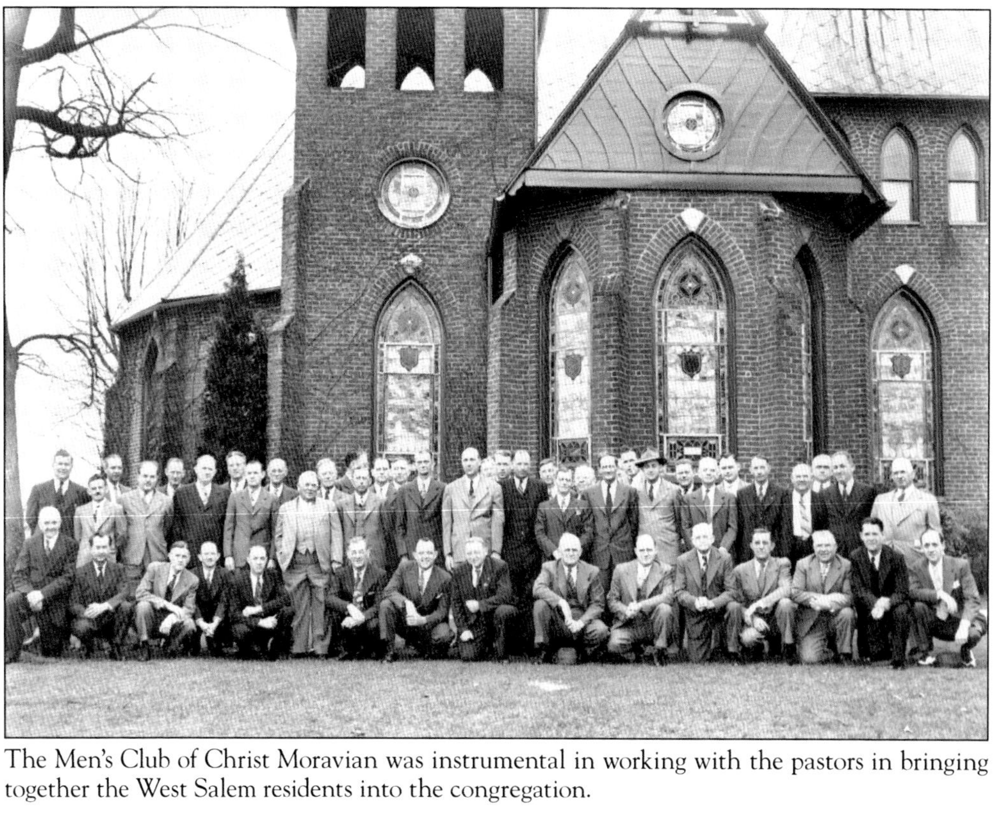

The Men's Club of Christ Moravian was instrumental in working with the pastors in bringing together the West Salem residents into the congregation.

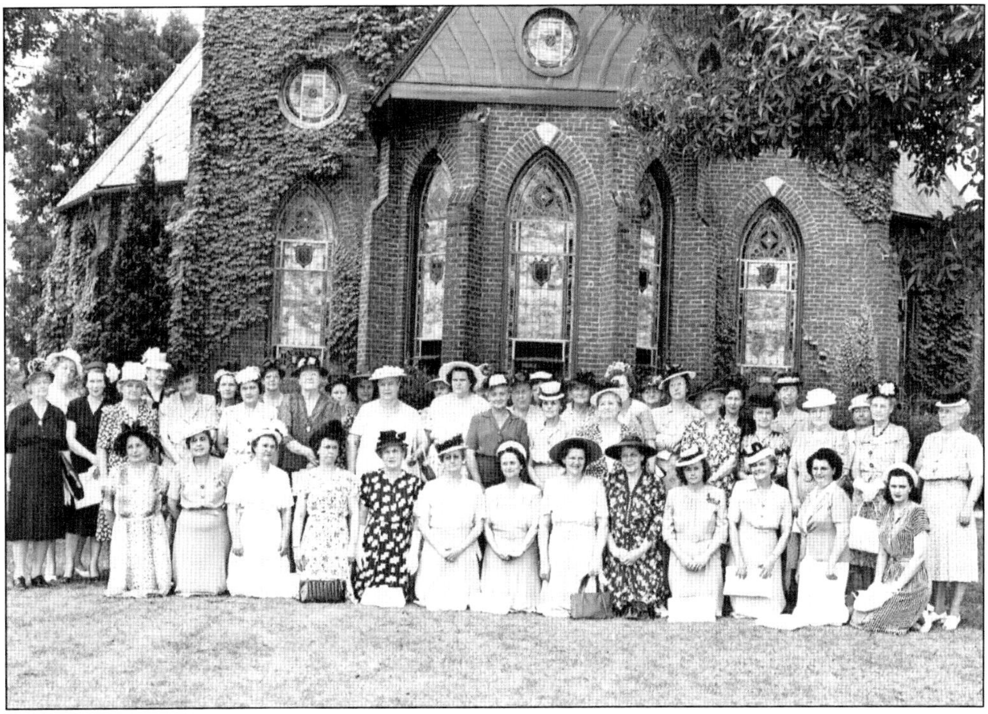

The Women's Club of Christ Moravian complemented the Men's Club in helping them ensure success of the Christ Moravian mission.

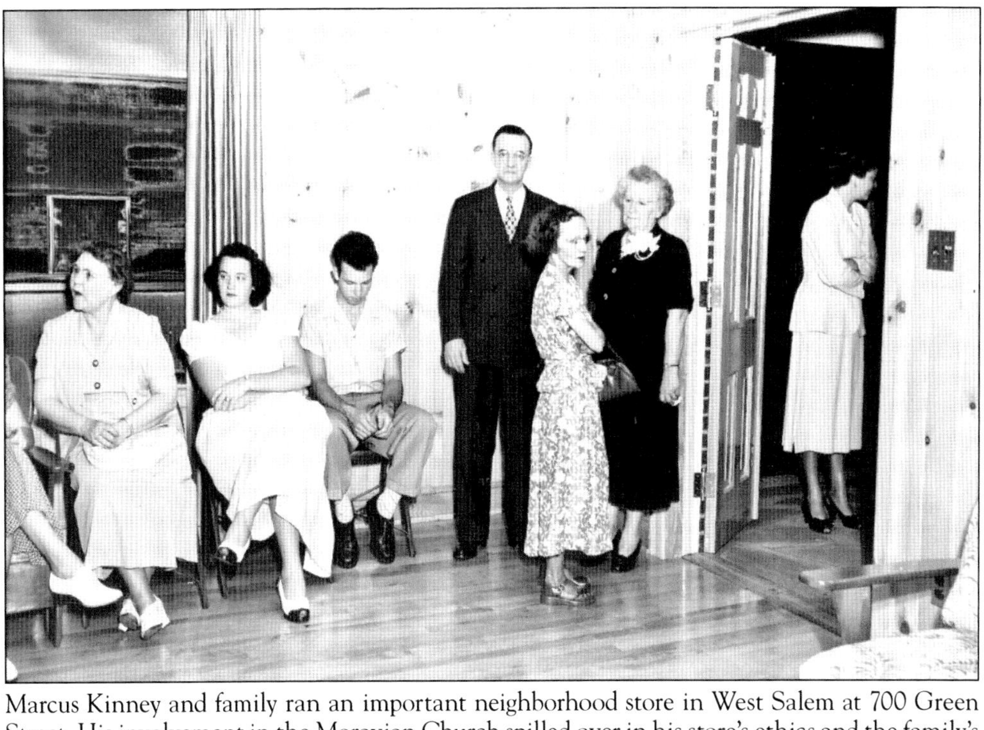

Marcus Kinney and family ran an important neighborhood store in West Salem at 700 Green Street. His involvement in the Moravian Church spilled over in his store's ethics and the family's neighborly attitudes toward his customers. Kinney resided at 750 Granville Drive.

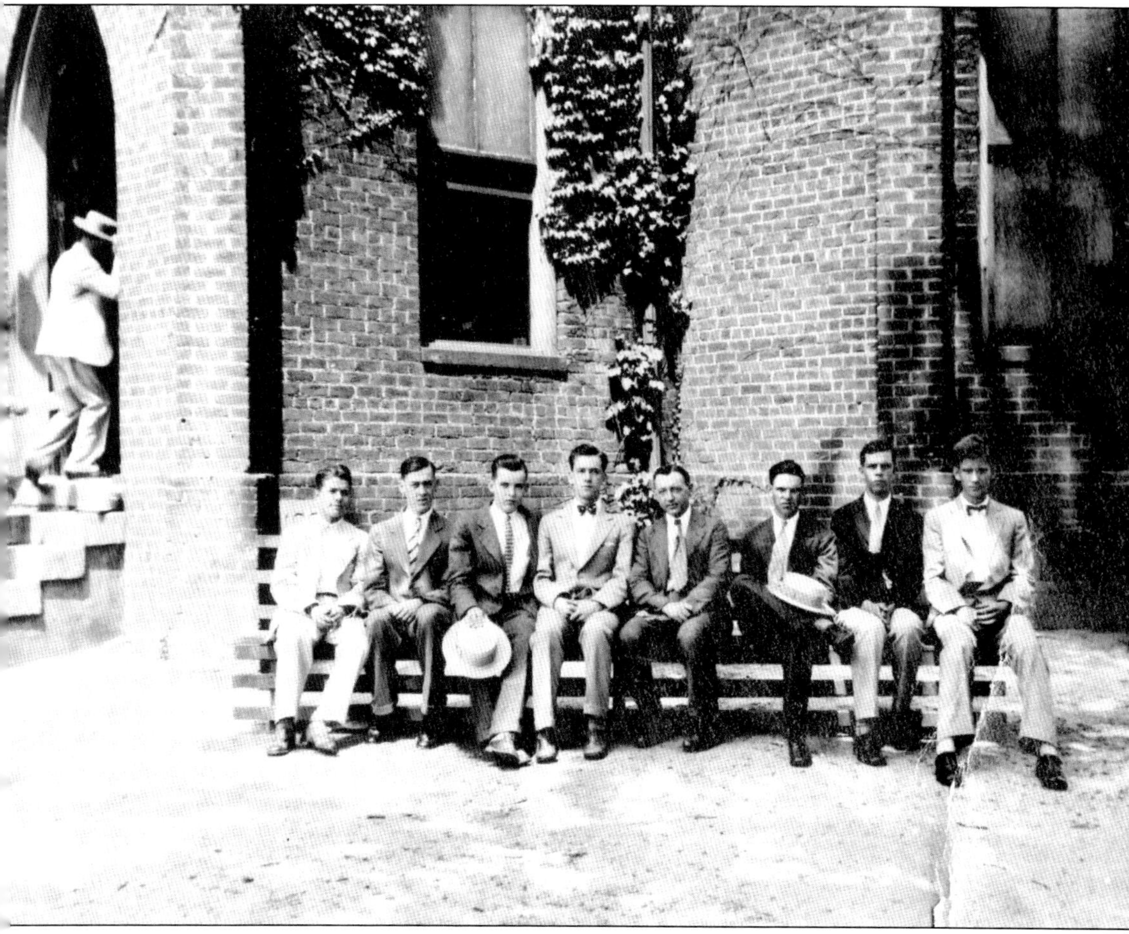

The Men's Club was formed with the beginning of the church. The ladies of Christ Church helped throughout the history. In 1919, the Ladies Aid Organization published a church directory: "On Palm Sunday 1920, 45 people were received into the membership of the congregation. Eleven joined by adult baptism, eleven joined by the rite of confirmation and 23 joined by letter of transfer."

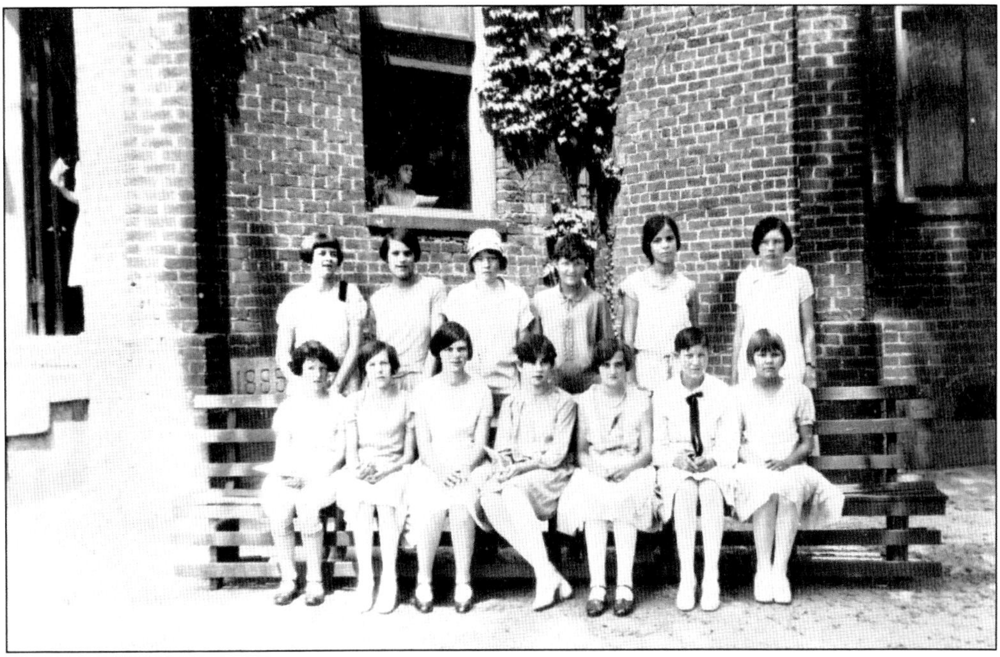

The year 1914 saw the church's largest increase in membership. This was due in great part to the opening of Granville Grammar School the same year. The school was honored by educators as one of the best grammar schools in the state. Many children enrolled, and Christ Moravian Church's youth programs were greatly enriched.

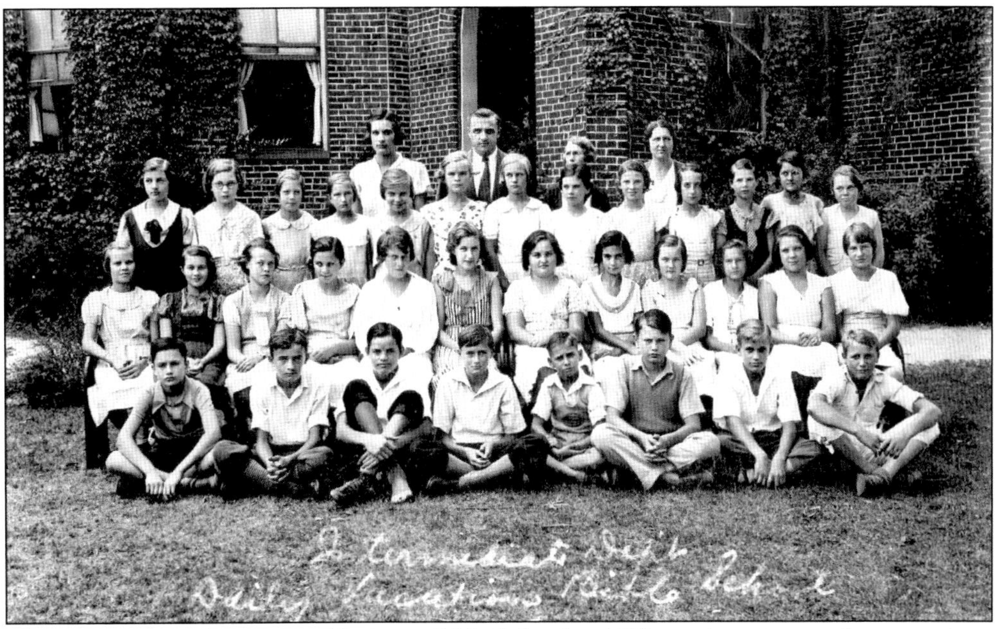

The intermediate department Vacation Bible School *c.* 1938 was in existence for some time. The year 1924 brought an updated brand of Sunday schools to the church. No longer did the intermediate or junior classes have to study their required hymns written on window shades. The junior department developed separately from the Sunday school. Several classrooms were created by using wooden partitions to separate the larger rooms.

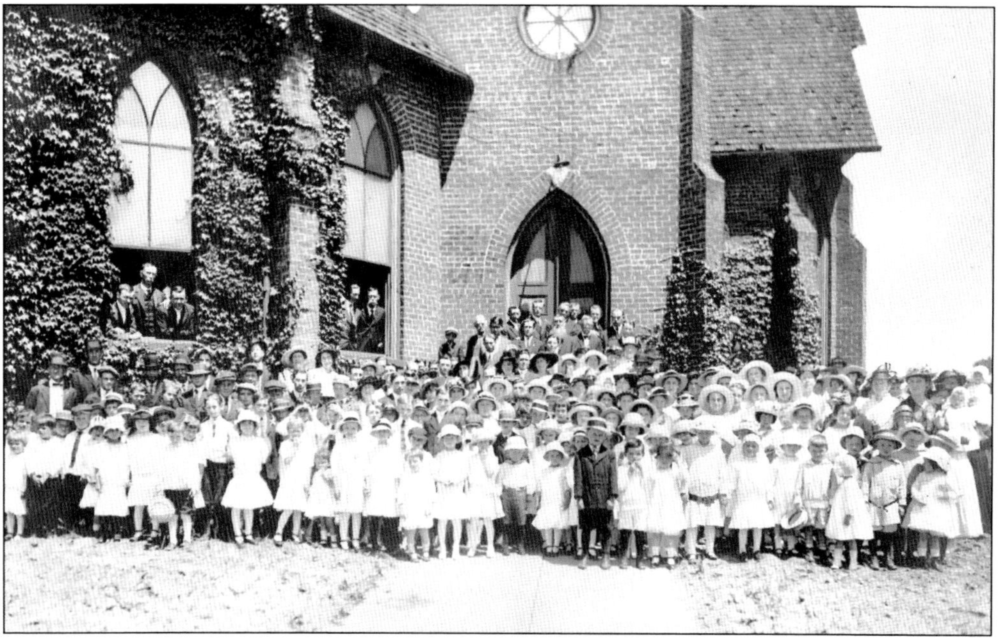

The first Vacation Bible School on a daily basis was held June 20–July 1, 1927, with an average attendance of 141 children. Christ and Home Moravian were the only churches of the Southern providence participating in this long vacation bible school format. The children enjoyed their time at church on holidays and at play. "In our Easter Bonnet" was the theme of vacation bible school, shown above. Watermelon, however, was the major topic on everyone's mind in the side yard of the parsonage. The house in the background at 918 Academy Street is the Pfaff house, shown below. It has been restored presently. The Pfaff family was instrumental in founding and settling the West Salem neighborhood in the late 19th century. The Pfaff family continues to serve the church and community today.

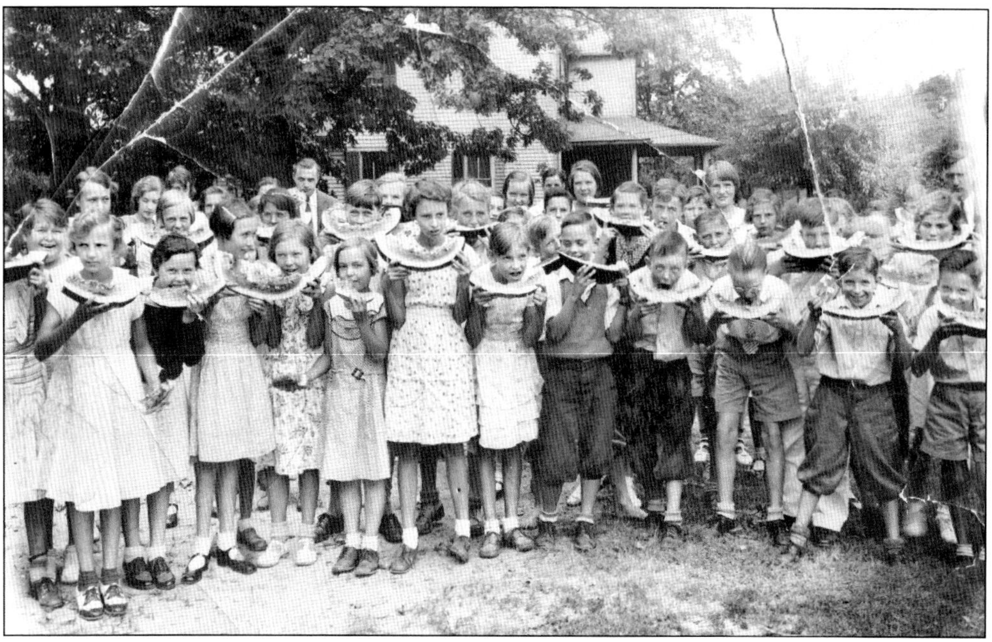

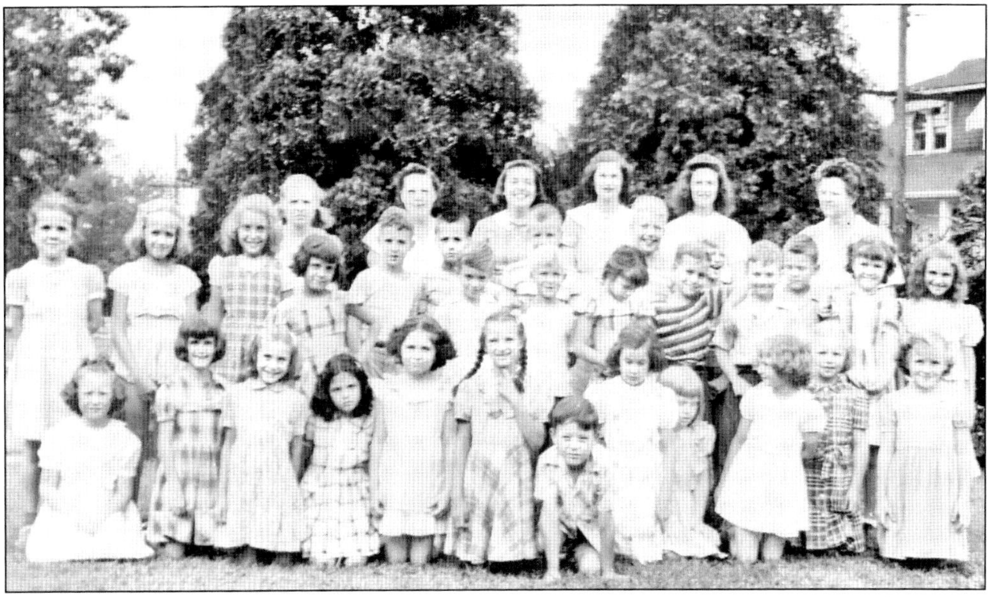

Approaching the 50-year anniversary of the Christ Moravian Church's founding, there were many positive changes. By 1940, Christ Moravian Church was the largest congregation in the Southern providence. Only Home Church and Calvary Moravian were larger. The congregation continued to change from simply a neighborhood church to an area church. New members came from other neighborhoods. Even though Christ Moravian Church had its beginning as a small chapel, the experiment was an overwhelming success. The above photograph includes Ruth Knox, Edith Tesch, and Gladys Talley. Mrs. Edith Tesch was the wife of Rev. Samuel Tesch. The photograph below includes Bobbie and Mickey Young, Alton Pfaff, and Alvin Disher. Youth groups were a mainstay of Christ Moravian Church. Bobbie and Mickey Young were residents of 733 Green Street.

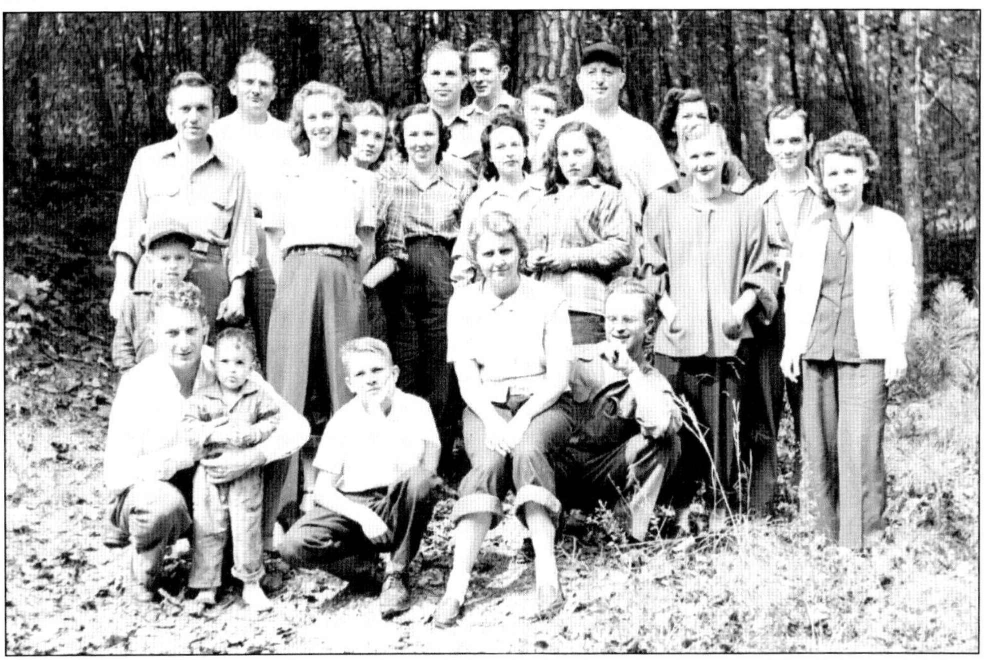

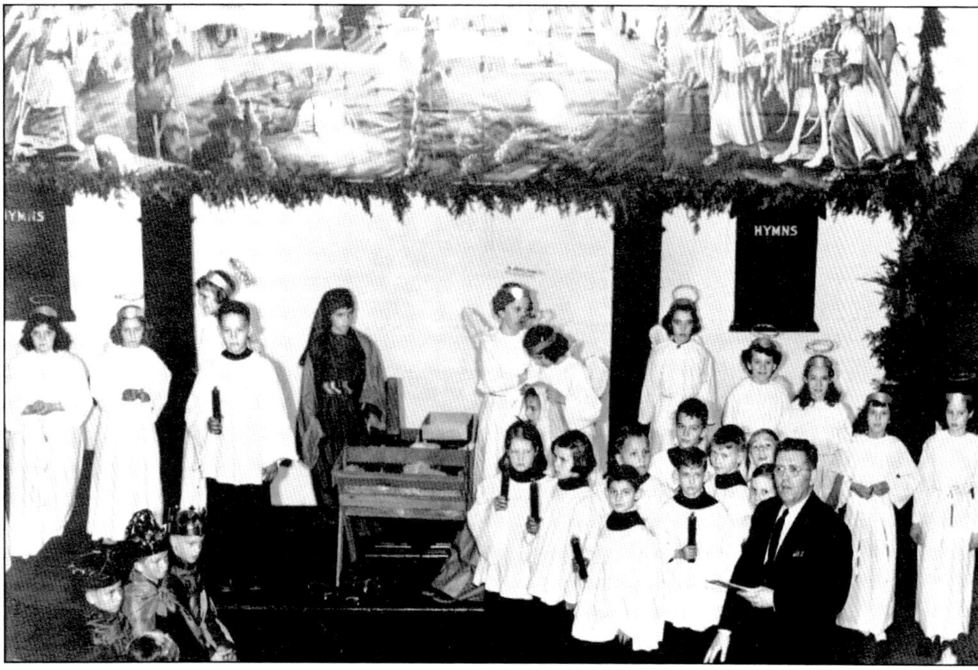

The Christmas program of 1952 brought the Christmas message to more members than ever before. The Fellowship building of Christ Moravian Church had aided in the attendance success. In the late 1940s, a group of young adults calling themselves the Trenco-Moravians developed and constructed the Fellowship building on the corner of Academy Street and Granville Drive. The homes shown in the bottom photograph are, from left to right, 936 Bank Street (at the intersection of Bank Street and Granville Drive), the former grocery store, Bailey's Cash Grocery; 935 Bank Street, the Bodenheimer home, *c.* 1920; 929 Bank Street, the Kriets home, *c.* 1920; 925 Bank Street, Saunder home, *c.* 1920; and 917 Bank Street, the Jane home, *c.* 1915.

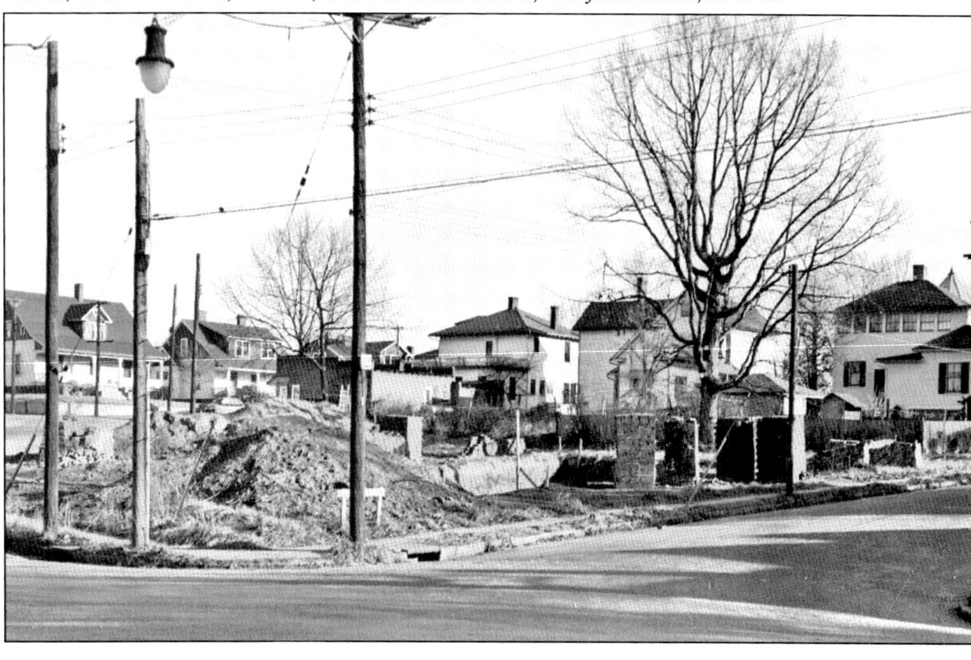

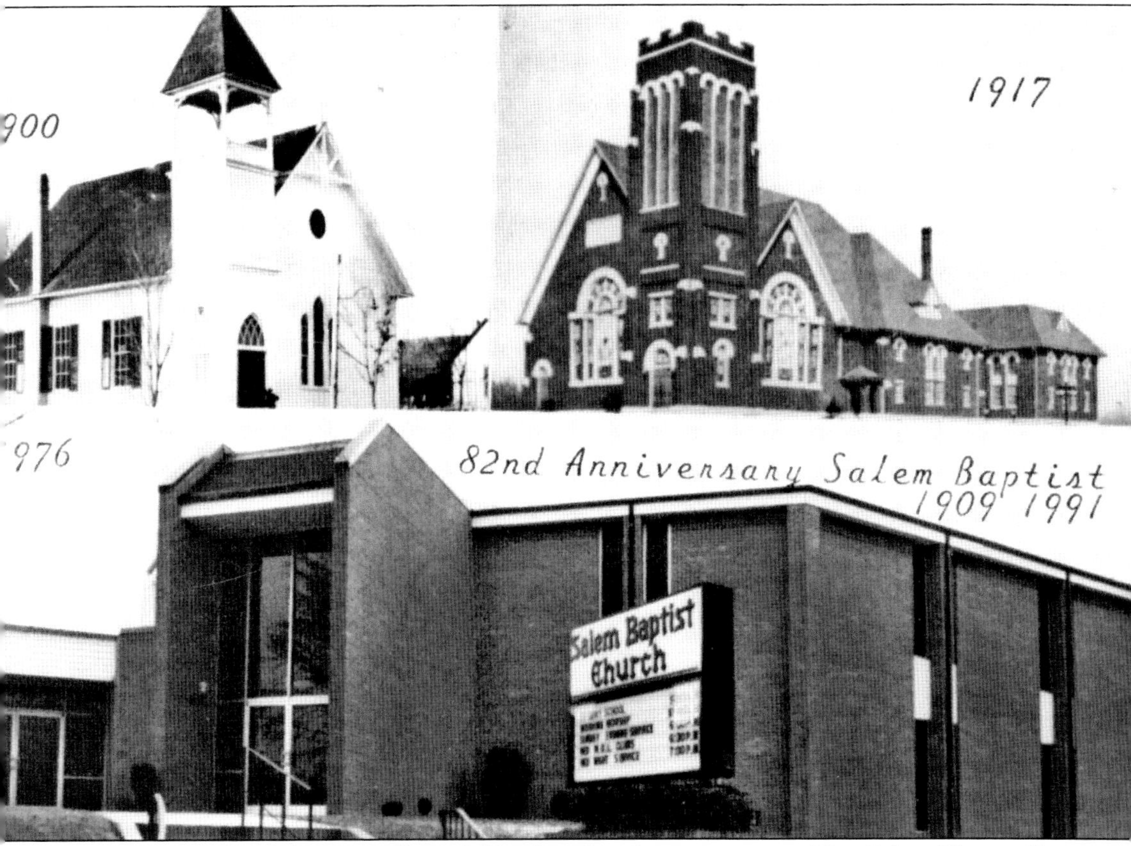

Salem Baptist Church began small, much like the other denominations in West Salem. The small Sunday school of Brother Sam Morton started in one mill house with 20 people in 1898. This church gained its strength from the large industrial development of the 1890s with the arrival of the Arista Cotton Mills. The Moravians were strong in Salem, North Carolina; however, the faith of the many mill workers, who came by the hundreds to live and work in the mills and factories, had added greatly to the neighborhood. Brother Sam Morton was the great Christian layman who was also the "Boss Weaver" of Arista Mills. Brother Morton studied the area around the mills on Sunday mornings. He concluded that the children and young people were left to roam the streets and play marbles while entertaining themselves on the Lord's Day. The Baptist movement of West Salem had begun.

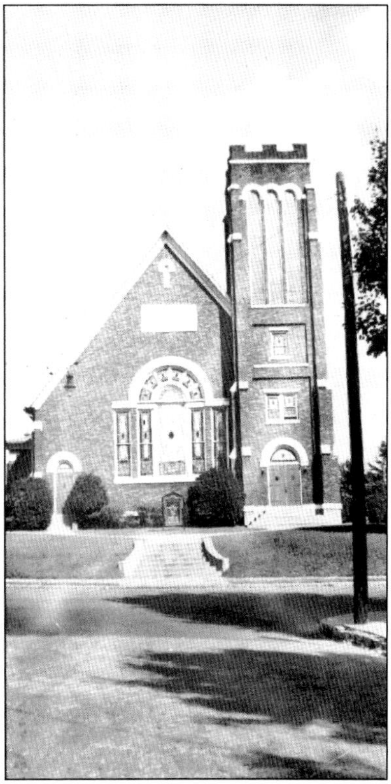

Within two years of beginning the Salem Baptist Sunday school, Brother Sam Morton, Dr. W. J. Conrad, and Lee Strange had made the arrangements to buy a lot on South Marshall Street for $150 in cash. The money was raised for the building, and September 16, 1900, the cornerstones were laid. By the first Sunday in November 1900, the building was erected and the debt paid with $300 in reserve. The first church was called the Salem Mission. On February 14, 1909, the church had grown and organized into the Salem Baptist Church. In a span of nine years from 1900 to 1909, the growth of members was impressive because of Brother Morton's organization of prayer meetings throughout the West Salem community.

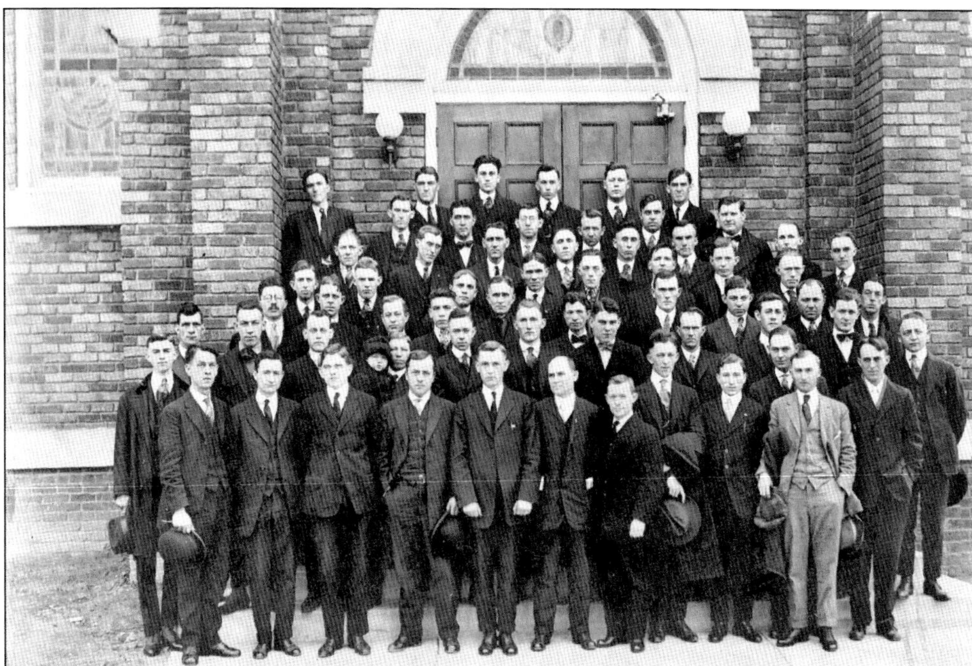

In 1917, the congregation had outgrown Marshall Street, and a 100-by-100-foot lot on Broad Street was chosen, and the new church erected. The church stood until the present church was built on the same site in 1976.

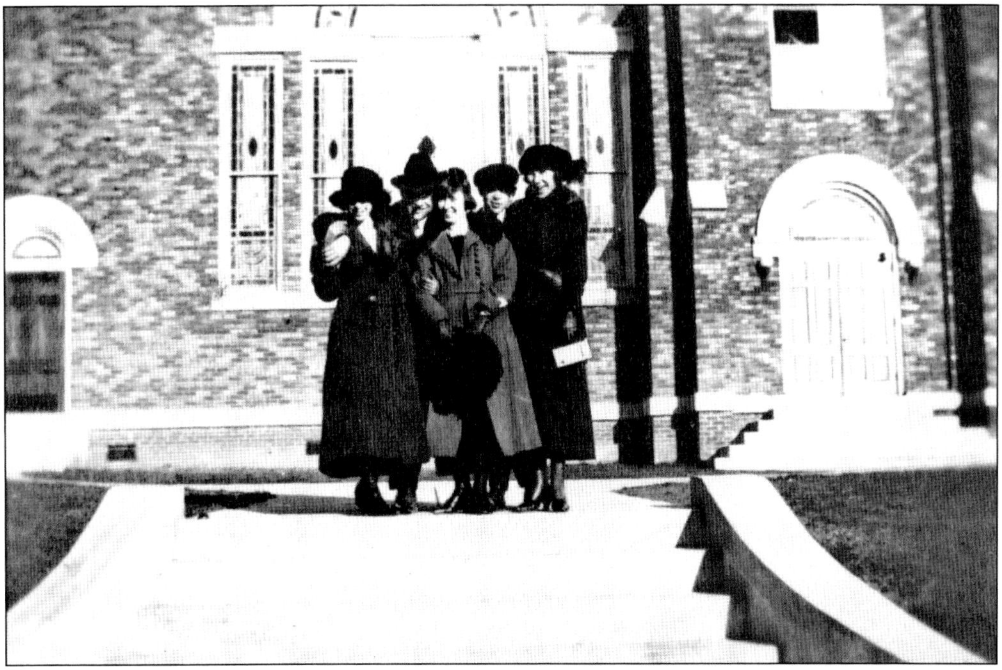

The Fries family was generous to the Salem Mission. The Fries were responsible for developing land along Marshall Street, Poplar Street, and Brookstown Avenue. The mill time in West Salem is responsible for much growth of Salem Baptist Church. The First Baptist Church in downtown Winston was also instrumental in 1900 to help with the founding of Salem Baptist Church. These ladies were proud of the accomplishments of the Salem Baptist Church.

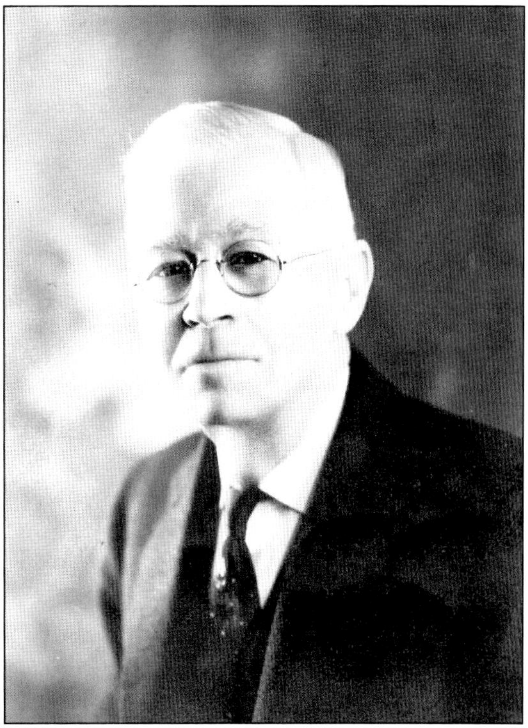

In 1900, four individuals came forward after a meeting with Sam Morton; Fred Day and B. F. Huntley were two of the four, who each gave $50 to begin the fund for the Salem Mission. Day, pictured, ran the Day Jewelry Store on Liberty Street. Huntley ran the B. F. Huntley Furniture Company on Patterson Avenue.

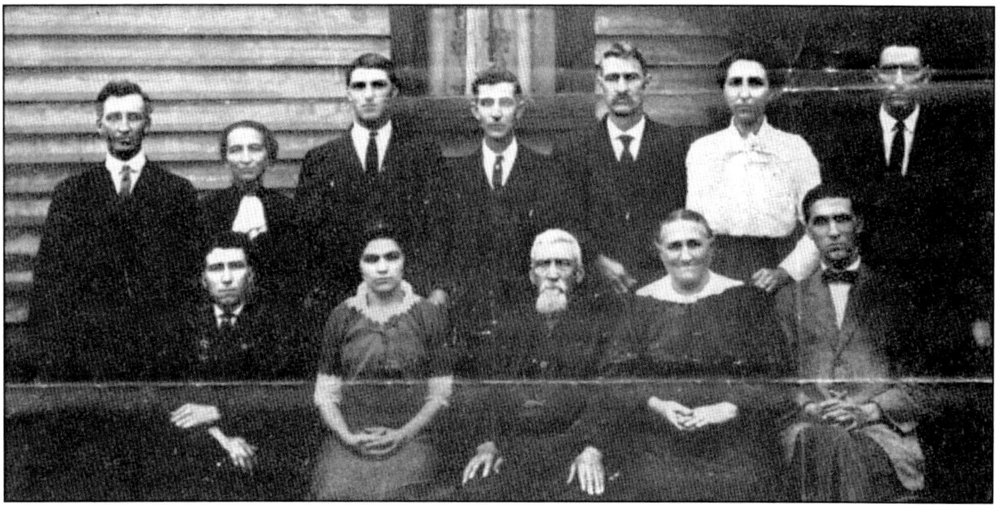

The Hemrick family was a pioneering family of Salem Baptist Mission Church. Seated above in the first row are Fletcher Hemrick (far left), Sallie Hemrick (second from left), and John Henry Hemrick (far right). The church members of Salem Baptist Church got together for the photograph below in 1961. Fred Day is in the first row, third from left, and Fred Lawrence Sr. is in the second row, far left.

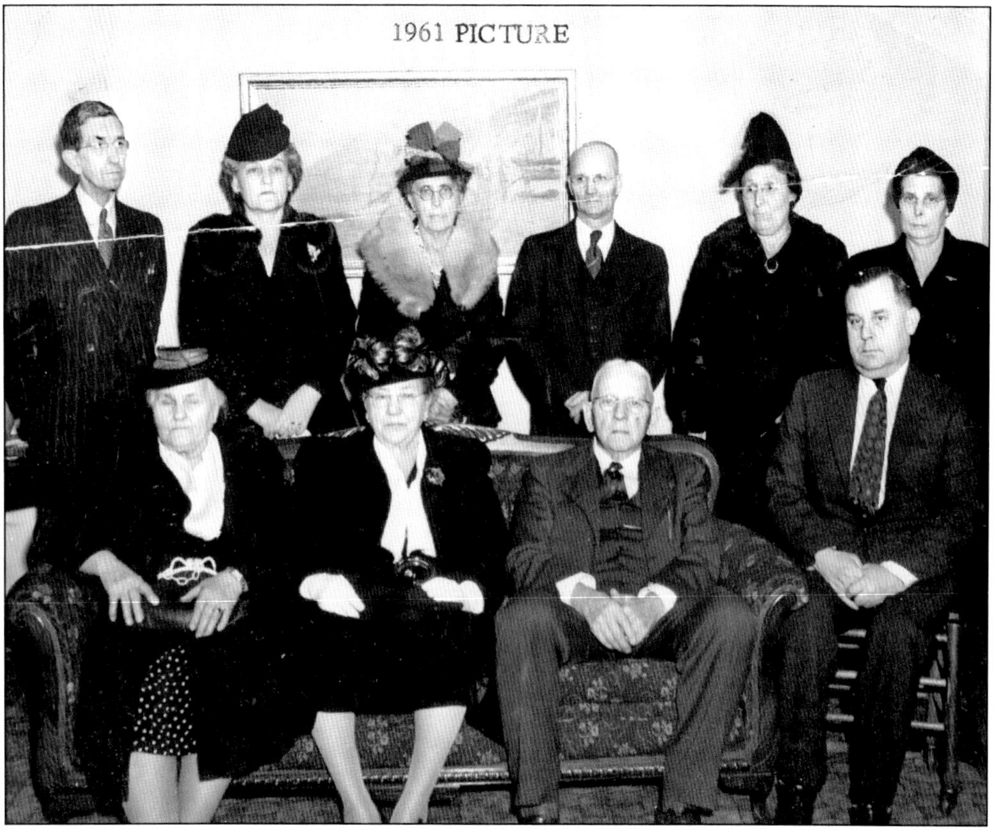

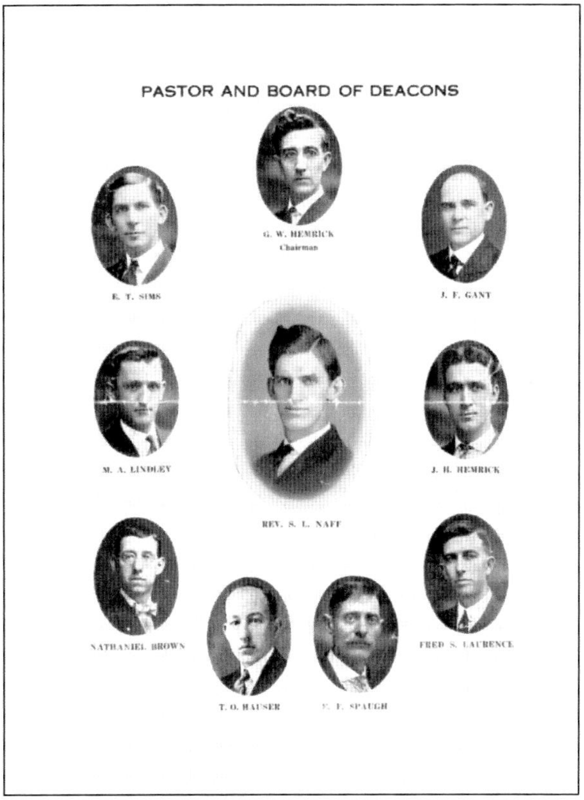

The pastor and board of deacons at Salem Baptist oversaw the building of Mission Church expanding into a larger congregational church. Their inspiration followed in the later years with the establishment of Piedmont Bible College and Salem Baptist Christian School.

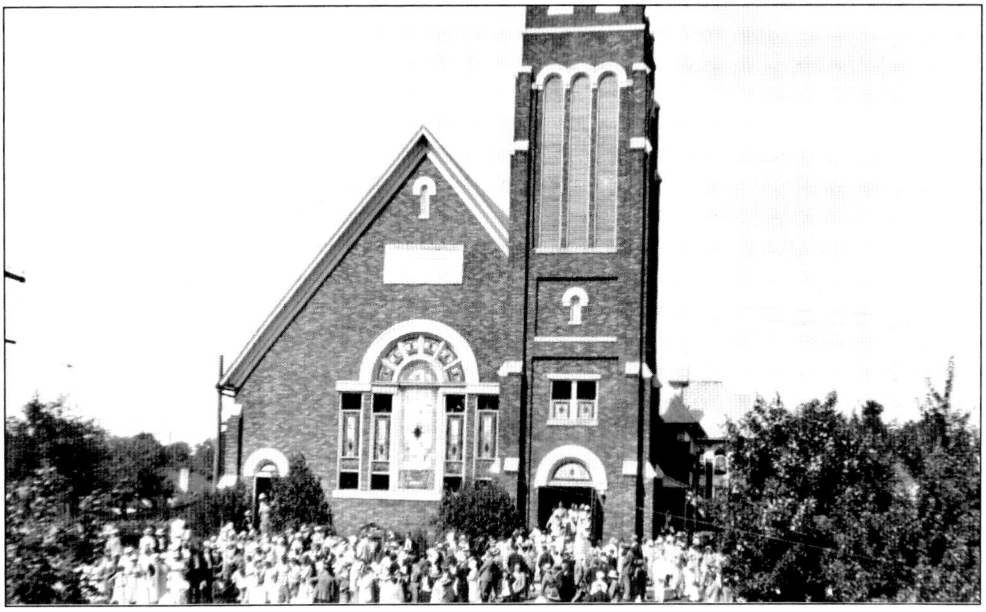

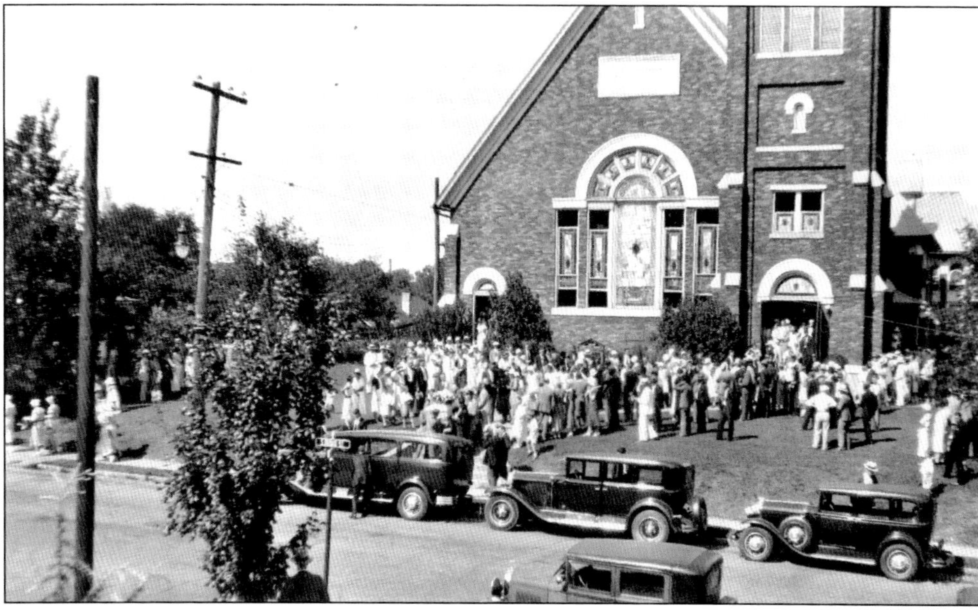

Death is a part of life. The funeral procession at Salem Baptist Church is shown as a solemn event; however, it was also a time to come together and champion the thought that the loved ones are at peace, and life goes on.

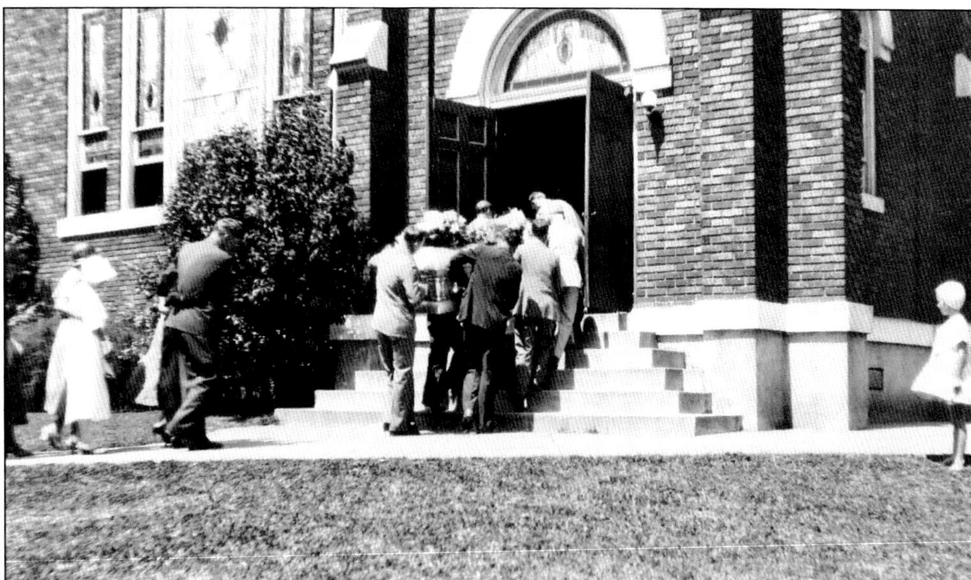

A weekly event was the adoption of the Salem Baptist Church's budget. This, a printed reminder, called for all members to heed the needs of the church with their monetary tithes.

SALEM BAPTIST CHURCH

WINSTON-SALEM, N. C.

Our Budget, per week, from July 1, 1923 to June 30, 1924, embraces the following items:

Pastors Support	$ 50.00
Janitors Support	12.50
Lights, Water and Fuel	10.00
Music	3.00
Repairs	5.00
Insurance	7.00
Incidentals	9.50
75 Million Campaign Fund	50.00
Street and Sidewalk Assessments	5.00
Stationery and Publicity	7.00
Furniture and Fixtures, including Musical	7.00
Building and Loan (present)	45.00
Building and Loan (extra)—Sunday School Annex	20.00
Support Missionary on Foreign Field	15.40
Total per week	$246.40

Each member is requested to read this budget carefully and make a subscription in keeping with it to be paid **weekly,** if possible, through the Envelope.

OBEDIENCE AND FELLOWSHIP PLEDGE

I hereby pledge to my Saviour faithful obedience to His will as He reveals it to me.

I pledge to the other members of the church the same Christian love and fellowship I wish them to show to me.

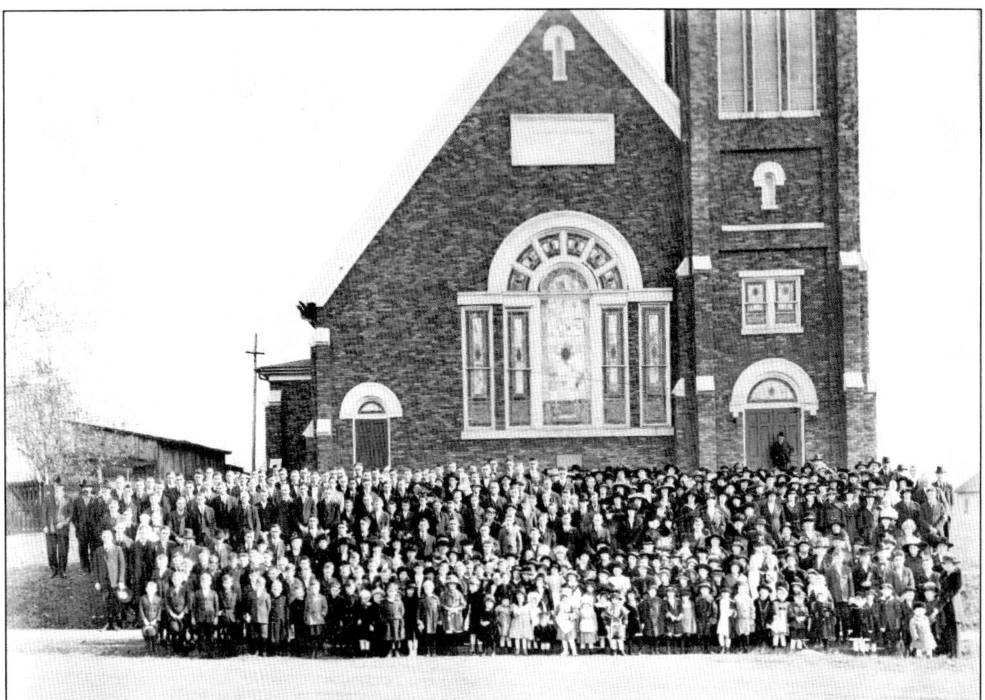

The complete congregation of Salem Baptist came together on this Sunday morning in the 1920s to show their strength in numbers.

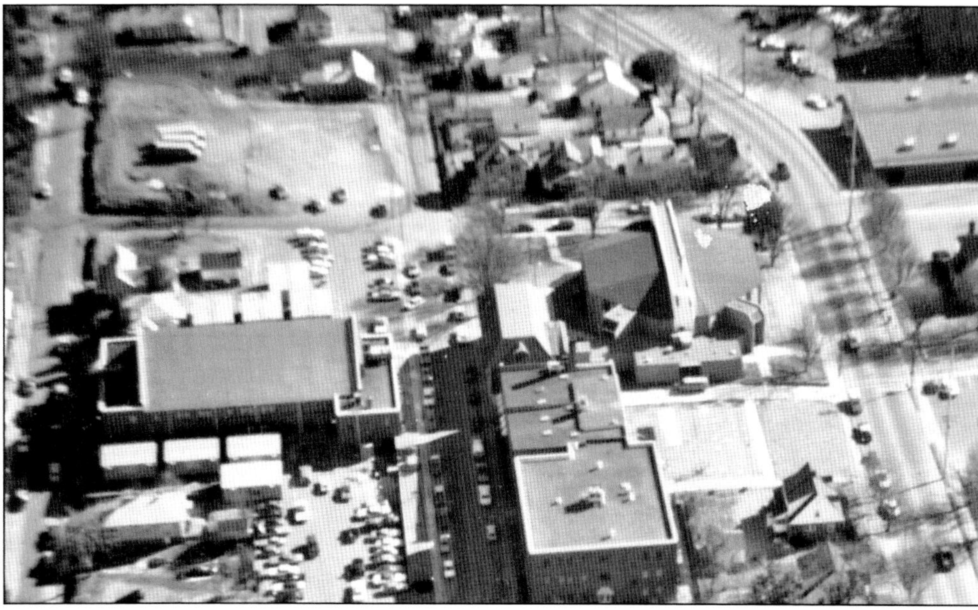

Salem Baptist and Piedmont Bible College are shown in an overhead view in the 1970s. The complex is home to a church, a private Christian school, and a college. The photograph was taken of the college and church to show its sponsorship of many missions throughout the world. The airplane that was used to photograph this picture was used to train missionaries. The airplane was the property of the school/college.

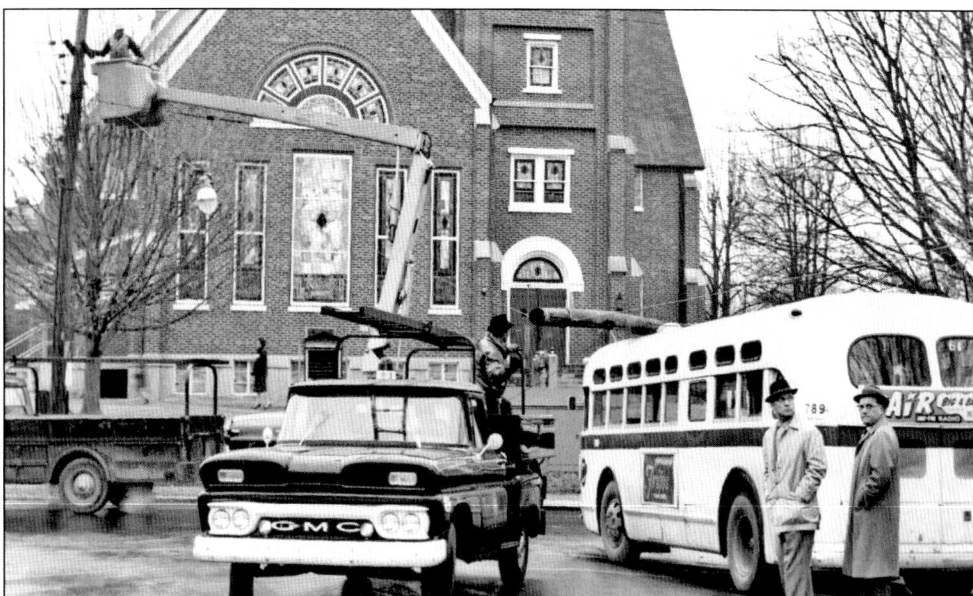

Salem Baptist Church grew from a prayer meeting in 1900 to a religious pillar of the West Salem community in the 20th century. Charles Stevens, a longtime pastor of the church, founded a nationally accredited school, Piedmont Bible College, in the 1940s. The Salem Baptist Church also founded Salem Baptist Christian School for children. That school also grew to prominence. Outside the walls of Salem Baptist is a busy Broad Street after a traffic accident in the early 1960s.

Charles Stevens and his wife, Grace, were instrumental in the growth of the church throughout the 1930s, 1940s, and 1950s. Reverend Stevens is responsible for founding Piedmont Bible College in the 1940s.

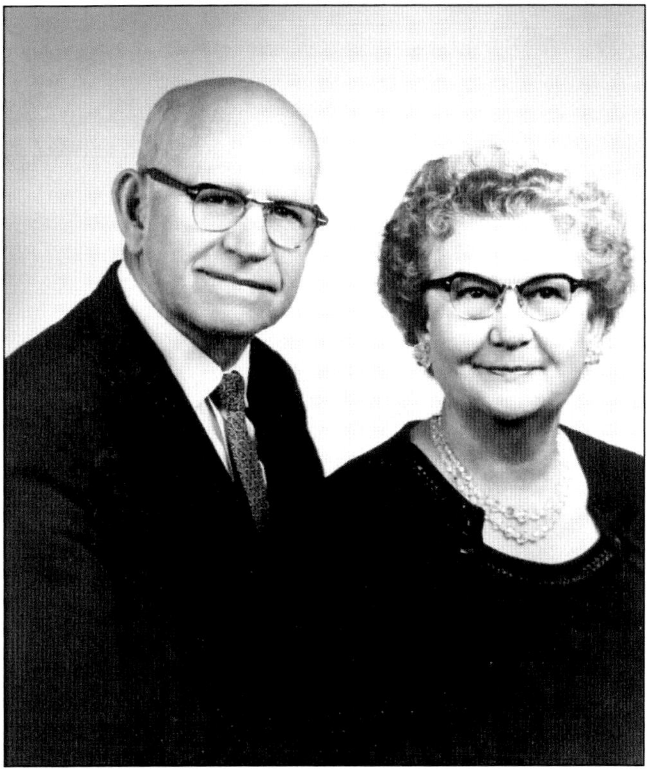

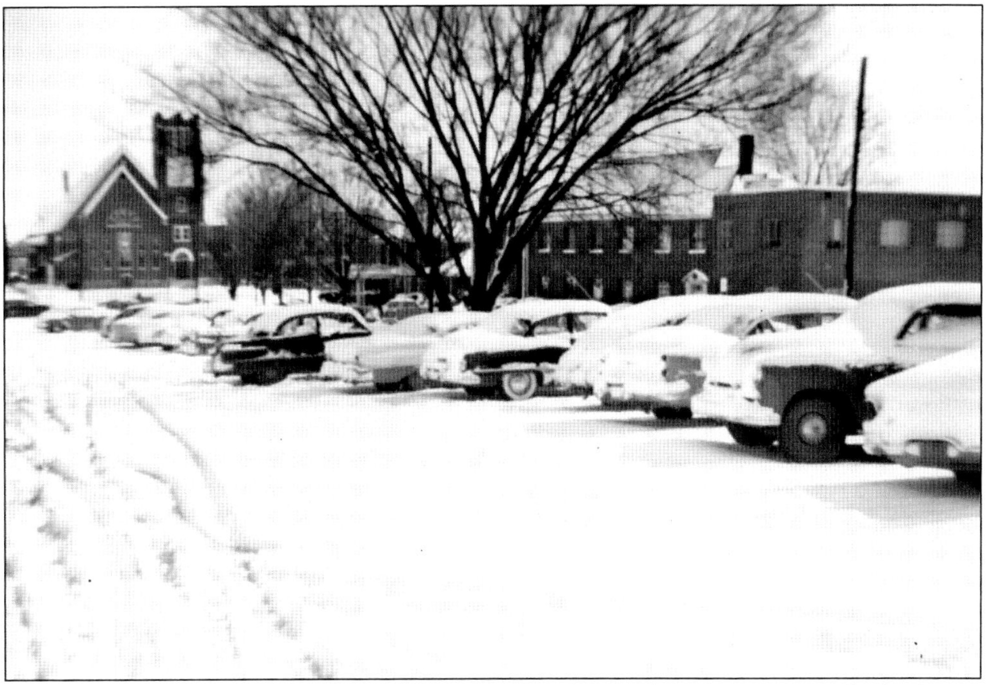

Piedmont Bible College and Salem Baptist Church are shown after a heavy snow. The landscape changed after the removal of the Kreuser-Brietz home *c.* 1818. The home was used as the college's dormitory before the present college dormitories were built.

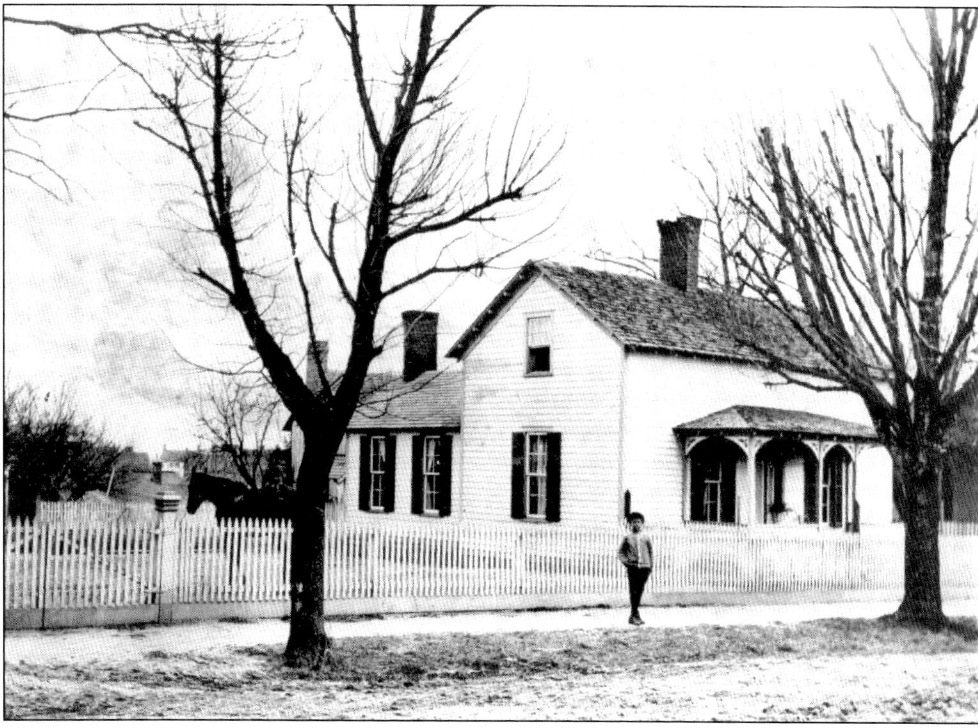

Joseph Chambers, the patriarch of the Chambers family, along with Rev. W. H. Willis, was the driving force in the organization of the first Methodist church in West Salem. Chambers allowed a tent revival in August 1902 in his side yard, and the Methodist church concept was born. His house was built in 1880 and served the family to the present day. In 1903, the first building was constructed for the Methodist church at the corner of Academy Street and Poplar Streets, shown below.

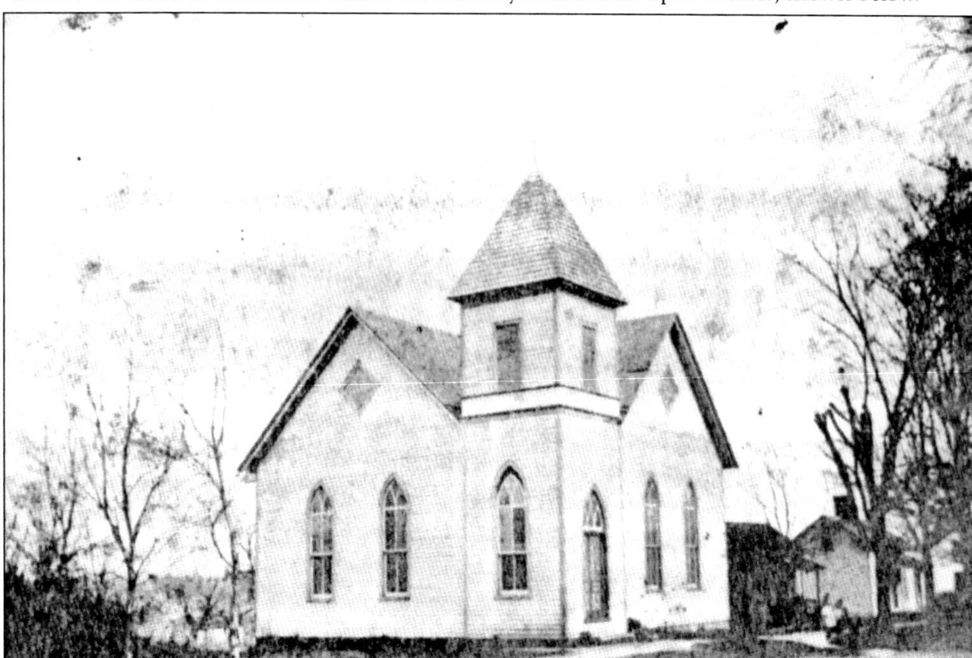

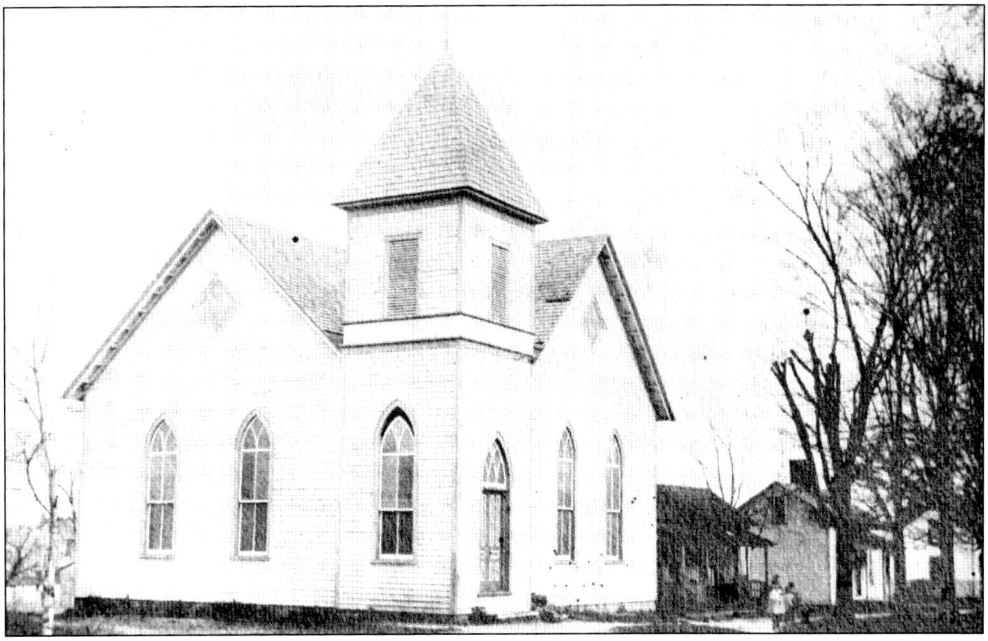

Interest was high from the beginning, and the Salem Methodist Episcopal Church, South, grew rapidly, averaging 15–20 new members annually. By 1909, three classrooms had been added to the sanctuary, two in 1908 and one in 1909. The church became a station, affiliated but independent, in 1913. The pastors during the first years of the church were students. Many stayed only one year. As most were unmarried, they roomed and boarded in the homes of members or rented. The first parsonage was not built until 1918. This photograph is in front of the First Methodist Church on Poplar Street.

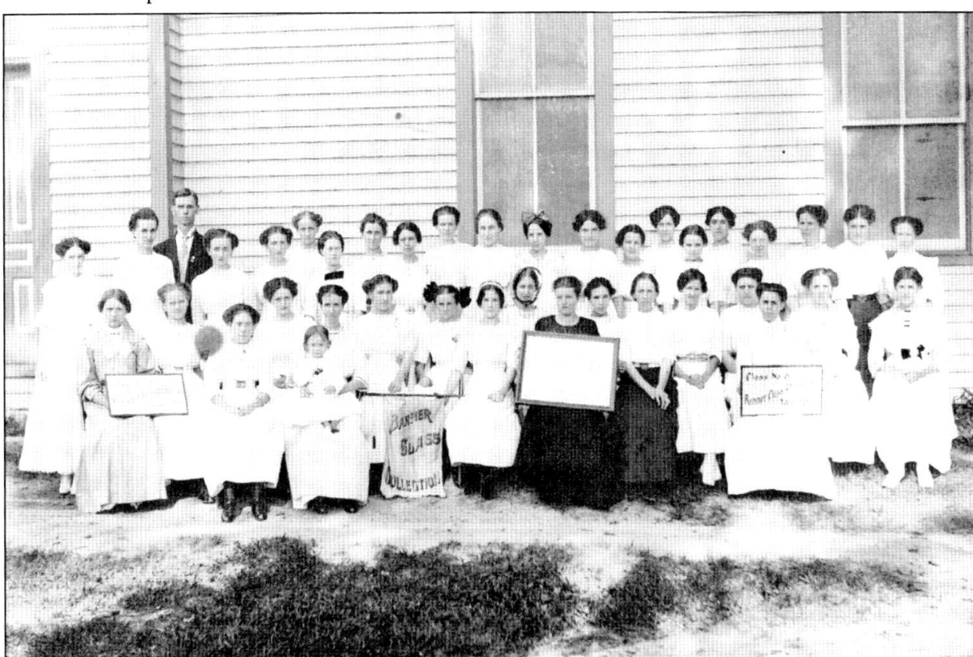

The Banner class in 1911 of the Women's club is shown in this *c.* 1911 photograph.

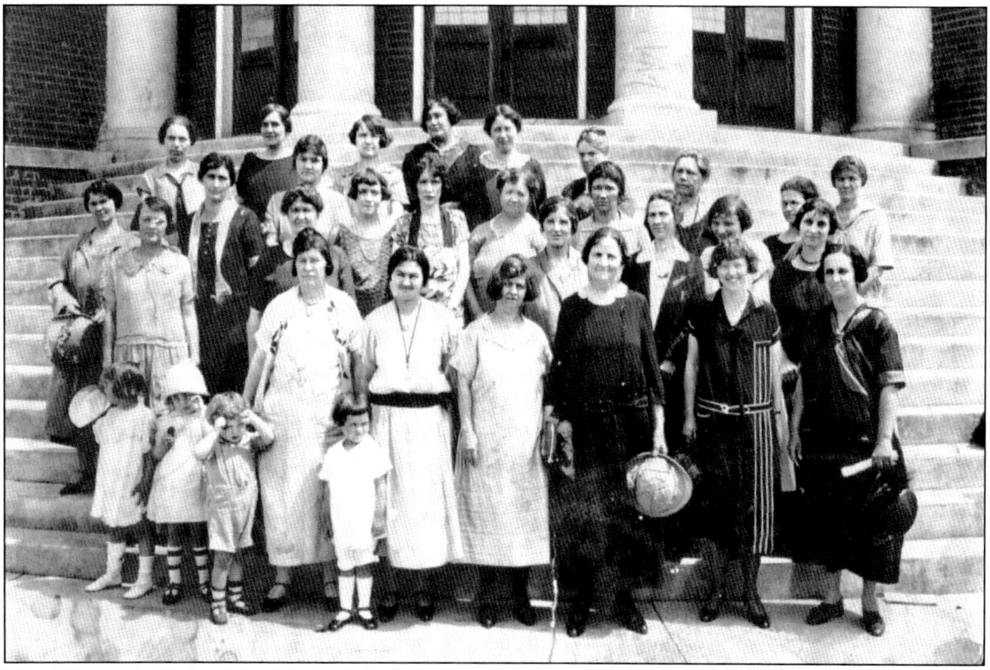

The Women's Club of the Methodist church c. 1920 was instrumental in setting the standard for improvements of the church. The congregation had grown, and the sights of the church were set higher with this club's involvement.

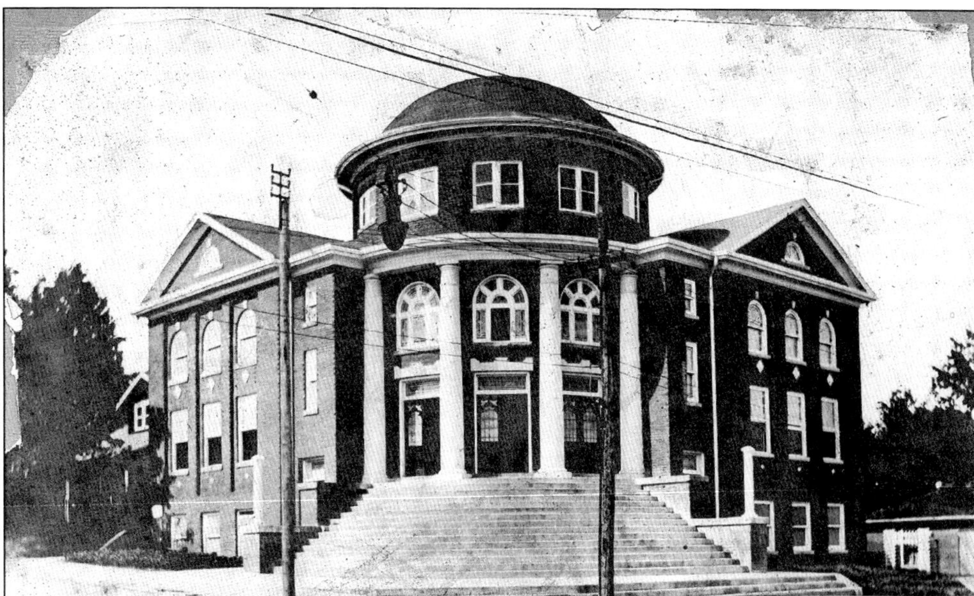

In 1920, the congregation faced new decisions. The church building was in a bad state of repair, and membership had grown to capacity. Again they made history by deciding to relocate to a lot on the corner of Green and West Streets. Construction of the new church, an Akron-style brick structure, began in 1921, the cornerstone being laid on June 19, 1921. Green Street Methodist Church is similar today except for the antique front doors. Pastor A. C. Swofford gave W. H. March this c. 1922 photograph for his services on the building committee.

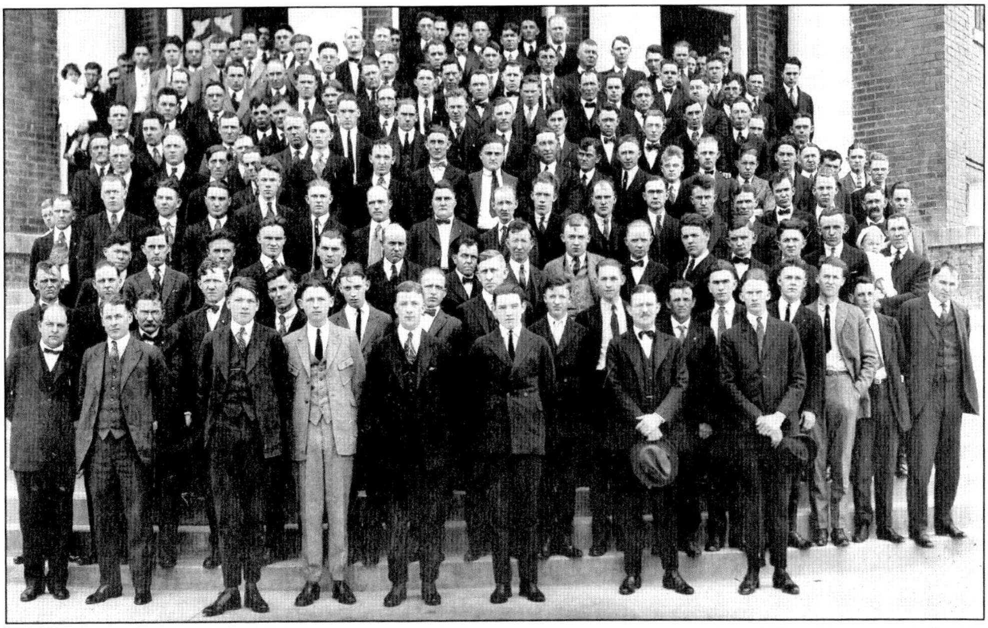

Services were held in the basement until the sanctuary was complete. The Reverend A. C. Swofford, the chief "architect" of this transition, reported in October 1921 that membership had grown to 302. A year later, there were 340 members. In October 1927, the mortgage was retired and the new church, now Green Street Methodist Episcopal Church, South, since its relocation, was dedicated. The Baraca class is shown c. 1922. Mr. and Mrs. B. F. Griffith, Mr. and Mrs. Lewis Griffith Davenport, and Mr. William Davenport are some of the members shown. Several of the Davenport family members resided at 223 South Green Street.

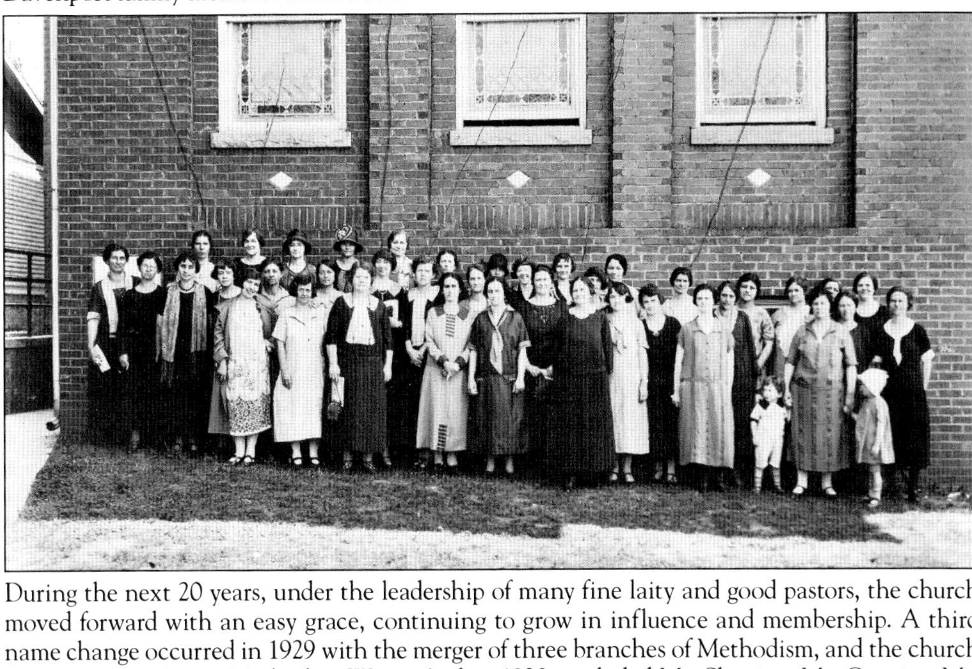

During the next 20 years, under the leadership of many fine laity and good pastors, the church moved forward with an easy grace, continuing to grow in influence and membership. A third name change occurred in 1929 with the merger of three branches of Methodism, and the church became Green Street Methodist. Women's class 1930s included Ms. Shuping, Ms. Coggins, Ms. Anna Davis, Ms. William Chambers, Mrs. Bob Miller, and Ms. Brandon.

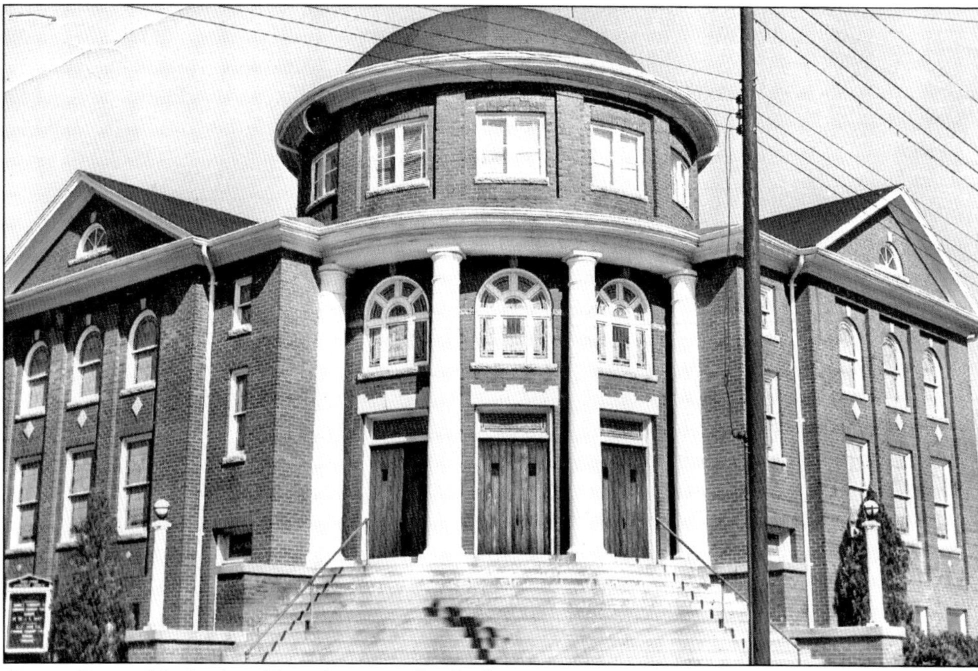

Green Street Methodist Church entered a fresh era in 1941 under the leadership of Rev. Cecil G. Hefner. During his pastorate, 1941–1945, the sanctuary was renovated throughout and the first organ installed. Additional property was purchased on Granville Drive and Shober Street, and a building fund started for an educational building. Rev. W. T. Medlin was the pastor for the church from 1960 to 1962.

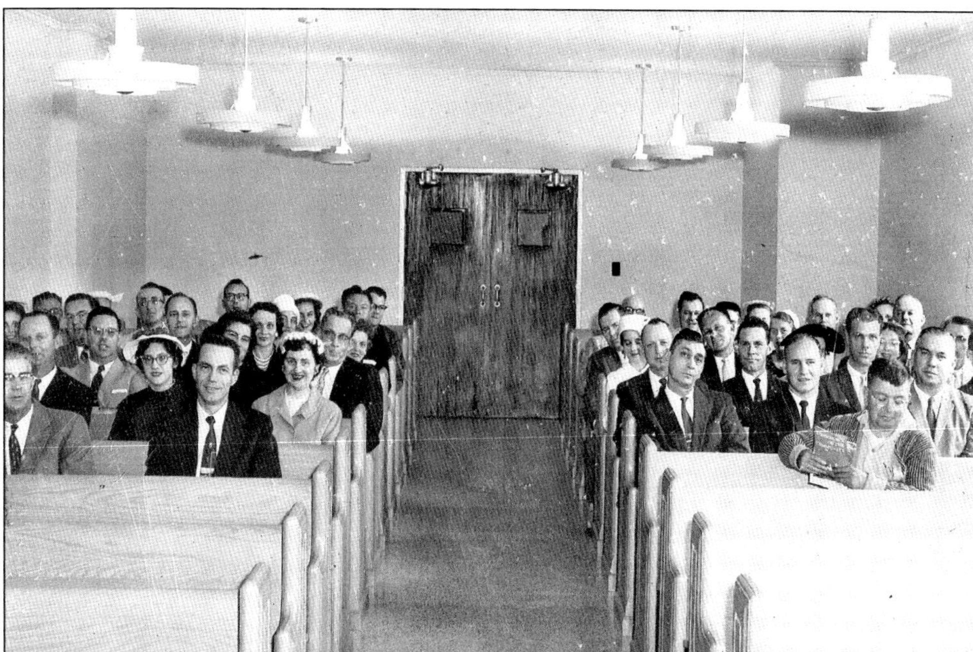

The inside of Green Street Methodist in the 1950s shows a quaintness associated with smaller churches and congregations. The lighting was good for Bible verses and hymn books.

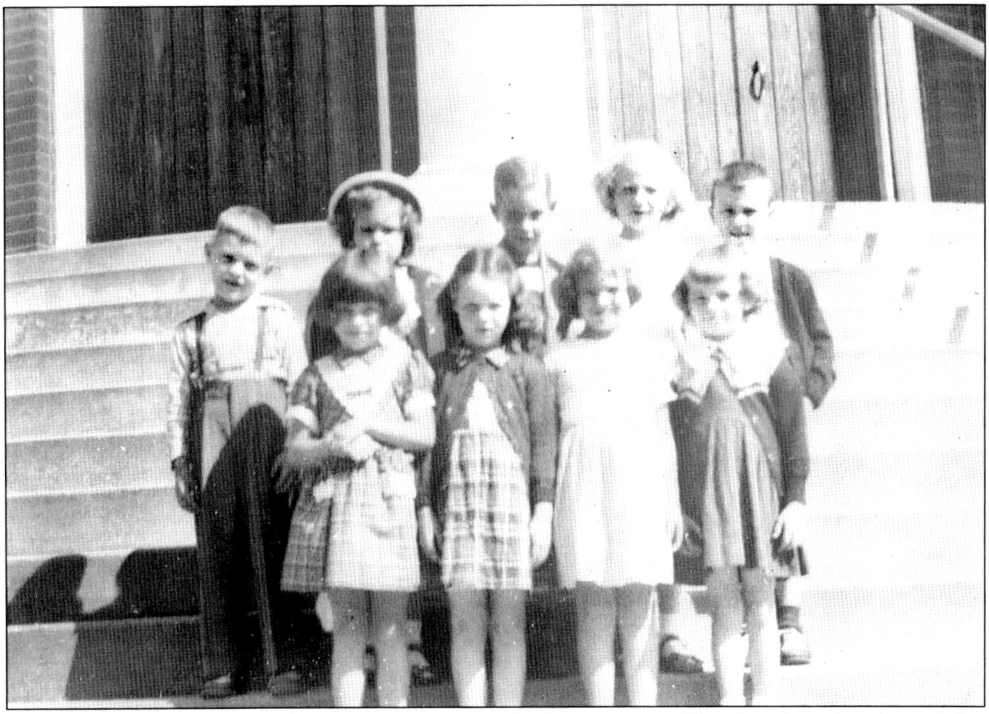

Children were central to the Green Street Methodist mission. The Sunday schools and the Vacation Bible Schools brought these West Salem children together.

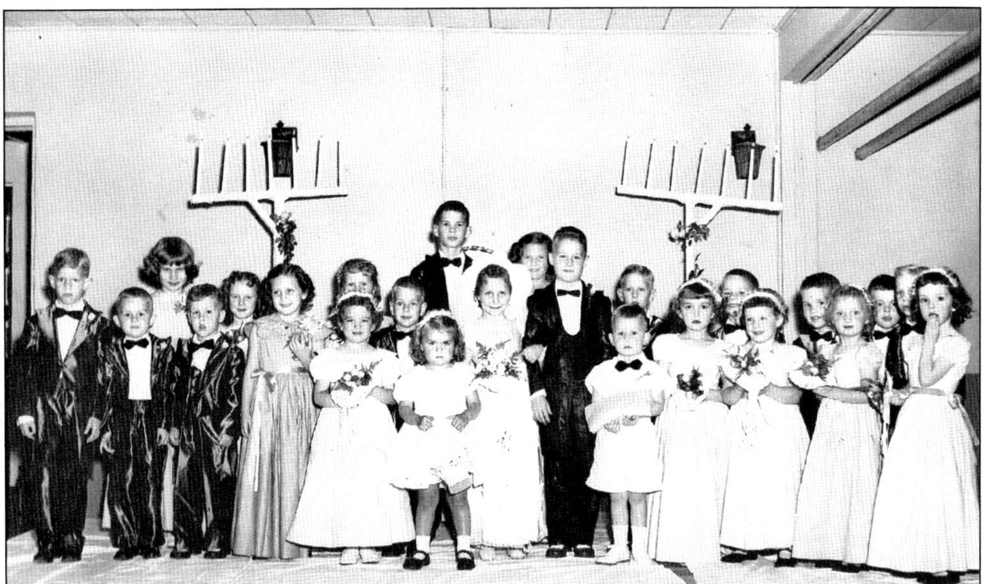

The Tom Thumb wedding *c.* 1954 was an example of an event that happened in the West Salem neighborhood throughout many years of the 20th century. A mock wedding was performed with all the participants being children. Included here are David VonCannon, Frank Froelich, Laura Evans, Joe Ellen, Beck Lanier, Susan Brown, Terry March, Tim Binkley Lynch, Steve Philo, Cynthia Chambers, Linda Brown, Phillip Froelich, Mike Froelich, Paul March, Clifford Chambers, Mary Jane Voss, Steve Ezell, Patsy Ezell, Joe Jones, and Wendy March.

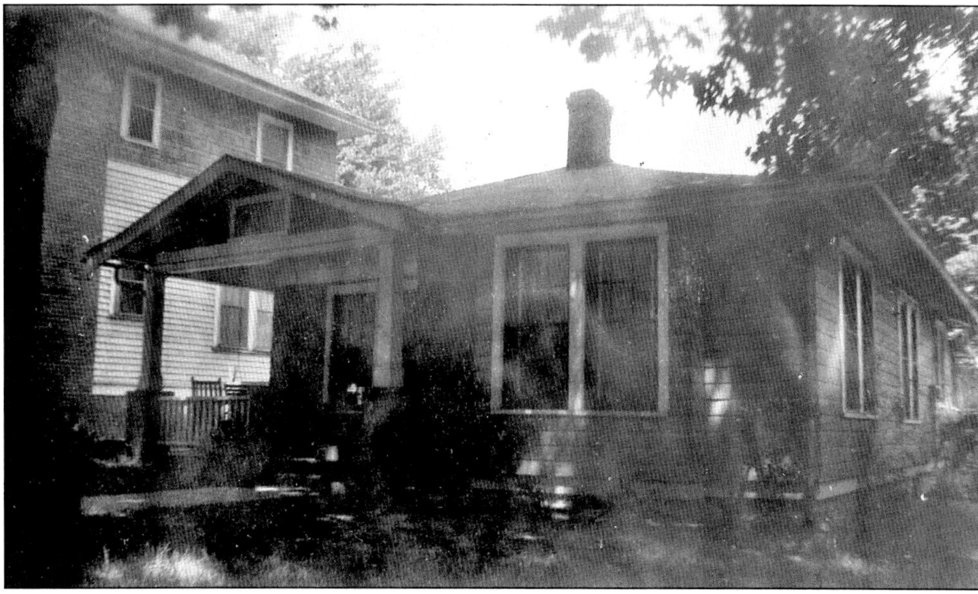

The streetscape of Green Street Methodist in 1947 shows a neighborhood with many trees and lush vegetation. The houses shown were beside the church and represent South Green Street.

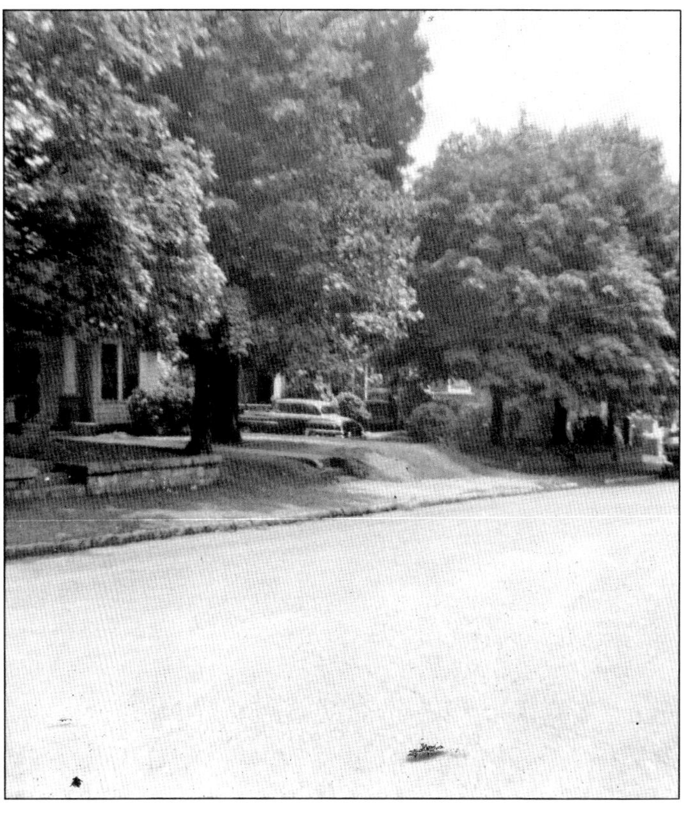

The church reached its zenith during the pastorate of Rev. Horace E. Bolick, 1951–1960. Membership mushroomed to over 600. Property was acquired across the street from the church, the present parking lot, and renovated for a parsonage. More property was purchased beside the church on Green Street, on which to build the education building. This streetscape of Green Street Methodist dates from September 1958.

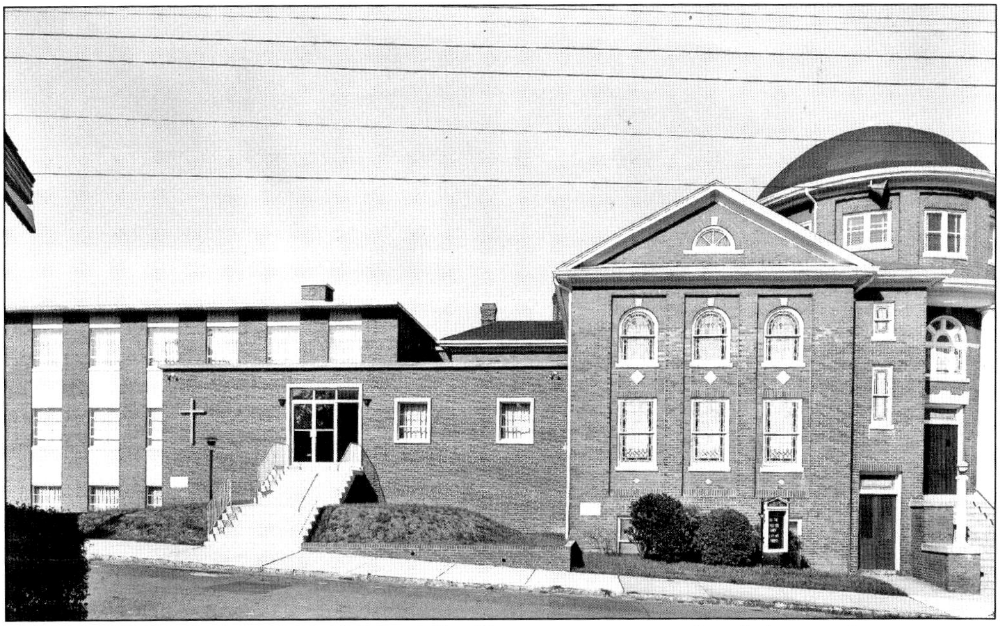

Construction began in 1958, and the new building was consecrated with laying of a cornerstone on Palm Sunday, March 22, 1959. It added 10 classrooms, a Scout room, a memorial chapel, and offices for the minister and secretary. A generous gift of $10,000 from Centenary Methodist Church helped to realize the long-awaited dream. The photograph shows the Green Street Methodist Church after additions were completed in 1959.

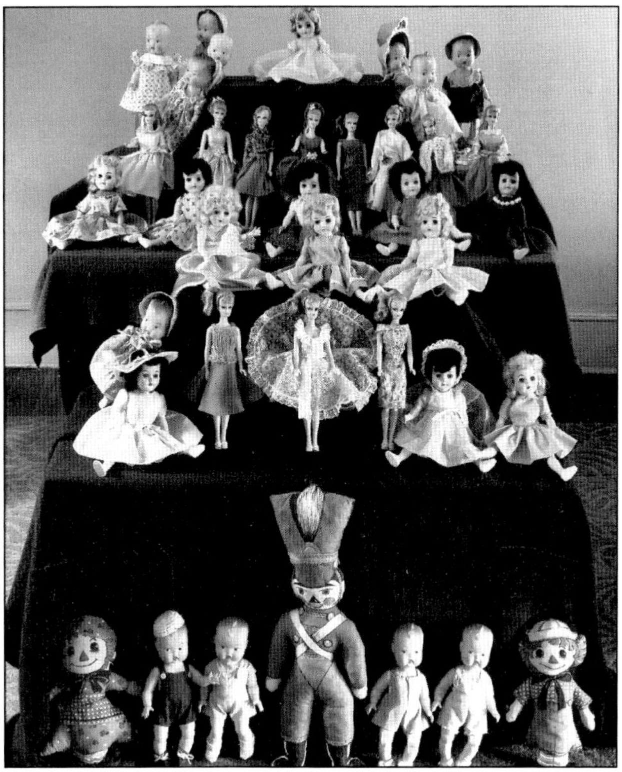

Fund-raisers have been used for many years by organizations to raise capital. The Toy Shoppe (shown at right), created by the women of Green Street Methodist Church, confirms the creativity of its church and neighborhood missions.

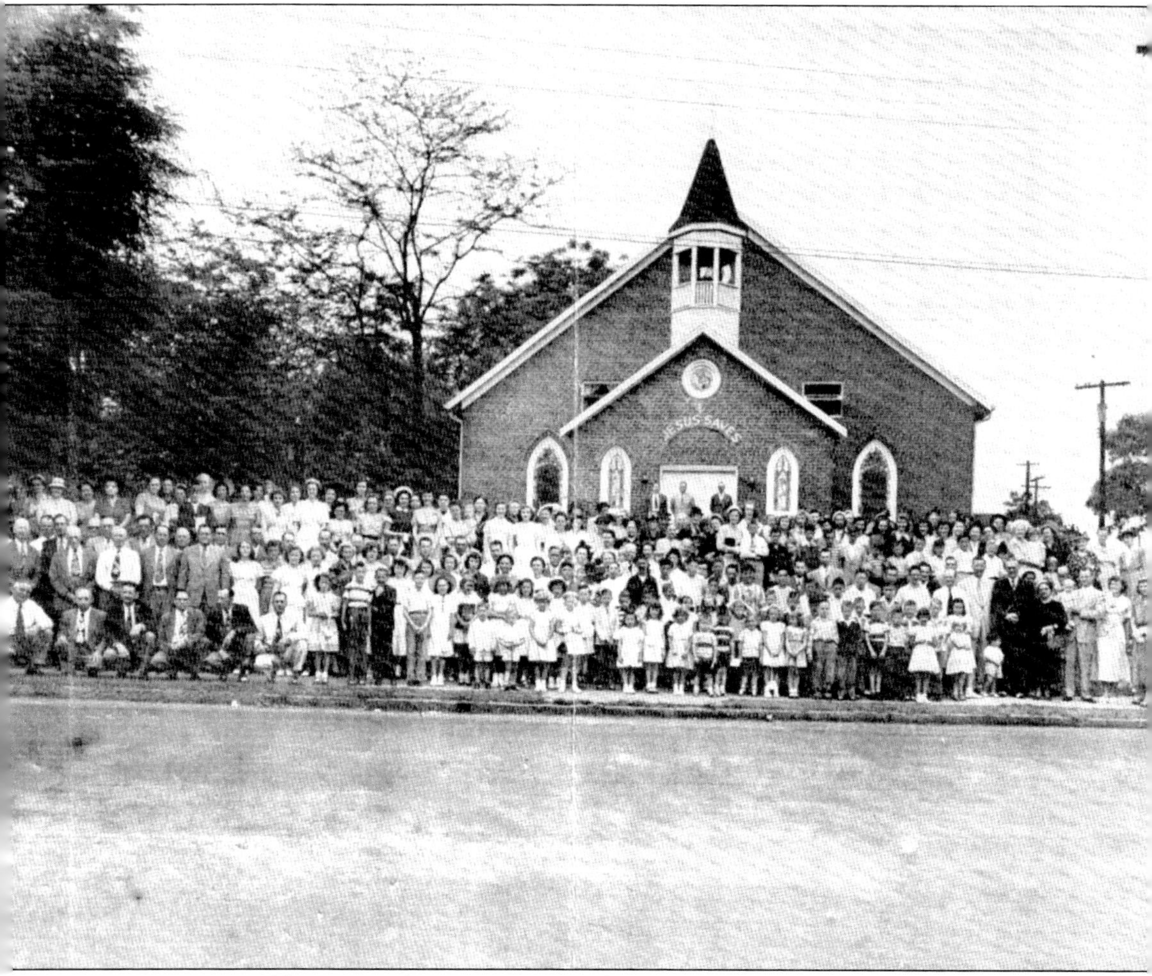

In 1908, M. B. Selder organized a congregation under a tent location on East Fifth Street. Reverend Selder and Rev. R. B. Jackson brought the message of holiness to Winston in 1907. Later in 1908, services were moved to the Fries Power House, located at the corner of Pine Street (Marshall Street) and Brookstown Avenue. The building is still standing today. From the Fries building, under the leadership of Reverend Gammons, a lot was purchased in East Winston, a tabernacle was built, and in 1909, a service was held in what was the first building in the city belonging to the Pentecostal Holiness Church. The church became a fixture throughout the East Winston neighborhood before arriving in West Salem. On July 12, 1912, a lot was purchased from Winston Development Company on Greenwood Avenue for the purpose of building an actual church building. In December 1936, a lot was purchased on the corner of Broad Street and Brookstown Avenue for a new church. The fourth Sunday in November 1937, the first service was held in what would become the Broad Street Church. The area around the church changed in the late 1960s; this church was being razed and the new one built on Hutton Street in 1970. Behind the church property on Green Street, a historical treasure was discovered in a small frame house before it was destroyed. The house was found to be a log cabin and contained the original free schoolhouse of West Salem c. 1847, which had been moved from Liberty Street and First Street in the late 1890s to this site.

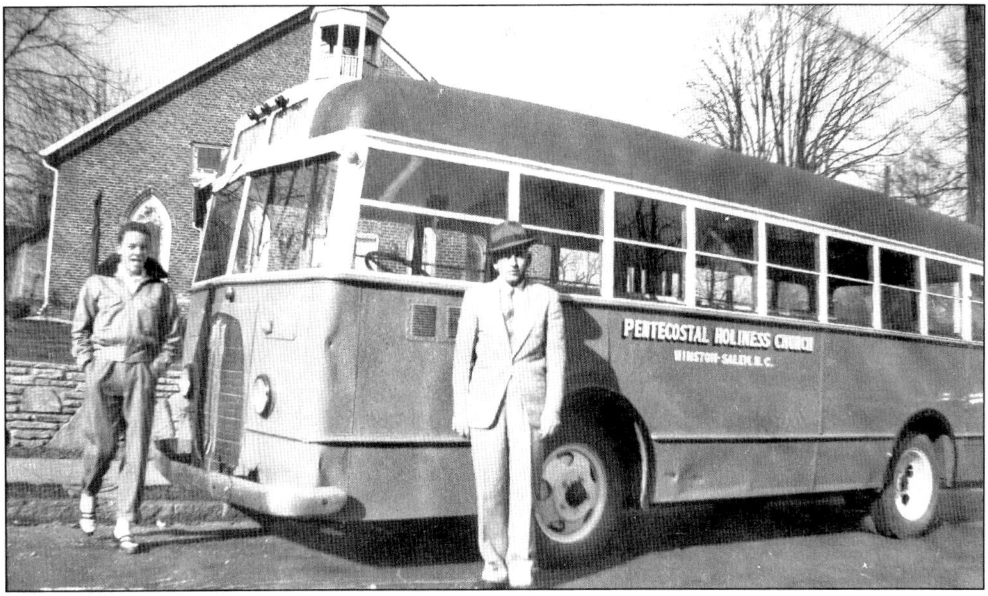

The church bus was an important player in the success of the West Salem neighborhood churches. Throughout the neighborhood's existence, transportation to church events brought out all types of vehicles to the neighborhood. Later buses were the normal transportation; however, wagons, bicycles, and even motorbikes served the residents in earlier days. King Brown of West Street told of his travels throughout the West Salem neighborhood by bicycle. He made sure all the children were awake and ready for Sunday school. The houses in the bottom photograph on the right were 128 and 130 South Broad Street. The style of houses was typical of the Broad Street homes in West End and West Salem, which were along this stretch of roadway.

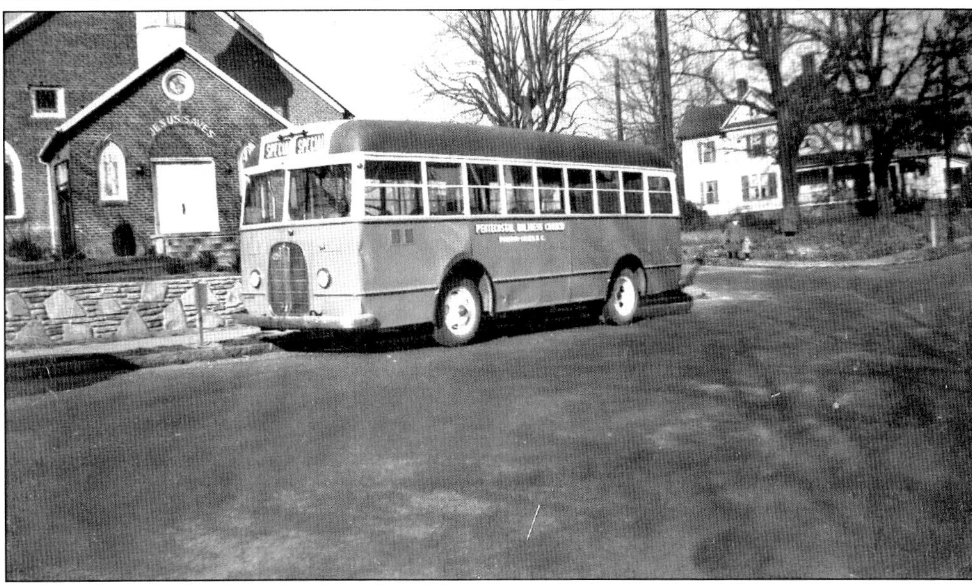

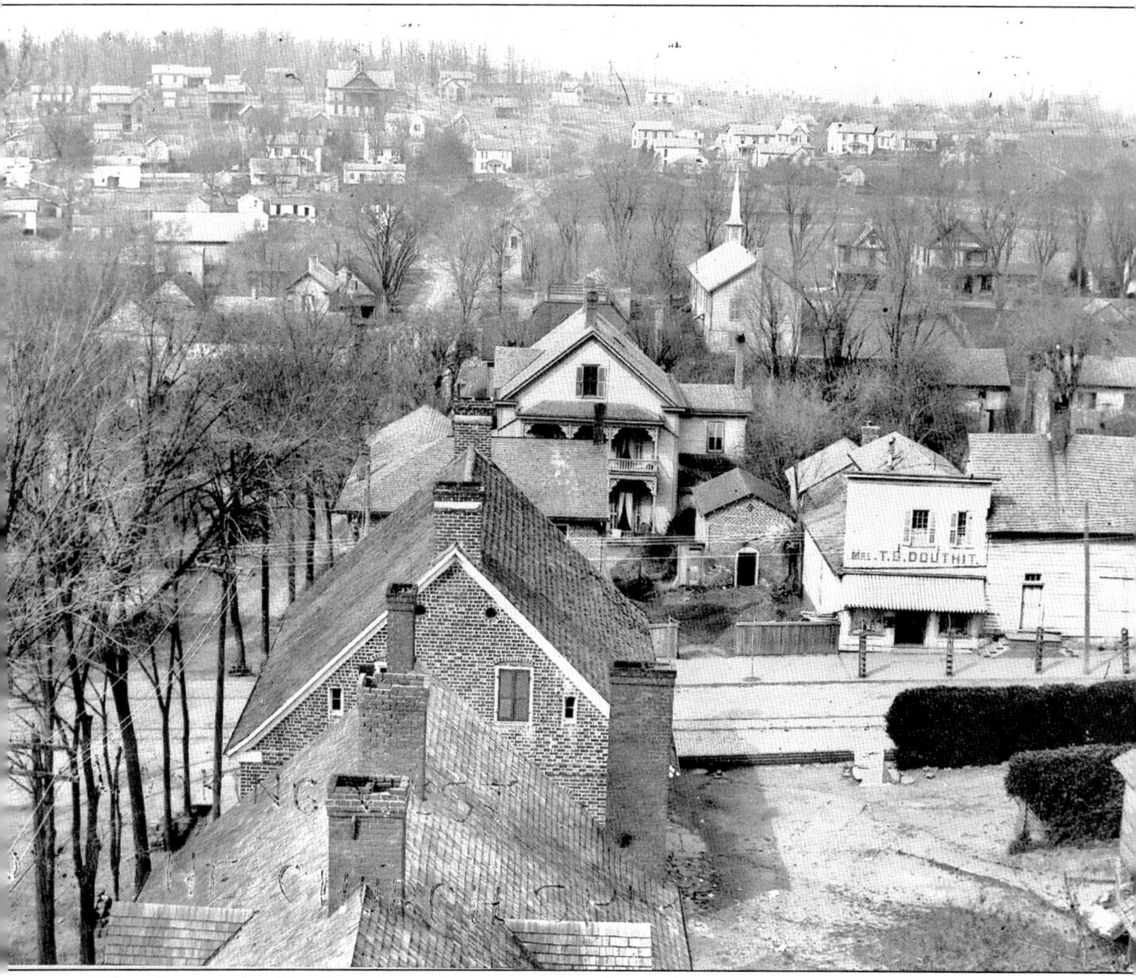

The photograph taken from Home Moravian Church on Church Street and Academy Street defines the landscape of West Salem in the 1890s. Education was found in two distinctive structures; the steeple of Elm Street Church can be seen located at the center of the photograph. Elm Church, *c.* 1867, housed a graded school after the close of the Civil War. Moving farther west at the center along Academy Street, the West Salem Graded School, *c.* 1890, can be found. This was the current grammar school at the time this photograph was taken. The expansion of West Salem is evident beyond Elm Street Chapel. The ridge in the uppermost part of the photograph is the developing streetscape of Green, Franklin, and Bank Streets. Research has also shown many residents resided in the peach orchards. The peach orchards were planted and harvested with other fruit trees by the early Moravians of West Salem in the 18th and early 19th centuries. A short time after this photograph was taken, Christ Chapel and Christ Moravian Church were built.

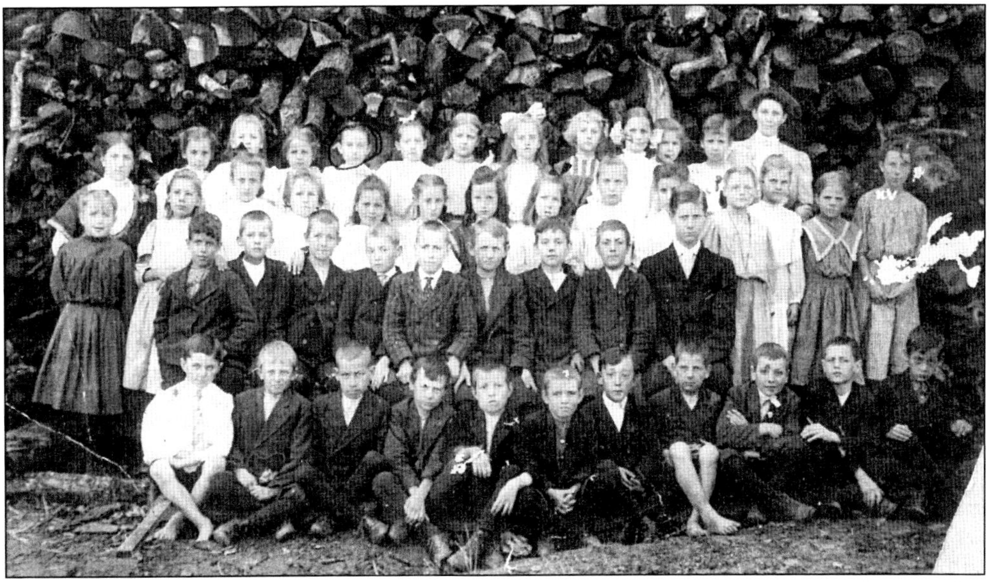

The following photograph, c. 1909, includes the third-grade class of the West Salem Graded School. Included here are teacher, Ms. Maggie Rierson, and students Lee Shore, Rosa Petree, Raymond Brinkley, Howard Brewer, Doug Lee, Paul Butner, Massey Shore, Maude Teshe, Dalton Orrell, Laura Monday, and Ruben Ziglar.

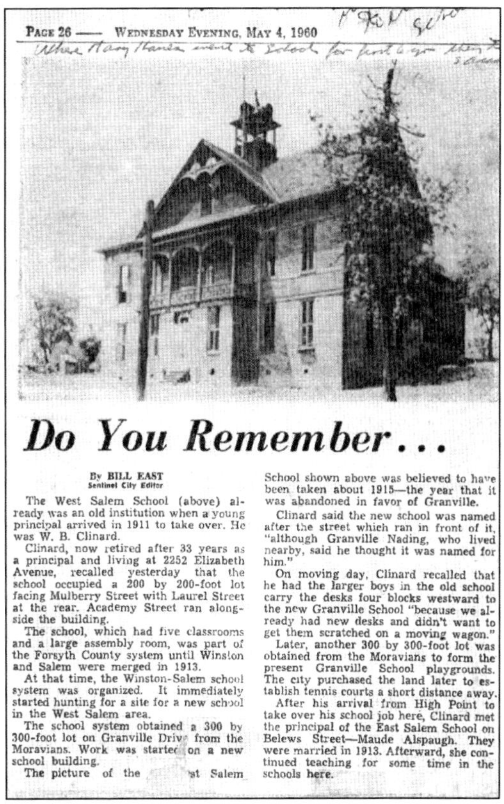

PAGE 26 —— WEDNESDAY EVENING, MAY 4, 1960

Do You Remember . . .

By BILL EAST
Sentinel City Editor

The West Salem School (above) already was an old institution when a young principal arrived in 1911 to take over. He was W. B. Clinard.

Clinard, now retired after 33 years as a principal and living at 2252 Elizabeth Avenue, recalled yesterday that the school occupied a 200 by 200-foot lot facing Mulberry Street with Laurel Street at the rear. Academy Street ran alongside the building.

The school, which had five classrooms and a large assembly room, was part of the Forsyth County system until Winston and Salem were merged in 1913.

At that time, the Winston-Salem school system was organized. It immediately started hunting for a site for a new school in the West Salem area.

The school system obtained a 300 by 300-foot lot on Granville Drive from the Moravians. Work was started on a new school building.

The picture of the [illegible]st Salem School shown above was believed to have been taken about 1915—the year that it was abandoned in favor of Granville.

Clinard said the new school was named after the street which ran in front of it, "although Granville Nading, who lived nearby, said he thought it was named for him."

On moving day, Clinard recalled that he had the larger boys in the old school carry the desks four blocks westward to the new Granville School "because we already had new desks and didn't want to get them scratched on a moving wagon."

Later, another 300 by 300-foot lot was obtained from the Moravians to form the present Granville School playgrounds. The city purchased the land later to establish tennis courts a short distance away.

After his arrival from High Point to take over his school job here, Clinard met the principal of the East Salem School on Belews Street—Maude Alspaugh. They were married in 1913. Afterward, she continued teaching for some time in the schools here.

"Do You Remember" articles were an invention of Bill East in the 1950s and 1960s. He was a writer for the *Winston-Salem Journal and Sentinel*. One of his specialties was as a lay historian in Winston-Salem history. This article gave information on West Salem Graded School, c. 1890.

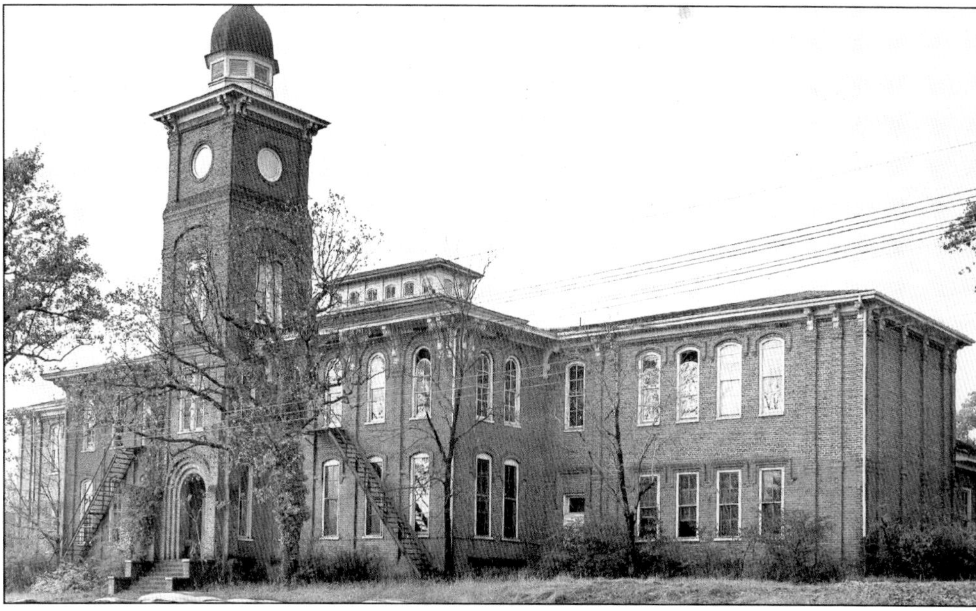

Winston Graded School on Fourth Street was the first graded school, championed by Calvin H. Wiley. His seven-year endeavor to bring the school into existence paid off in more ways than one. Literally a neighborhood grew around the school. Along Broad Street and Green Street, the first West End neighborhood developed. Broad and Green Streets ran through to the West Salem neighborhood. The link between West End and West Salem was apparent with large, 1880s-era mansions. Winston Graded School changed to West End School around 1900. Wiley continued in education and became the most progressive state superintendent in the South.

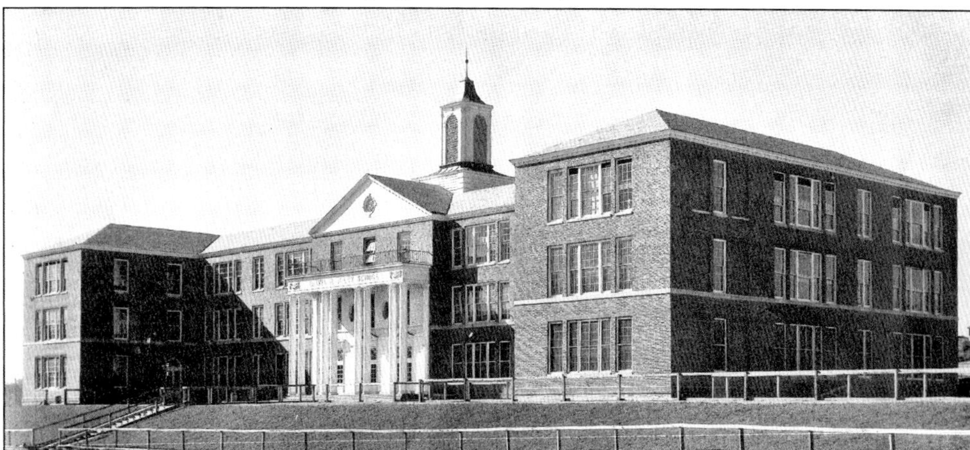

Calvin Wiley was a pioneer in education after the Civil War. He championed public and state-supported schools for all people. Wiley School was named in his honor. The school sat on the ridge above Hanes Park and was constructed in the 1920s at the same time as Reynolds High School and Reynolds Auditorium on Northwest Boulevard. Wiley School was a grammar school with grades one through eight. The educational facilities of Wiley School and Reynolds High School next door brought an educational usage to the former West Salem 18th and 19th industrial outlets of Brother Gottlieb Schober and his son-in-law, Brother Niemen Van Zeverly. The photograph was taken at Wiley School's opening by Mr. Matthews, a professional photographer who resided in Winston.

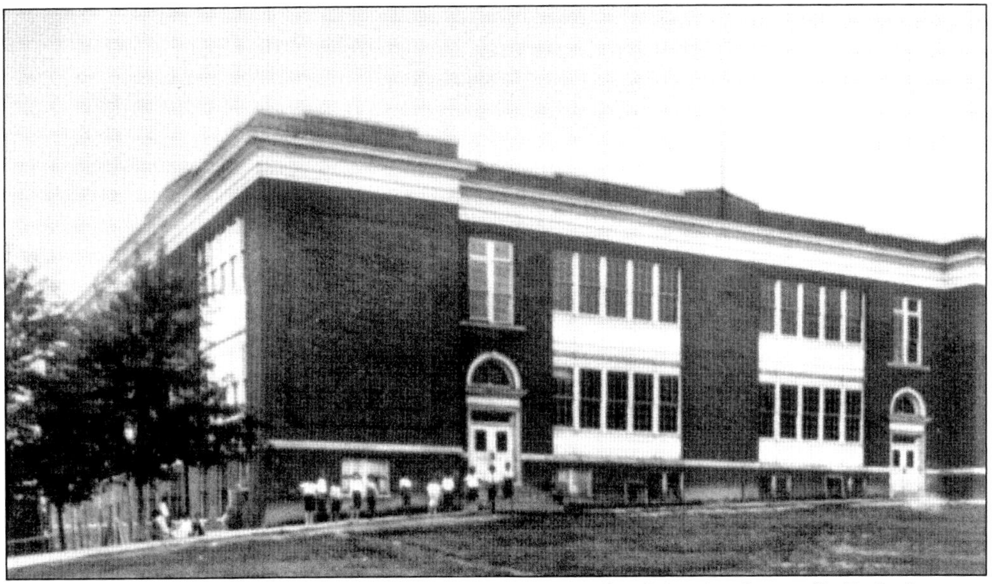

Granville School was built as the permanent grammar school for the Granville Park division, c. 1914, in West Salem. The school was credited by state educators as one of the best grammar schools in the state.

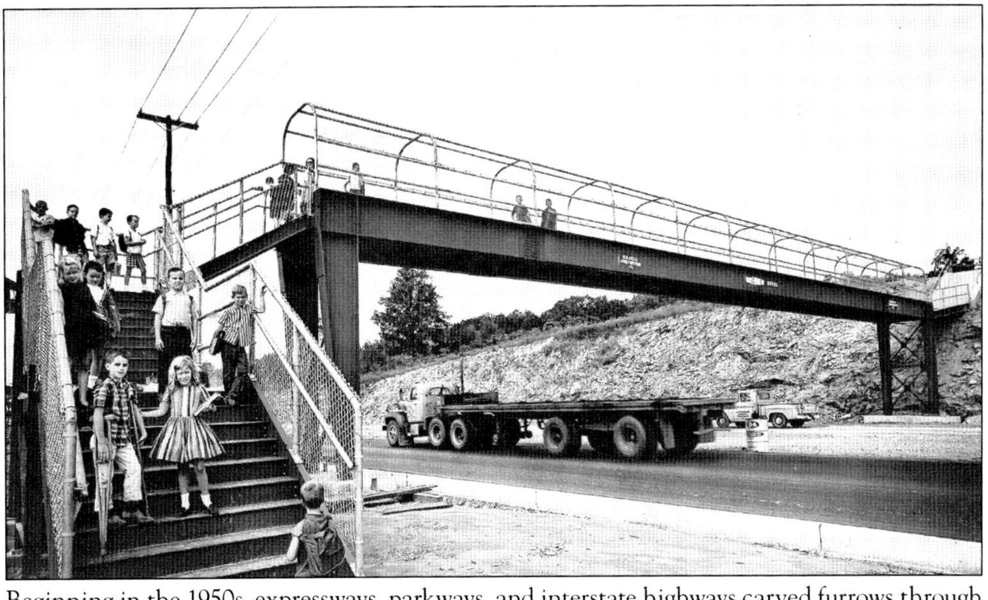

Beginning in the 1950s, expressways, parkways, and interstate highways carved furrows through our city's landscape. This early-1960s photograph shows a steel walkway bridge, which extended above the newly constructed Peters Creek Parkway. The parkway bridge connected the eastern side of the Ardmore neighborhood with the western edge of West Salem. The main usage of the bridge was to safely bring Ardmore children to West Salem to attend Latham Elementary School on Hutton Street. Latham School had recently replaced Granville School as West Salem's neighborhood school. Ardmore children were assigned to the school, and in its early days of the 1950s, Latham School was called the Ardmore–West Salem Elementary School. The bridge was taken down 30 years later, and the ties that once bound Ardmore and West Salem students were also severed.

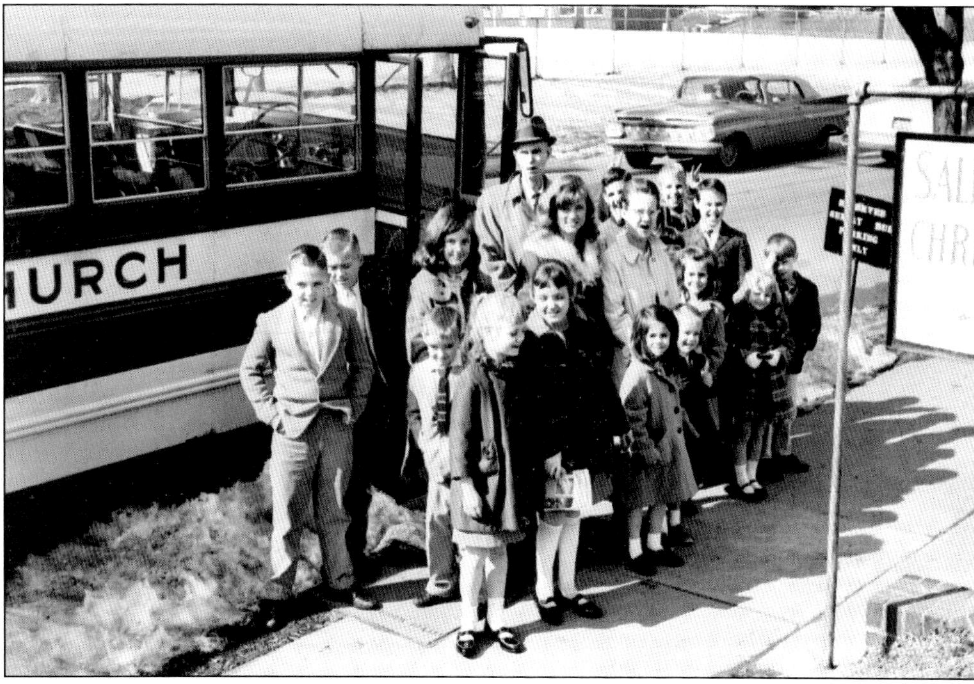

The above photograph shows the front of Salem Baptist Christian School on Broad Street in the 1960s. Notice the fencing in the background of the photograph. This was the time when West Salem lost one of its oldest historic structures, the *c.* 1818 Kreuser-Brietz house, which was directly across from the church. The bottom photograph shows the rear of the church along Spring Street at the same time as the top photograph.

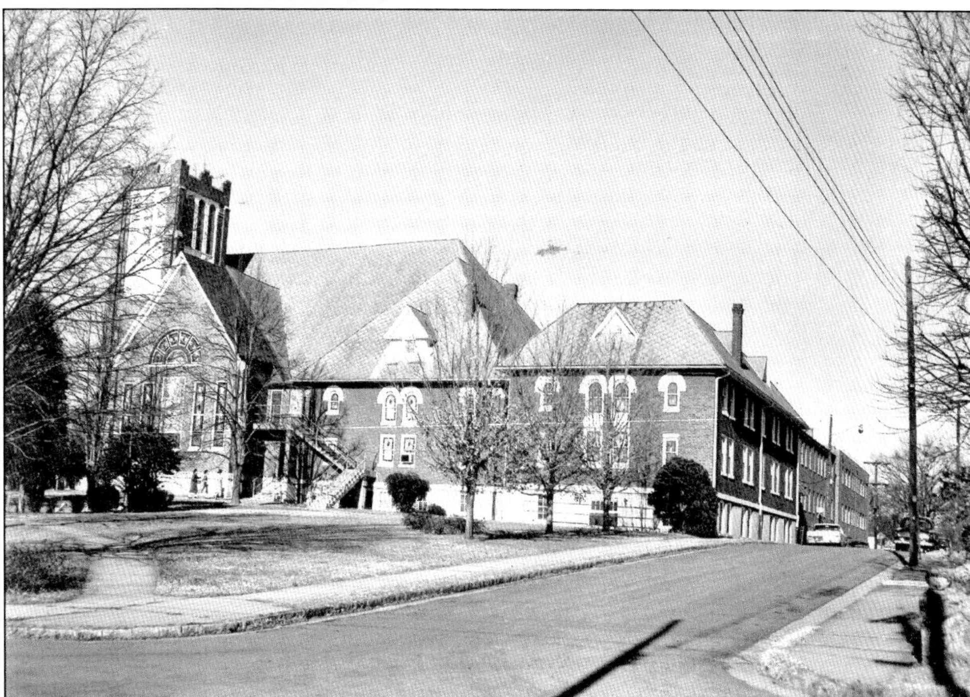

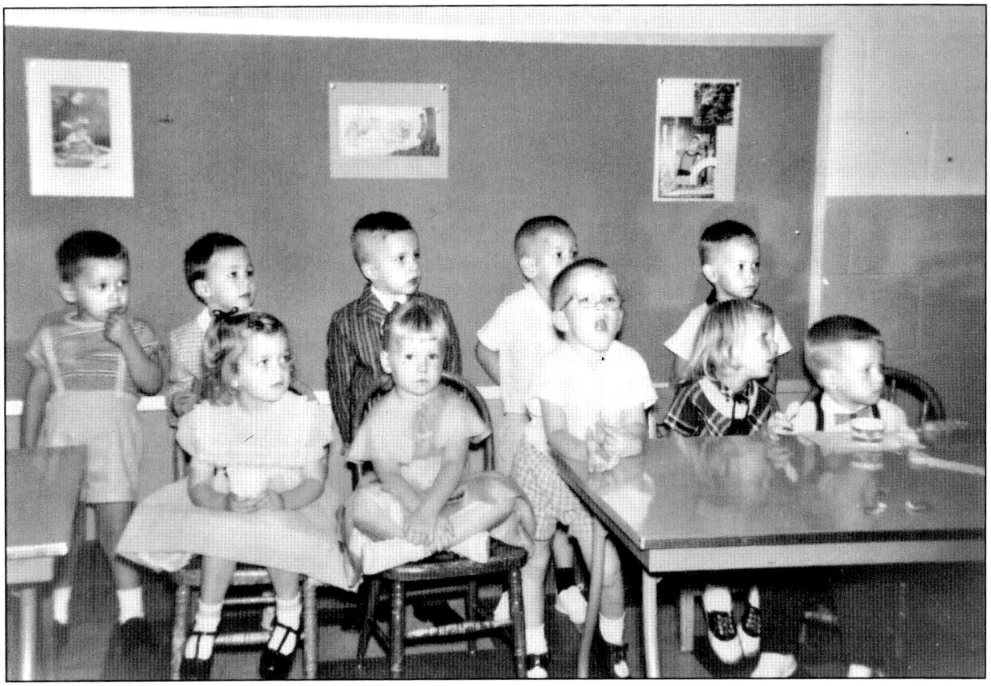

The West Salem neighborhood has been blessed with many schools of higher learning. The West Salem Educational facilities were added to with the beginning of Salem Baptist Christian School on Broad Street. An early class is shown above. Mr. King Brown of West Salem, 921 West Street, is credited with beginning the Piedmont Bible Book Store on Trade Street downtown. The bookstore was an offspring business of Bible College on Frankin Street in West Salem.

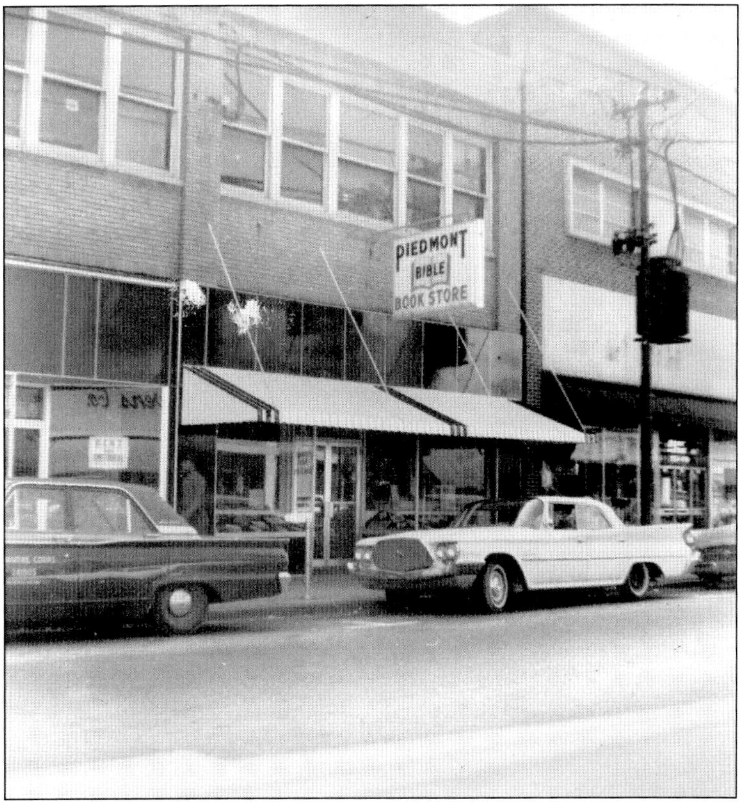

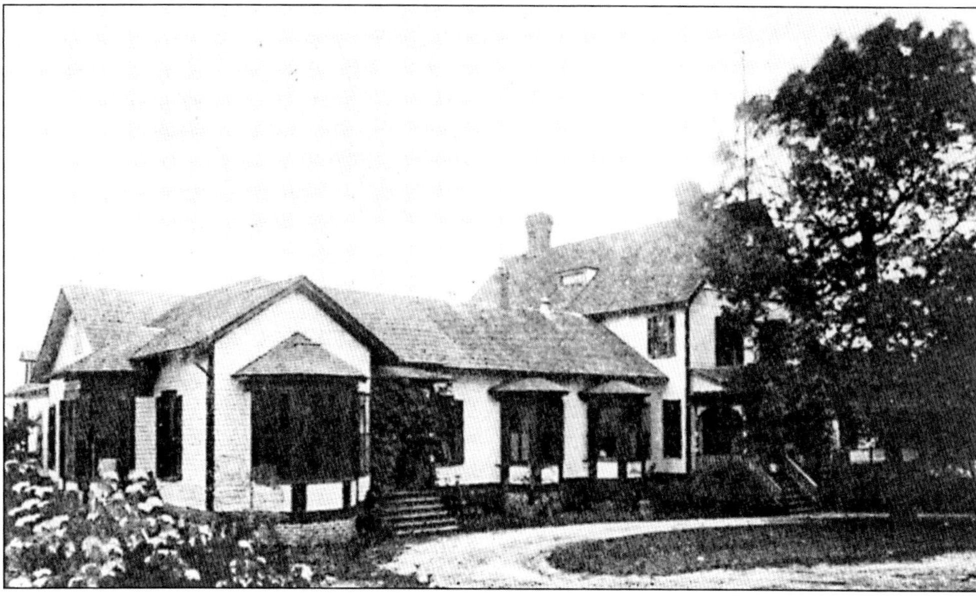

Twin-City Hospital and teaching facility is shown. The establishment of a public hospital began by a group of women in 1887. They formed themselves into the Twin-City Hospital Association at the residence of Dr. Henry Bahnson. The old Martin Grogan home on Liberty Street was their first facility, c. 1887. The Grogan house became inadequate, and the Twin-City Hospital was moved to a one-story frame building on Brookstown Avenue. It contained one ward and three private rooms, with a total accommodation of 17 beds. The time frame of the hospital on Brookstown Avenue had the facility on the border of West Salem. Brookstown Avenue was the northern border of West Salem and Winston's West End neighborhood.

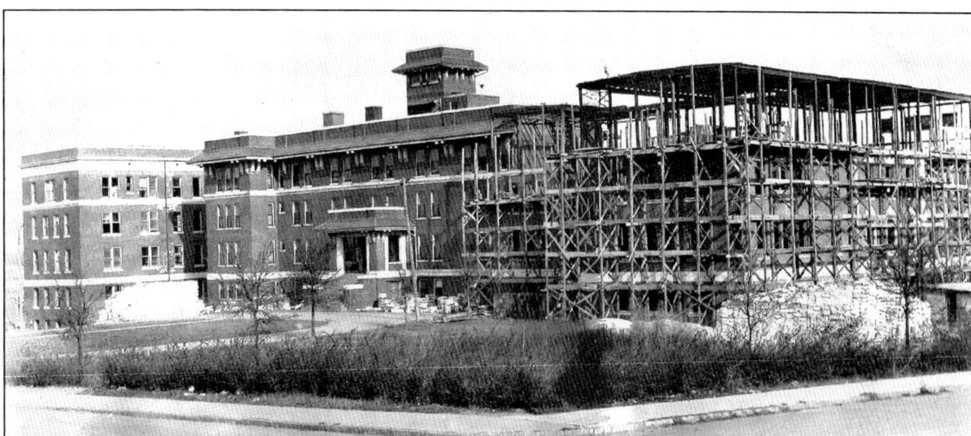

City Hospital and teaching facility is shown. The Twin-City Hospital on Brookstown Avenue became obsolete, and in 1914, the City Hospital was built. In 1915, a nurses' home was built by the ladies of the Twin-City Hospital Association after the sale of the building on Brookstown Avenue. Tobacco magnate R. J. Reynolds gave $240,000 to the city for building two additions to the hospital. In 1922, the North Reynolds Wing for black patients was completed, and in 1924, construction on the South Reynolds Wing was finished. In 1930, a nursing school was added. Many nurses and hospital workers called West Salem home.

Three

Residents Shape the Neighborhood and City

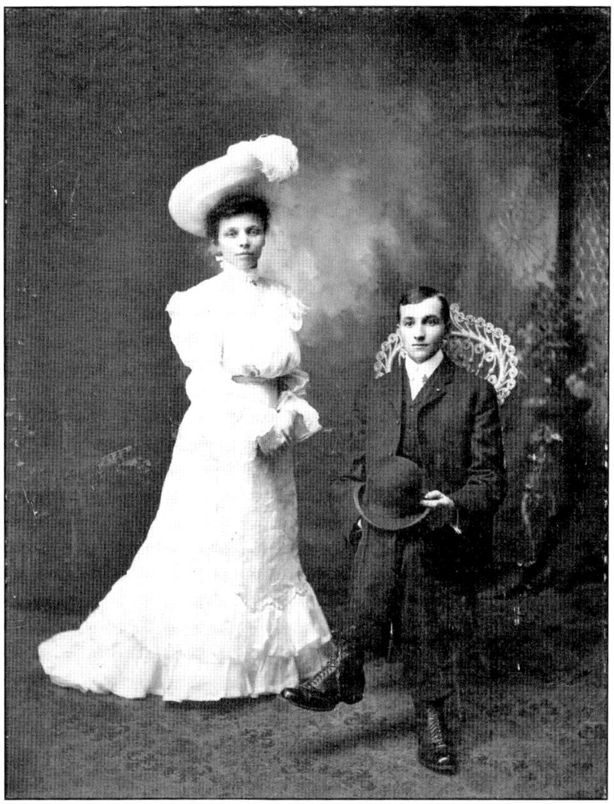

The Fries family was instrumental in shaping, developing, and building Salem and Winston. Much like the Fries family, the Ruff family played an important part in shaping and developing the homes and businesses in West Salem land. Ida and John Ruff Sr., pictured, were the pioneering patriarchs of the Ruff family, who began the task of reclaiming West Salem's history.

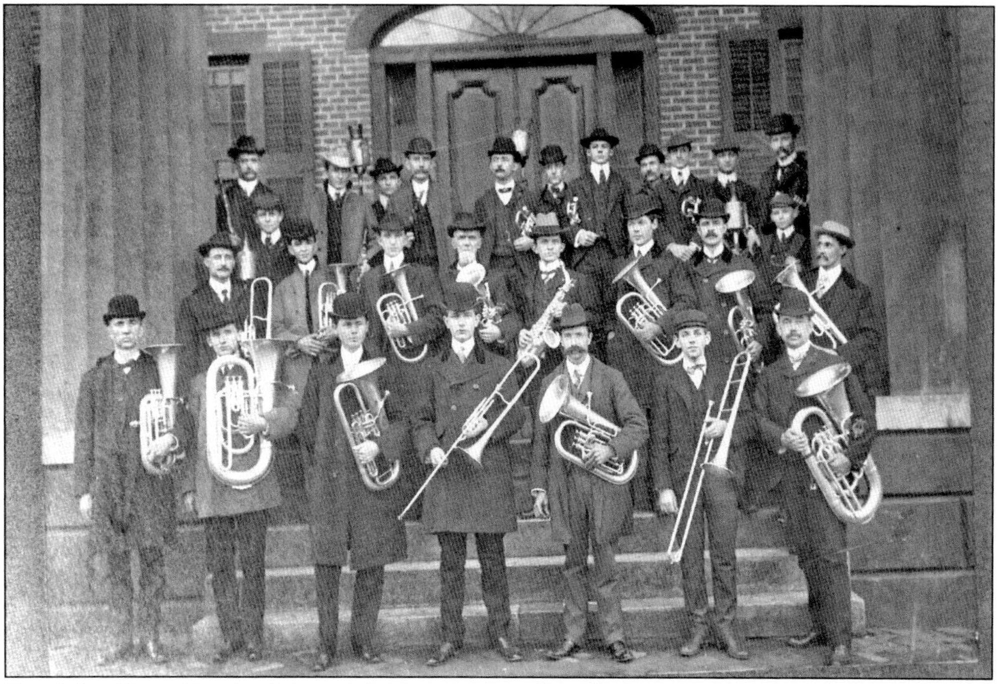

The Salem Easter Band is shown with participant and Civil War veteran Sam Mickey (second row, center, with the beard). Mickey resided in the West Salem neighborhood and was commissioned as a captain in the Confederate army.

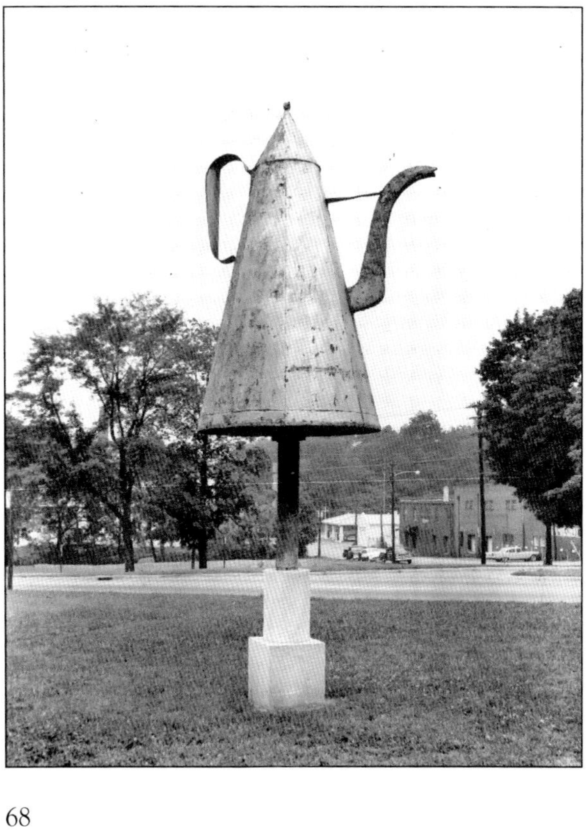

The symbol of the city, the Salem coffee pot, was moved to this location in the 1950s after the opening of Interstate 40. The coffee pot had survived nearly three-quarters of a century at its location on Main Street. J. E. Mickey and his brother, Harry Mickey established their business on Main Street with the coffee pot as their symbol. Harry resided in West Salem in his later years at 613 West Street.

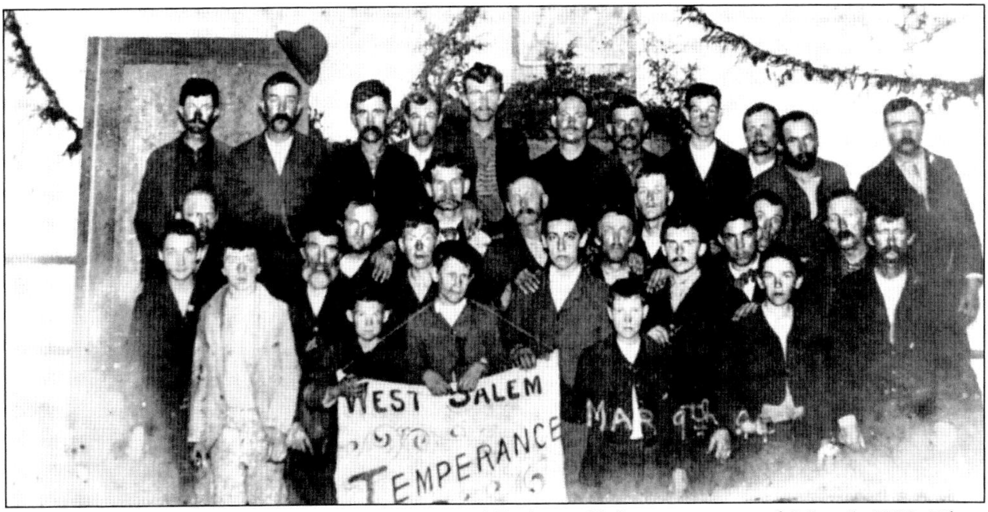

The West Salem Temperance Association and Reform Club was organized May 5, 1893. They met at the Elm Street Hall. L. W. Seabait, president, worked as a salesman in stoves and cooking supplies. His home was on Franklin Street. W. G. Knight, vice president, was a shoemaker and resided on Wachovia Street. T. C. Hege, secretary, was involved in the ownership of Salem Iron Works, and his home was on South Liberty Street. W. F. Hailey, assistant secretary, was a shoemaker who lived on South Green Street. J. W. Linebach, treasurer, was a dyer, and his home was on S. Green Street. R. N. Paige, sergeant at arms, was retired. W. M. Binkley was the chaplain. The West Salem Temperance Association helped in the organization of the Prohibition movement of the early 20th century.

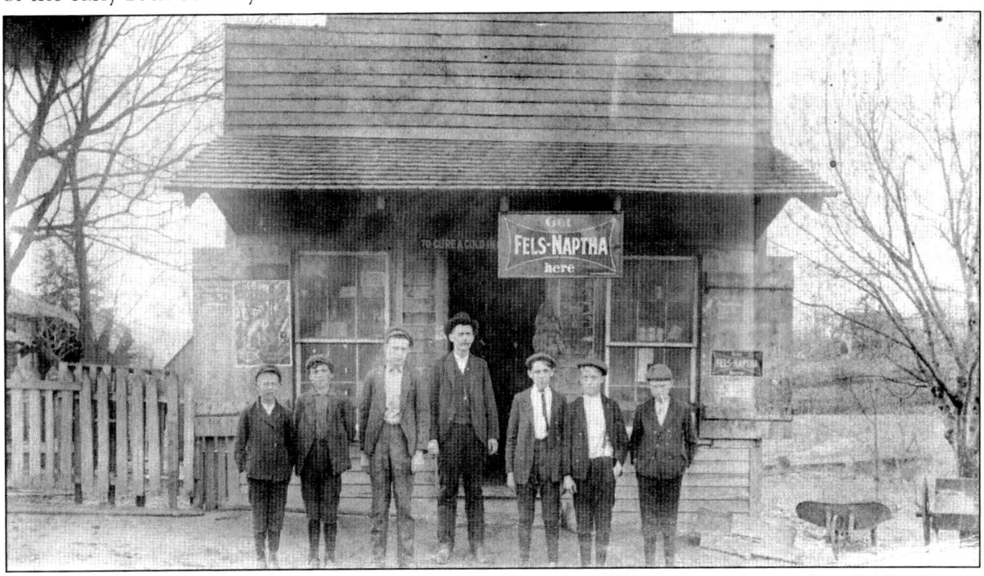

A. W. Pettycord built this store in the early 1900s. Pettycord's home was located at 618 Mulberry Street. The house is a 19th-century structure that exists today. The store was later owned by Virgil Joyce, who resided at 607 South Green Street. Joyce was remembered by older residents as one who provided deliveries in his Model T Ford. The store shown was located at 300 West Street. Today the property is owned by Philip Vanhorn. Vanhorn has done extensive landscaping on his property and found a partial-brick foundation underground in the area where the store existed. The address in present day in 510 West Street.

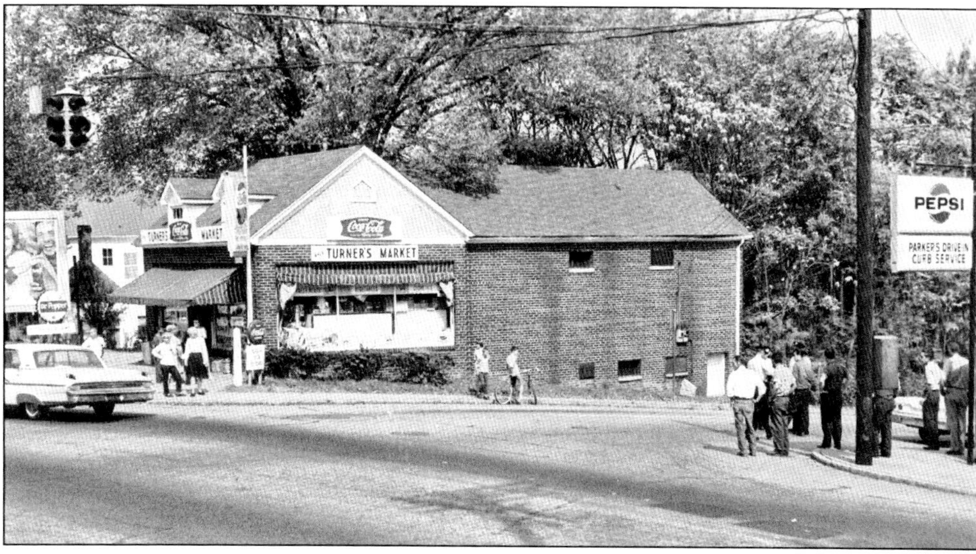

The Greenfront Grocery Store is a neighborhood store built in 1924 at the corner of Broad and First Streets. This store in its early years was run by Mr. and Mrs. Robert Turner. Turner had started his employment in the produce and general store business in the 1900s. The 1918 City Directory of Winston-Salem shows nearly 150 "ma and pa" grocery stores in town. With the limits of the town encompassing only the older neighborhoods of today, a grocery store on every corner was feasible.

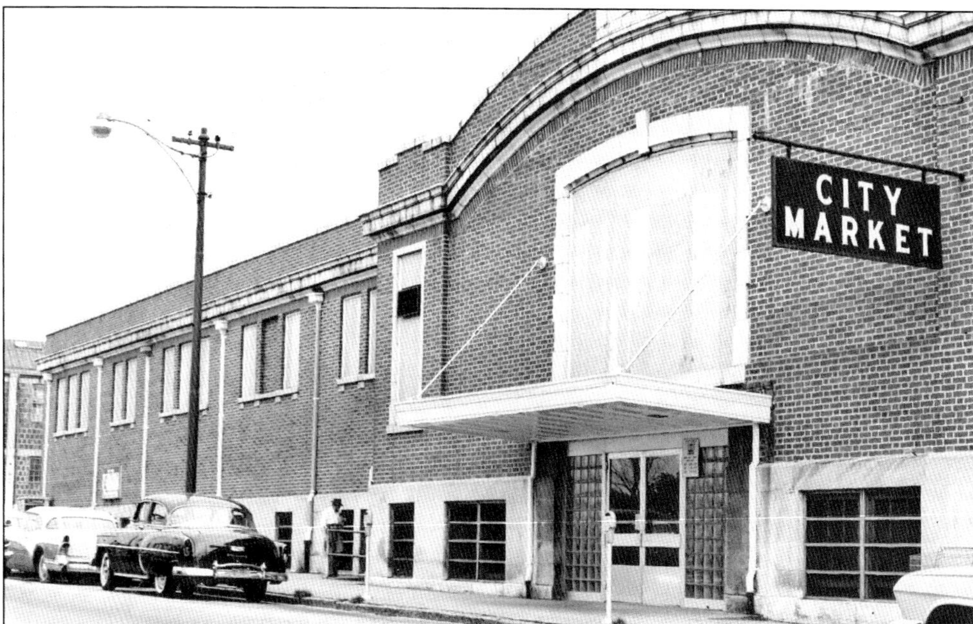

New construction began on the City Market at the corner of Cherry and Sixth Streets. It was completed in 1925. Many West Salem residents had businesses at the market. One such business owner was John Ruff Jr., whose business, Twin City Packing Company, incorporated the bottom level of the City Market. Ruff was credited in the market's later years with saving it from the demolition ball. The business served several more years, and presently it is home to the Downtown Elementary School as well as serving during the summer and fall as a Farmer's Market.

John Ruff Jr., here with his daughter, Patricia, became the patriarch of the 600 block of Poplar Street. He was a pioneer in preserving one of the most beautiful and historic blocks in the city. The 600 block is unique because of its different representation in seven decades of West Salem history. Beginning in 1840 with the Ackerman house, houses represent 1850, 1860, 1870, 1880, 1890, and 1900, all within one city block. This is unique even in North Carolina history.

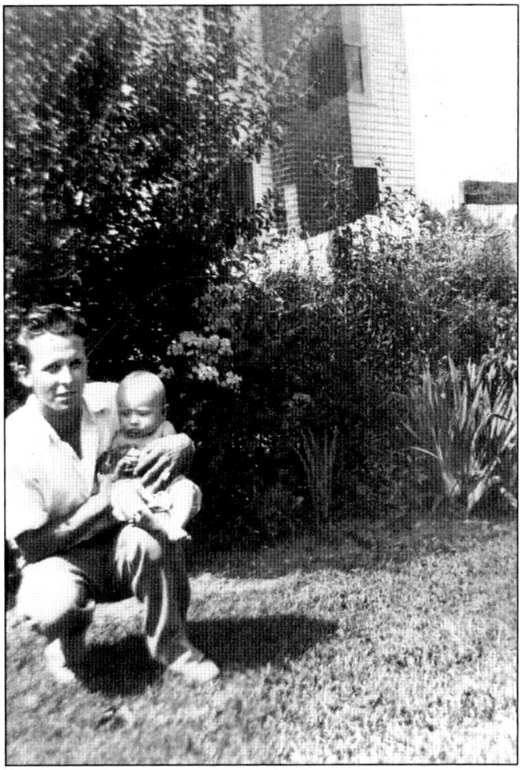

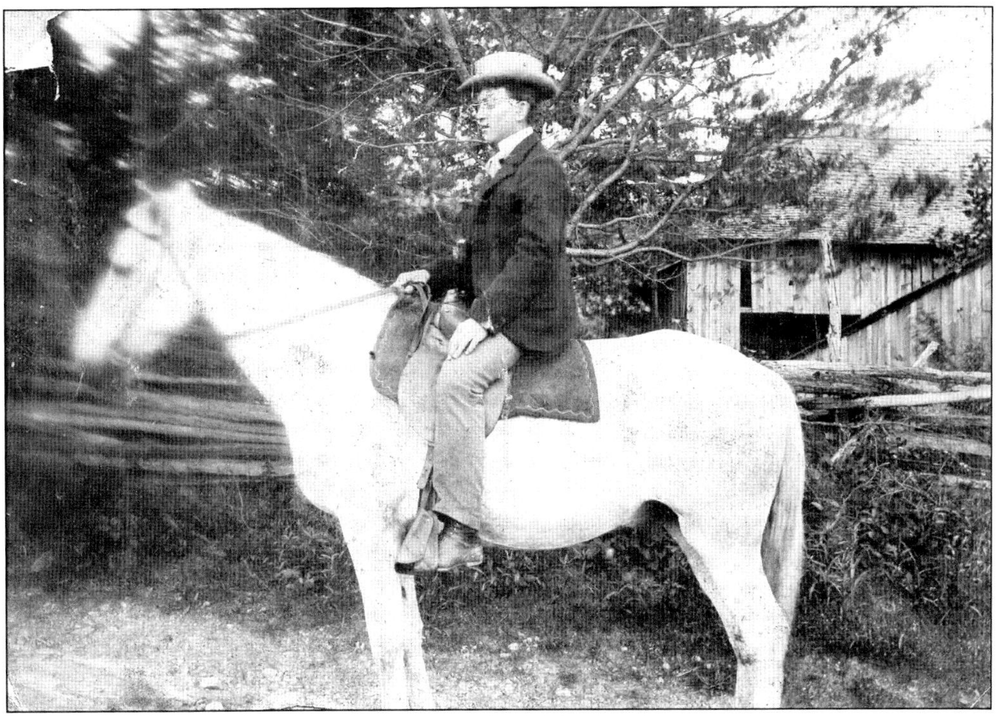

Robah Snyder, born May 5, 1884, is shown in this photograph when he was 16 years of age. He would ride his horse to work on North Liberty Street.

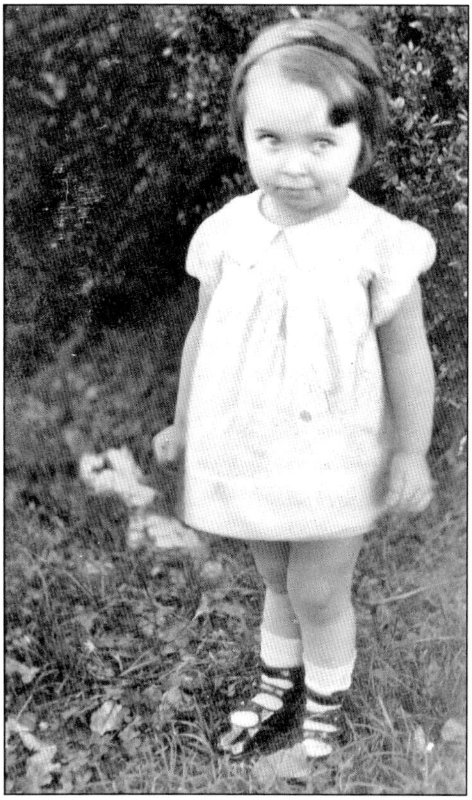

Bobbie Ruff, daughter of John Ruff Jr., is shown in the backyard of her parents' home at 608 Poplar Street in the 1930s. Bobbie Ruff and her sisters followed in her father's footsteps in preserving the 600 block of Poplar Street. She is active in the Washington Park neighborhood as well.

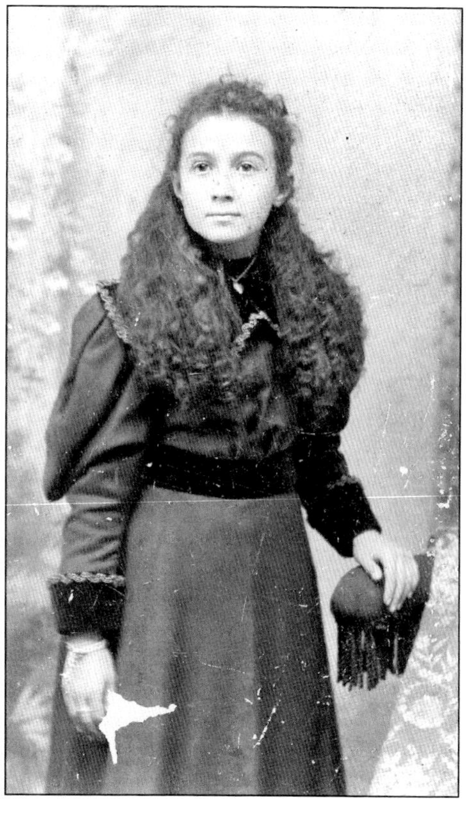

Ida Snyder, pictured, was the wife of John Ruff Sr. She helped her husband in preserving the West Salem heritage by cooking for many functions in the Old Salem district. Her German style of cooking was well known. Her husband was an ironworker for Salem Iron Works.

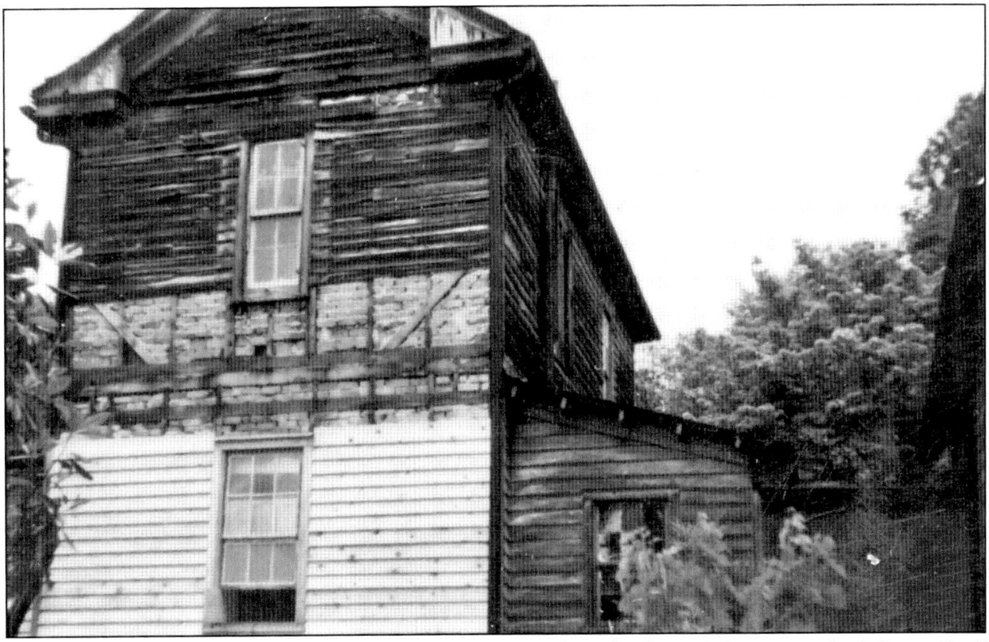

The homes of 600 block of Poplar Street were restored in the late 20th century by Johnny Ruff Jr. He was known as the master craftsman of Poplar Street. The photograph shown is the Tesh-Butner-Bryant house under restoration for a Ruff family member, Mrs. Marilyn Ruff-Clemmons. One should note the exposed brick walls with the crossbeams showing the 18th-century German architecture. The brick German architecture is prevalent throughout the Poplar Street homes; however, much of this is covered with siding.

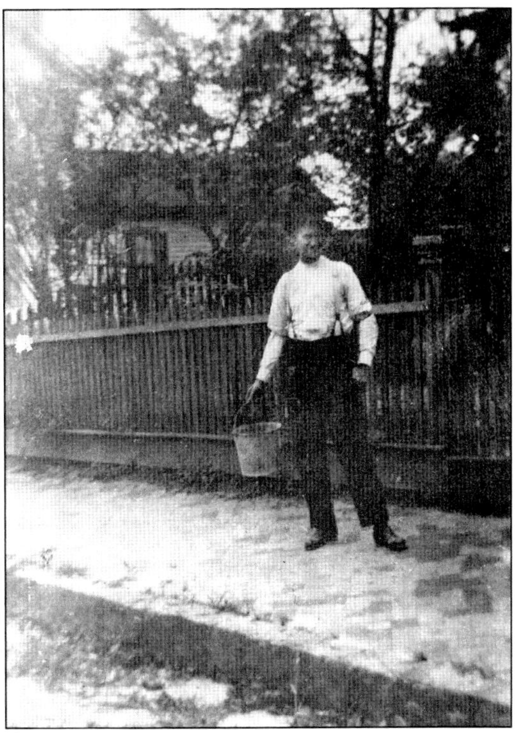

W. C. Grunert, in a c. 1910 photograph, is shown in front of his establishment and home. Grunert built his home in 1884. The West Salem Greenhouse was a floral business in the early 20th century run by W. C. and his son, Robert E. Grunert. Robert later sold the floral establishment to John Ruff Jr. The floral business continues today as Ruff's Florist and is run by Marilyn Ruff-Clemmons and her husband, Jack.

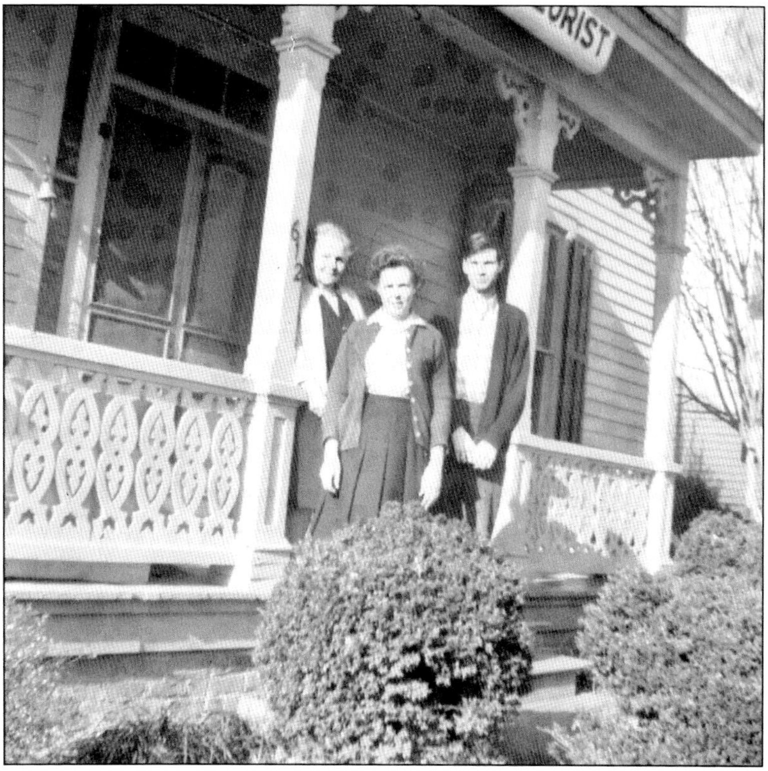

The West Salem Florist Shop is shown in this 1960s photograph. Pictured from left to right are Della Snyder, Lib Bennett, and Harry Beal. They were workers for the florist. Mrs. Lib Bennett resided at 925 Hutton Street. Of note, the open porch has currently been enclosed as a foyer.

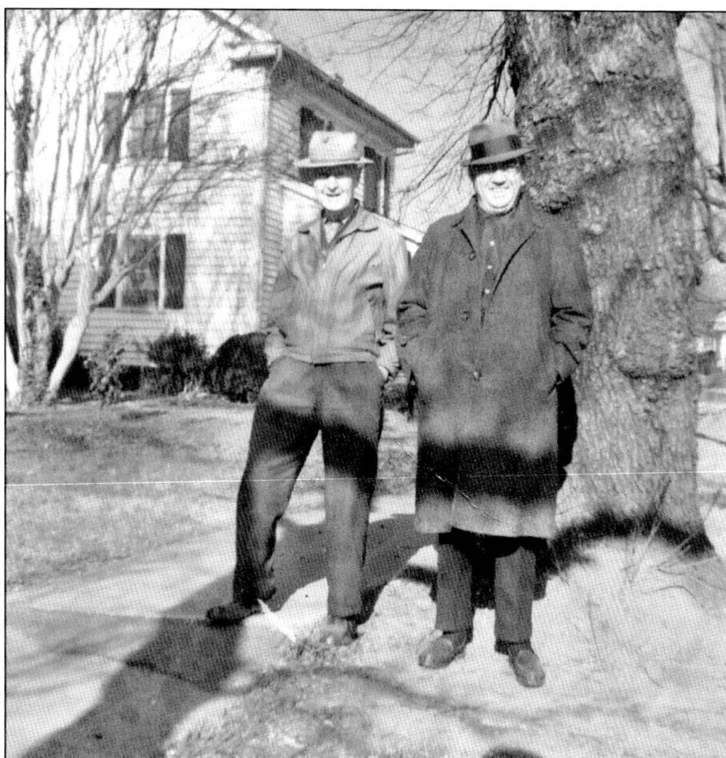

Robert Grunert (left) is shown in front of the West Salem Florist with the Ackerman-Reich house in background. "Chick" Ledford is pictured on the right.

Robert Grunert is shown inside the West Salem Greenhouse establishment. His legacy was followed by that of the Ruff family shortly after this photograph was taken.

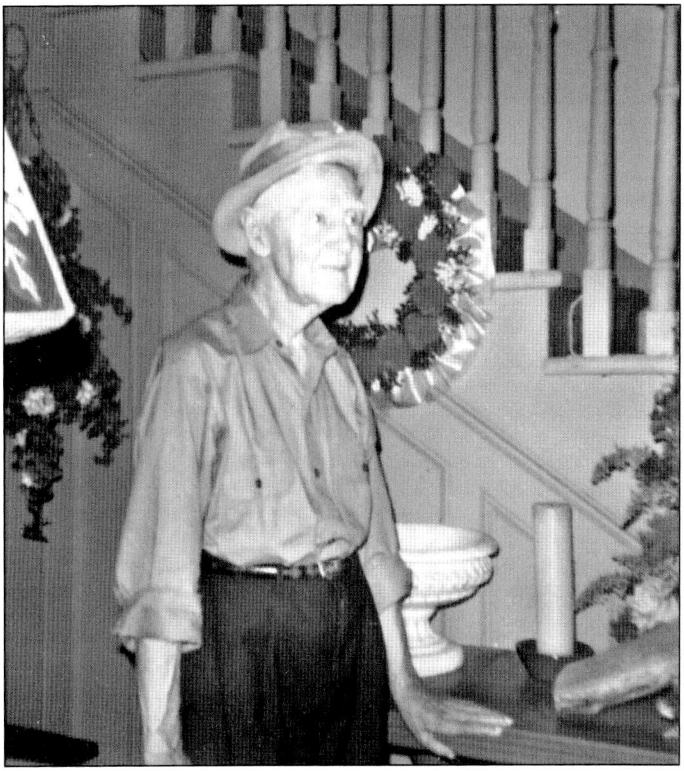

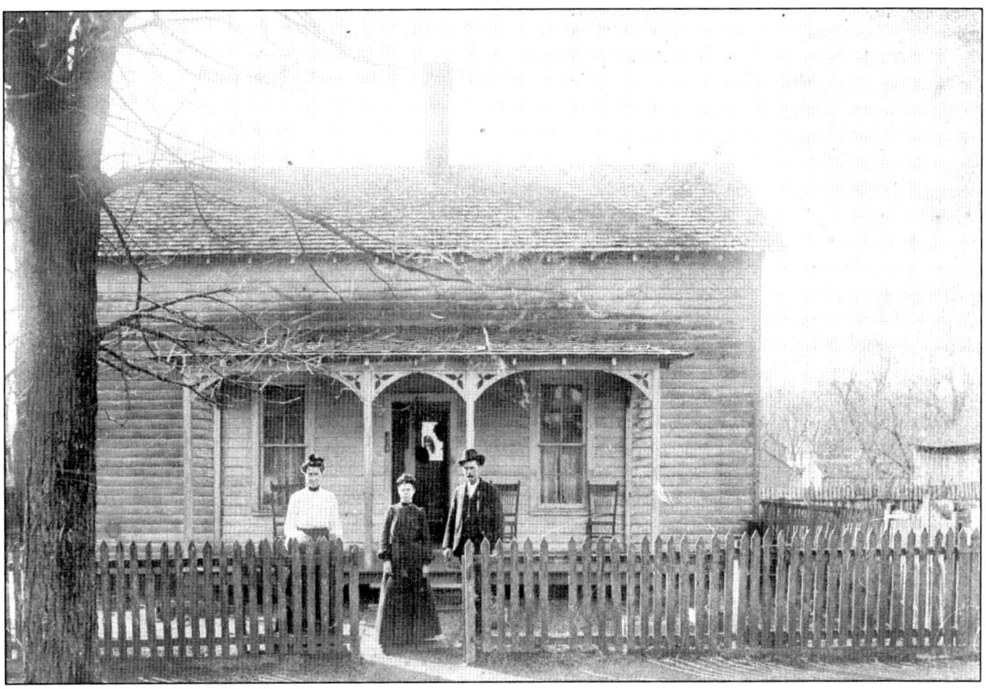

The Chambers were another pioneering family, who helped develop the West Salem neighborhood. The tent revivals on their land helped to establish the Green Street Methodist Church. The family also owned the Peerless Ice Cream Company in Salem.

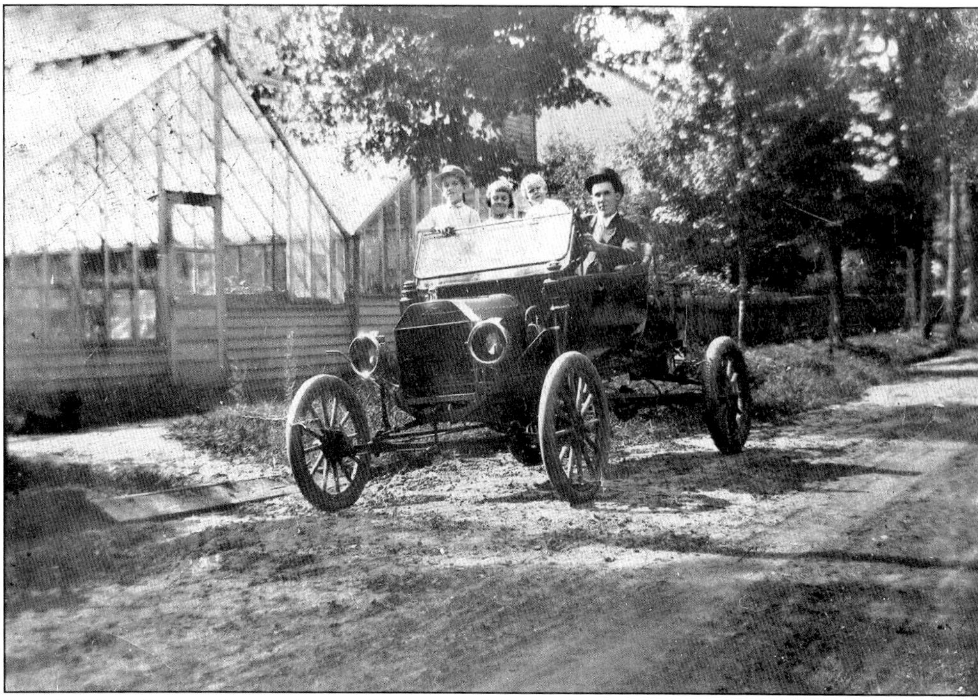

Joseph Chambers is shown driving his automobile by the early greenhouses of the West Salem Greenhouses in the 1920s.

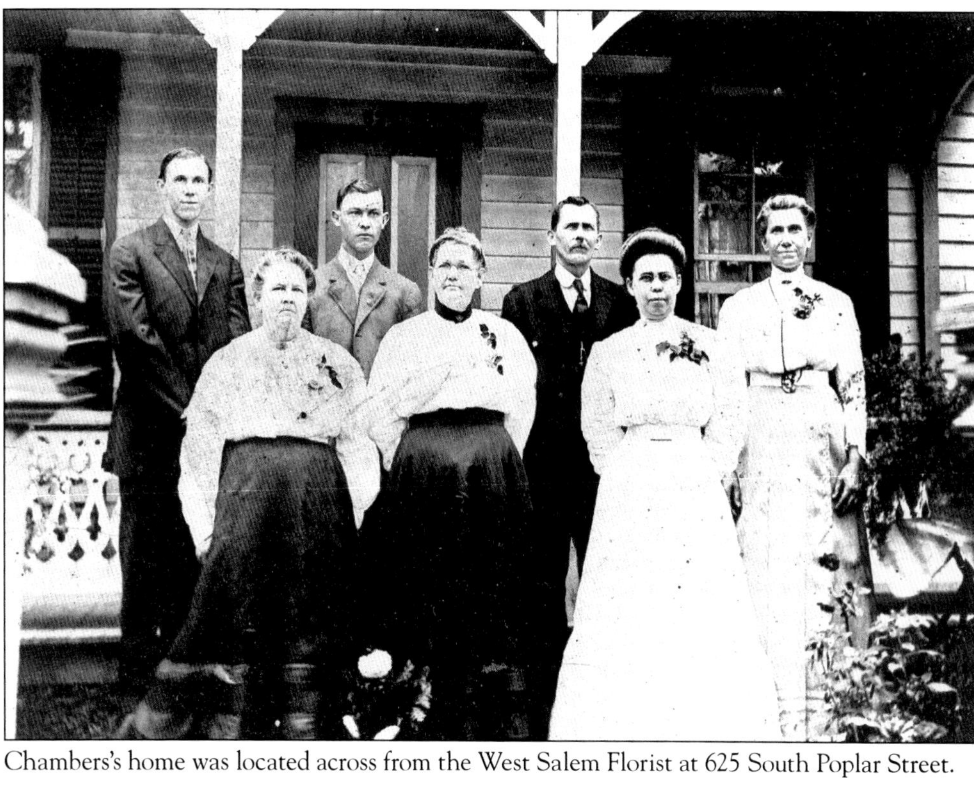

Chambers's home was located across from the West Salem Florist at 625 South Poplar Street.

Grandma Chambers is seen in one of her favorite places, sitting in the garden by the house. The old chair could tell some tales.

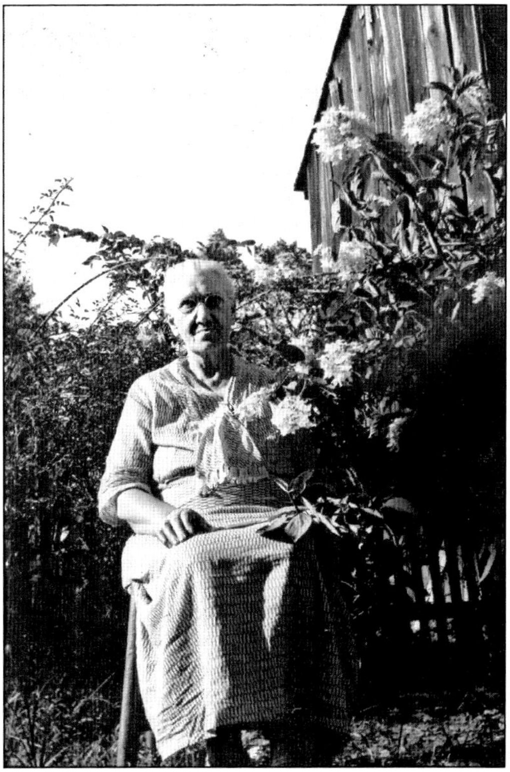

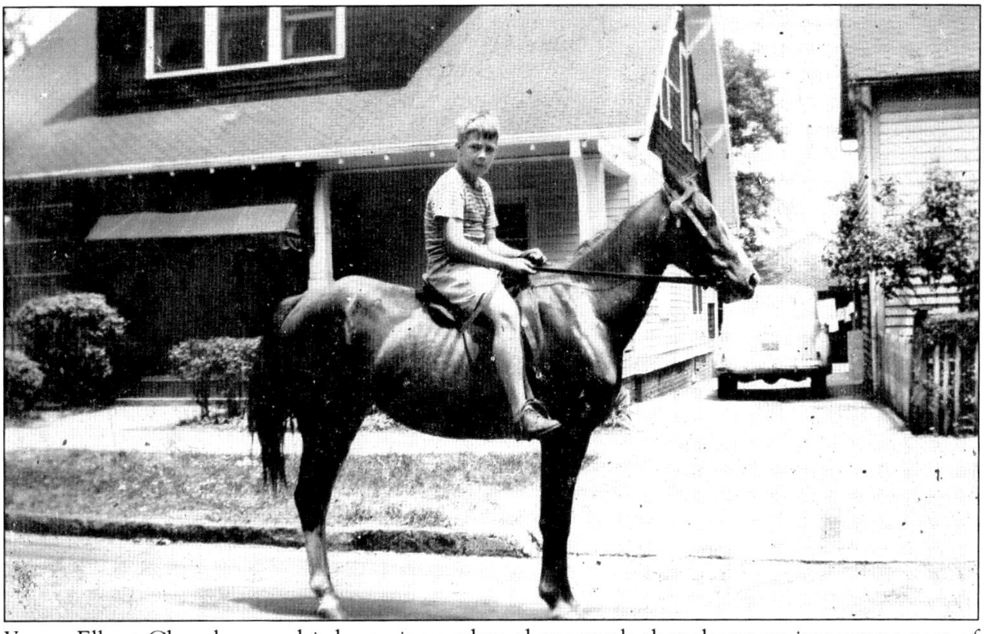

Young Elbert Chambers on his horse is another photograph that shows an important part of West Salem entertainment. The Ruff family tells of many stories with their horses as they rode the back roads of the West Salem neighborhood. The second industrial area, c. 1790, along what is now Peters Creek Parkway, had been reclaimed by nature and made for good horseback riding terrain.

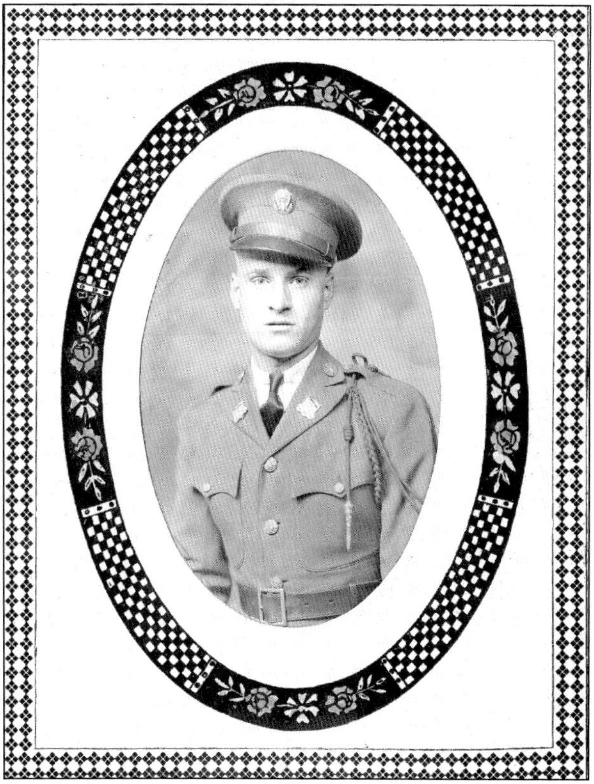

Robert Lee Martin and family resided at 105 Fayette Street near the intersection of West First Street. The Martin family epitomized the families of mill and industrial workers. The Martin family led West Salem beyond its borders to the Great Wars, World War I, and World War II.

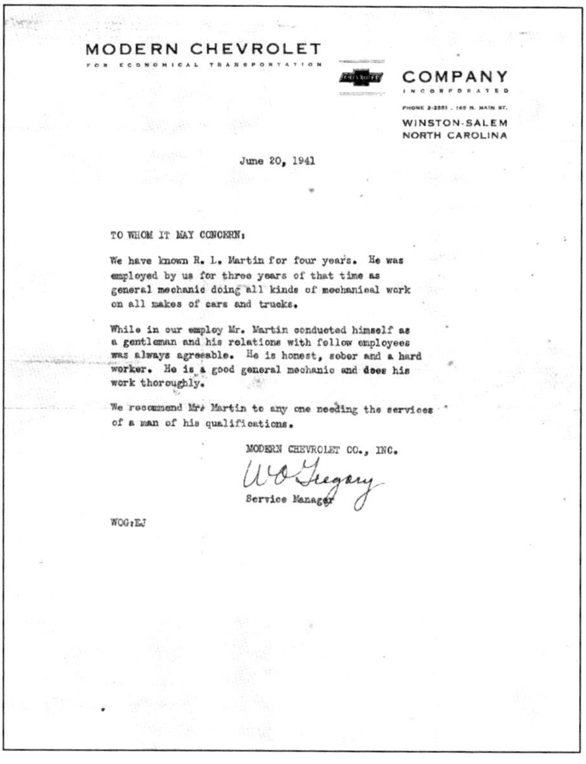

MODERN CHEVROLET
FOR ECONOMICAL TRANSPORTATION

COMPANY
INCORPORATED

PHONE 2-2551 . 145 N. MAIN ST.
WINSTON-SALEM
NORTH CAROLINA

June 20, 1941

TO WHOM IT MAY CONCERN:

We have known R. L. Martin for four years. He was employed by us for three years of that time as general mechanic doing all kinds of mechanical work on all makes of cars and trucks.

While in our employ Mr. Martin conducted himself as a gentleman and his relations with fellow employees was always agreeable. He is honest, sober and a hard worker. He is a good general mechanic and does his work thoroughly.

We recommend Mr. Martin to any one needing the services of a man of his qualifications.

MODERN CHEVROLET CO., INC.

W O Gregory

Service Manager

WOG:EJ

In this letter from Modern Chevrolet on Main Street, Robert Martin is rewarded for his service as a mechanic. With the help of Martin and his fellow workers, the business grew and moved to Fourth Street at Broad Street as part of the West End fixture, which would survive into the 21st century. Modern Chevrolet had the Winston-Salem Police Department contract for maintenance on the police cars.

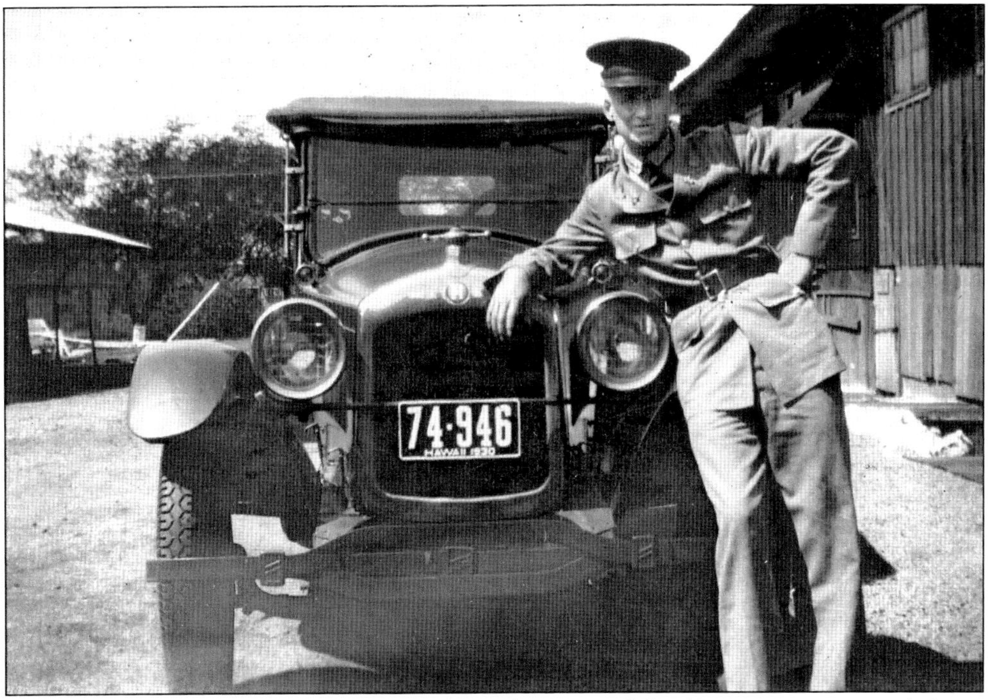

Robert Martin's mechanical skills were not limited to automobiles. His experience extended into the mechanics of airplanes and ships as well. His fascination as depicted in this airplane formation led him to pursue flying and owning his own aircraft.

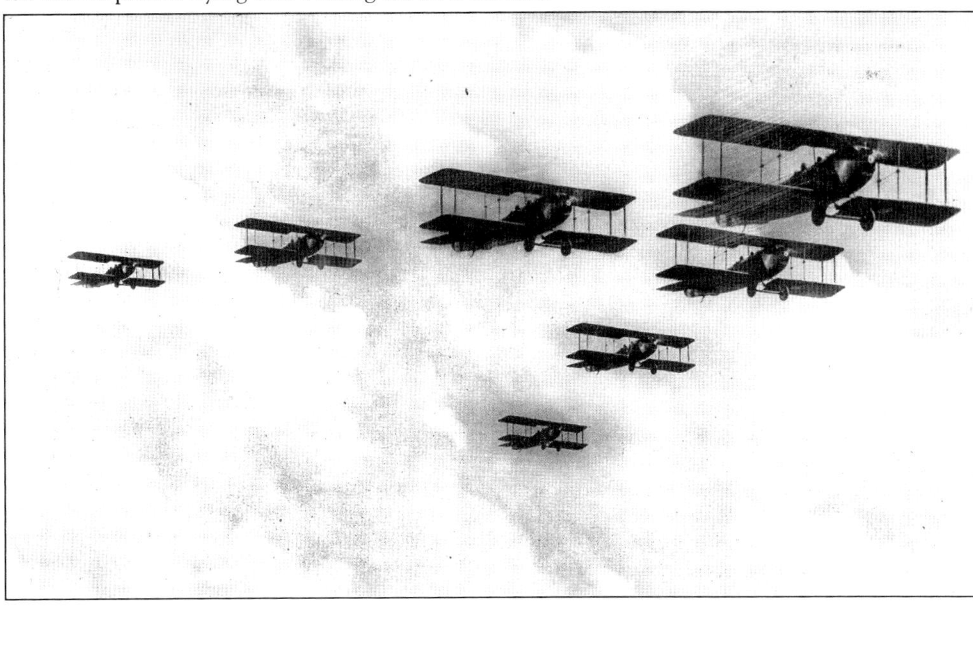

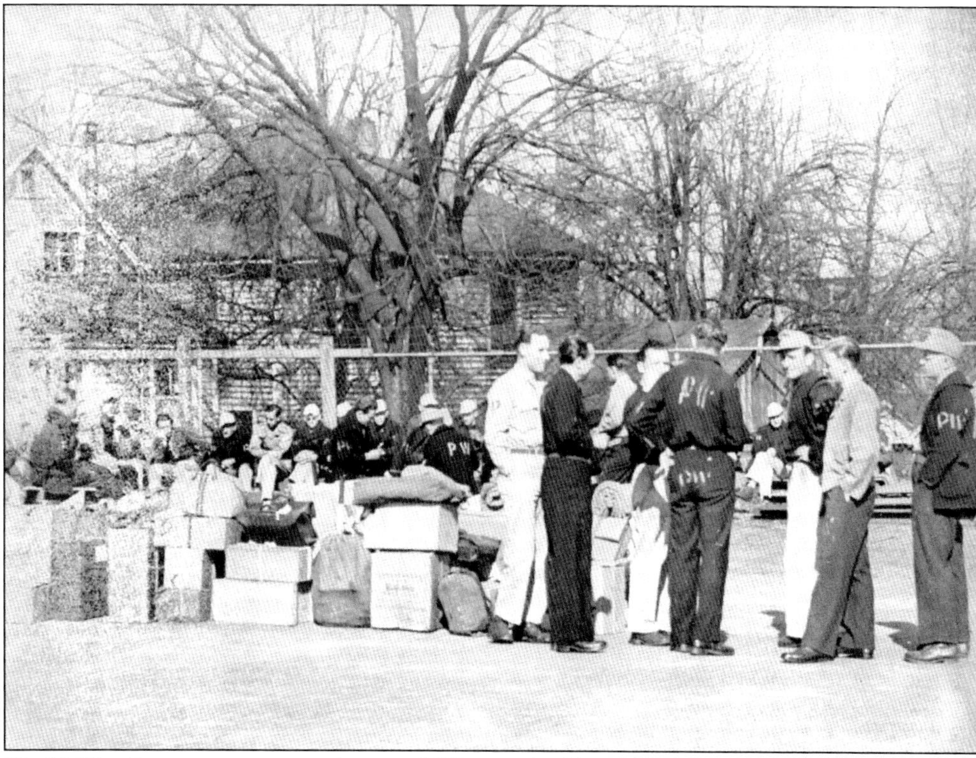

World War II was coming to a close, and Winston had been home to many German prisoners. The prison camp was located on Patterson Avenue. Many West Salem residents, as well as other neighborhood residents, visited this area to see the prison camp of Winston-Salem. Stories and an occasional cigarette were exchanged between the prisoners and visitors.

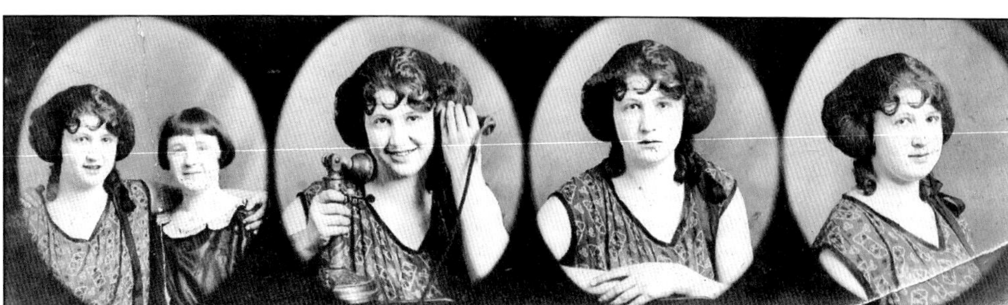

Sarah Shoaf is pictured above. Stereo photographs were introduced in 1849 and became popular in the United States by 1858. These consist of two or more photographs mounted side-by-side, showing the same subject from slightly different perspectives. Stereo photographs continued to be popular well into the 20th century.

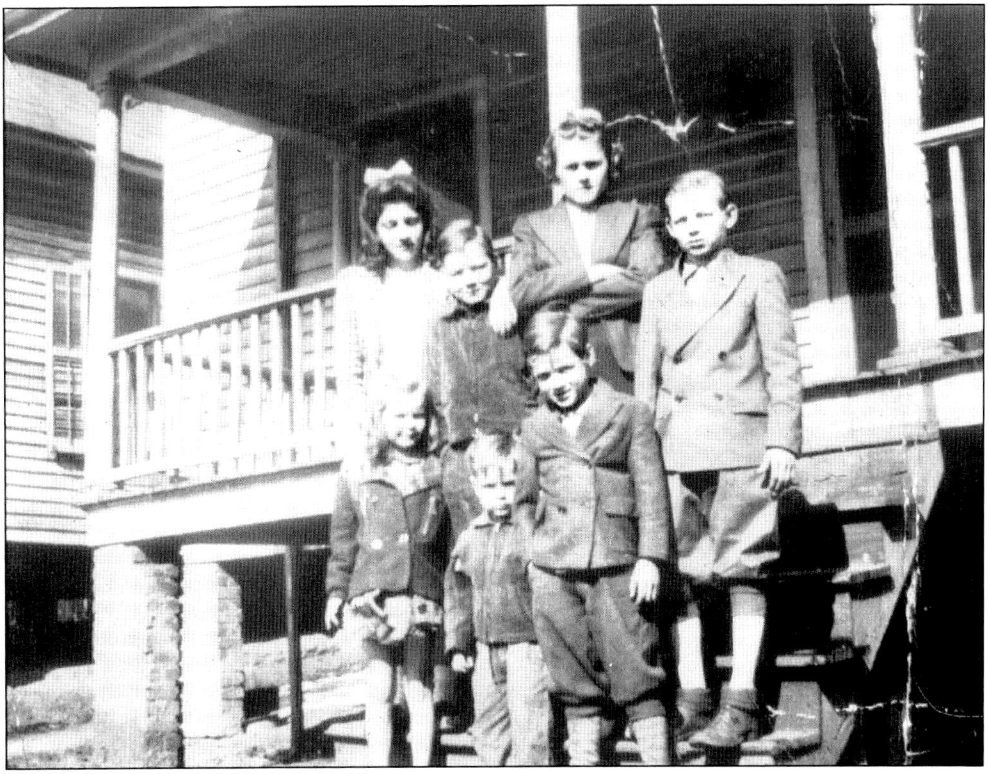

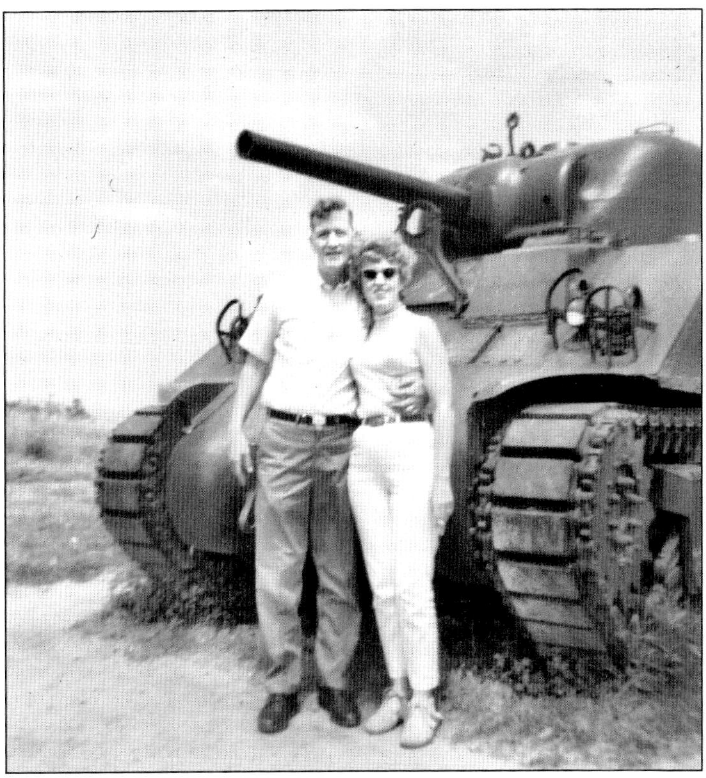

The Thomas and Lillie Howell family resided at 712 South Broad Street. The Howell children attended the West Salem Graded School and enjoyed going to camp at the Salvation Army. The boys grew up to be carpenters, machinists, truck drivers, and military men. Thomas and wife Shelby Howell are pictured below. They were members of Salem Baptist Church. Thomas Howell was a 35-year veteran in the Armed Forces, serving in Korean and returning as a sergeant in the army.

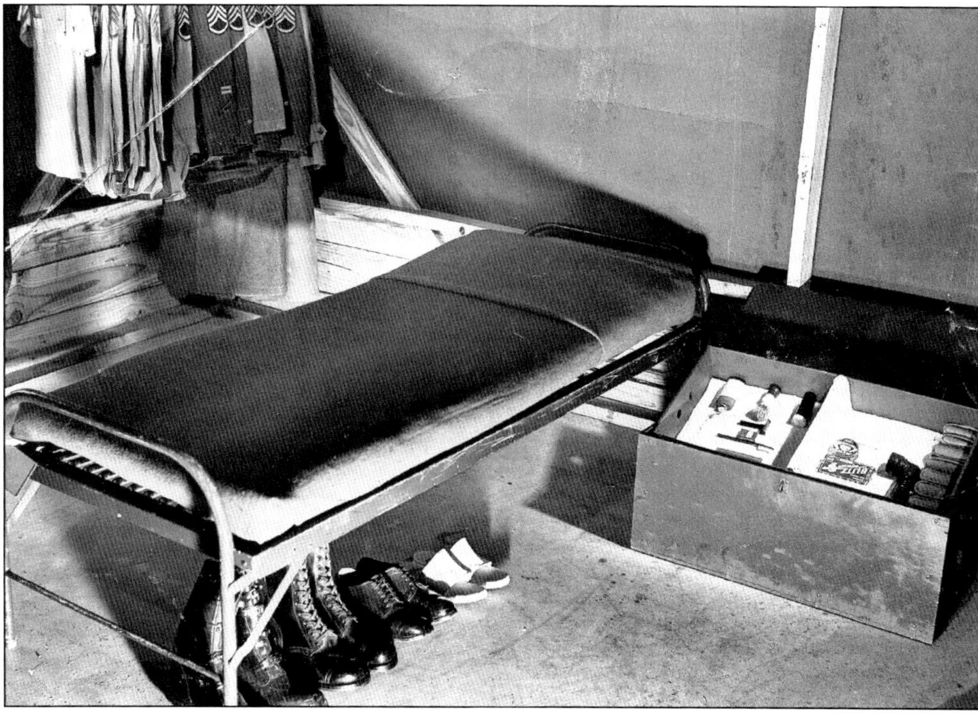

Illustrating the equipment of an army officer, Sgt. Thomas Howell's barracks are pictured. Sergeant Howell is an example of the dedication found in West Salem residents throughout the neighborhood. For over 200 years, service to our country has been a mainstay, generation after generation.

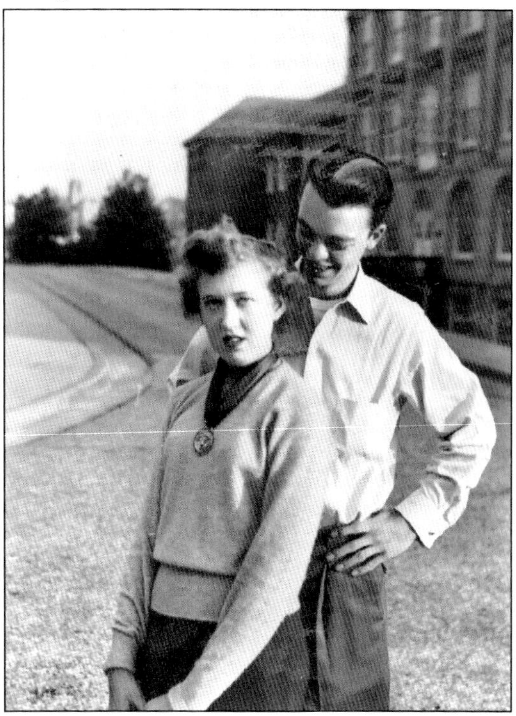

Mrs. Shelby Martin Howell is shown in front of Reynolds High School at the end of school *c.* 1950s. Reynolds High School and Gray High School were important high schools for West Salem residents. Shelby relates, "My friends were found at Reynolds High, Gray High, and Hanes High. The schools were rivals in sports, of course."

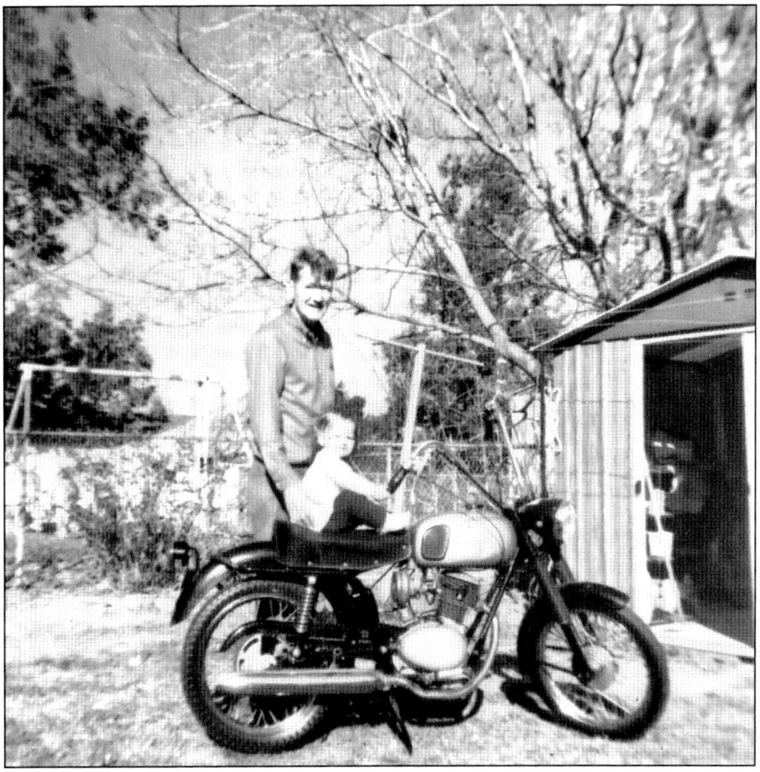

Thomas Howell is pictured with his prized motorcycle and daughter on board. Howell, or Sarge, as he liked to be called, was at home on motor vehicles from motorcycle to large 18-wheelers. He retired from a unionized trucking company but never gave up his love of the open road.

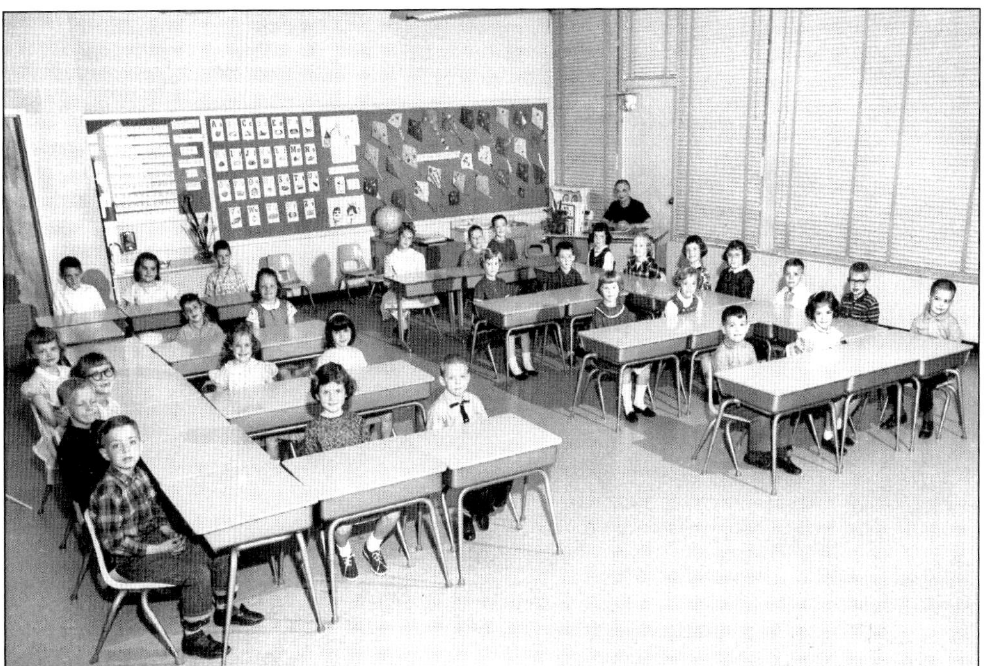

The class of 1963 at Brunson Elementary School is another example of a wonderful elementary school, which was shared by West Salem, Andmore, and West End children. Brunson Elementary School opened in 1959. It was built in a flood plain along Peters Creek at Hawthorne Road.

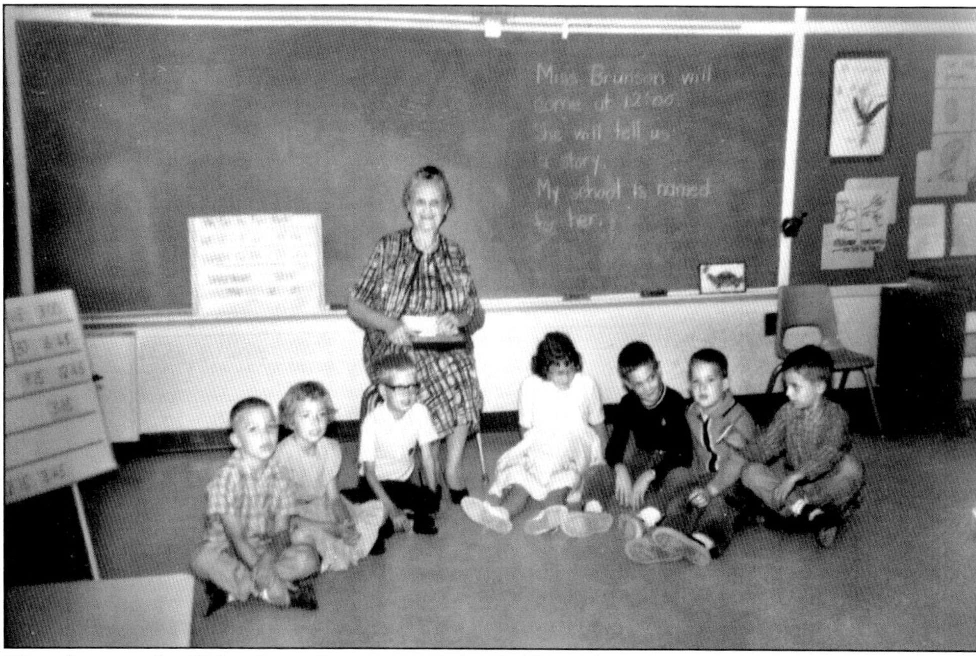

This photograph of Miss Grace Brunson and the children of Brunson Elementary School was taken shortly before her retirement from the public school system. Miss Brunson was a beloved teacher; thus, the elementary school received her name. Tommy Lee Howell, third from right, was the son of Thomas and Shelby Howell. The author also attended this school from 1960 to 1966.

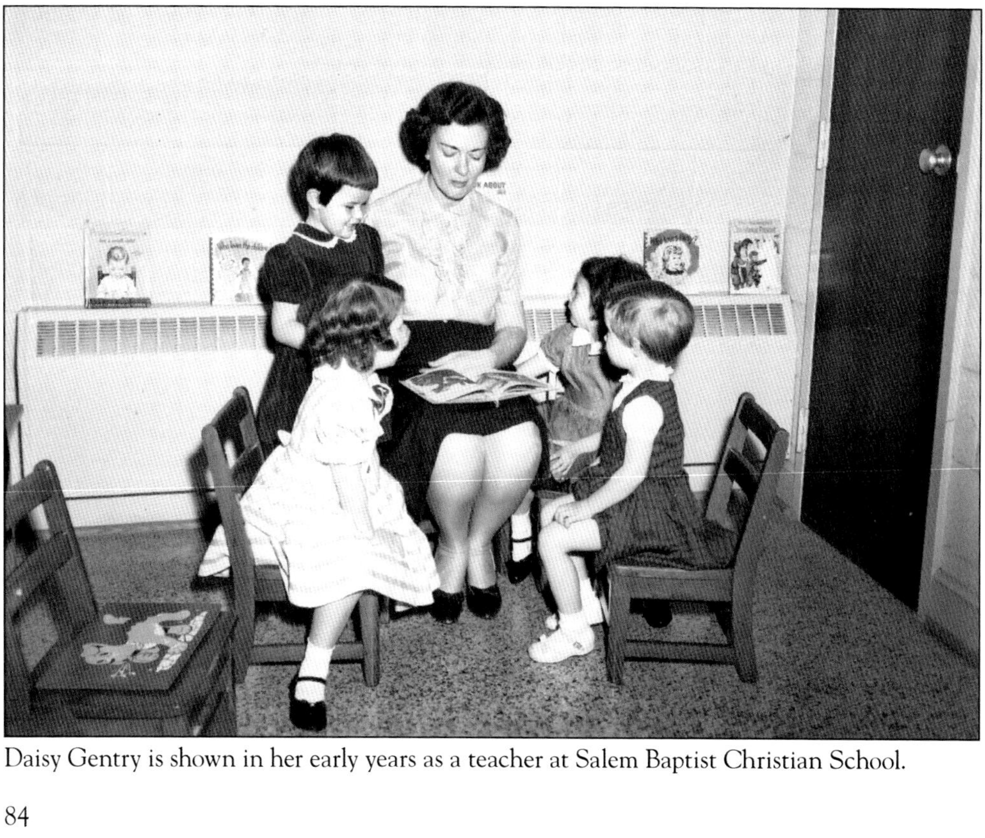

Daisy Gentry is shown in her early years as a teacher at Salem Baptist Christian School.

Daisy Gentry celebrates her 100th birthday in 1980 at Wesley Nursing Home in Charlotte, North Carolina.

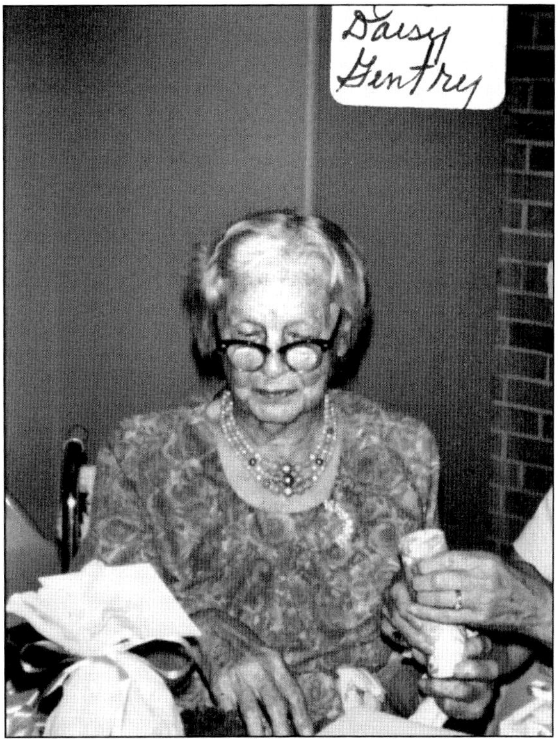

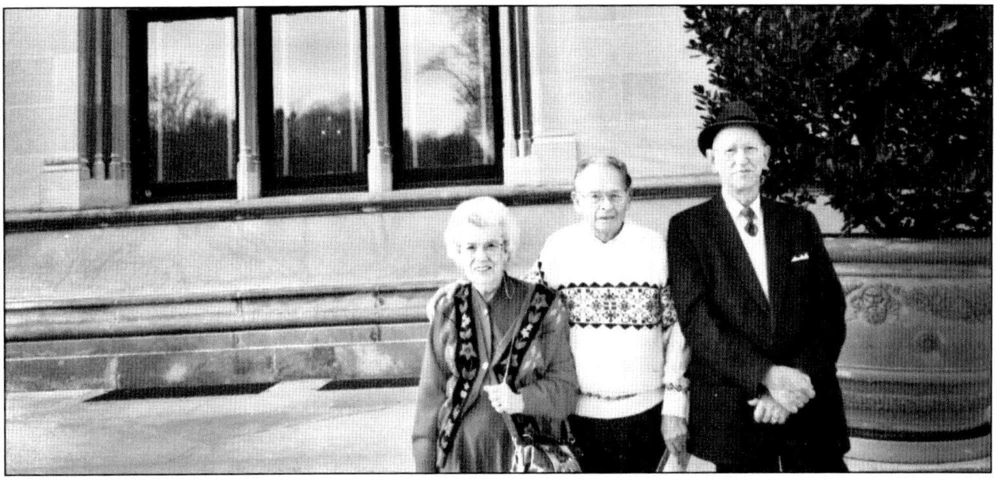

Hal (middle) and Vergie (right) Church are shown on one of their many church bus excursions, compliments of Salem Baptist Church. Hal Church, 93 years young, shared much of his memories of West Salem dating back to his arrival in Winston in the 1930s. Mr. Church has had residences on Washington Avenue and Marshall Street. He remembers many of the houses in the Granville Park area, where he now resides. Many of the homes in this area were built before World War II. He relates that World War II was a tough and lean time. The rationing of food and gasoline supplies along with the practiced electrical blackouts were regular occurrences in West Salem during wartime. One example of wartime in West Salem was the use of blinders placed around the headlights on all motor vehicles. This helped to keep the light focused on the road, so unnecessary light would not escape outward. In theory, this was done so no overhead enemy aircraft could spot heavily populated areas.

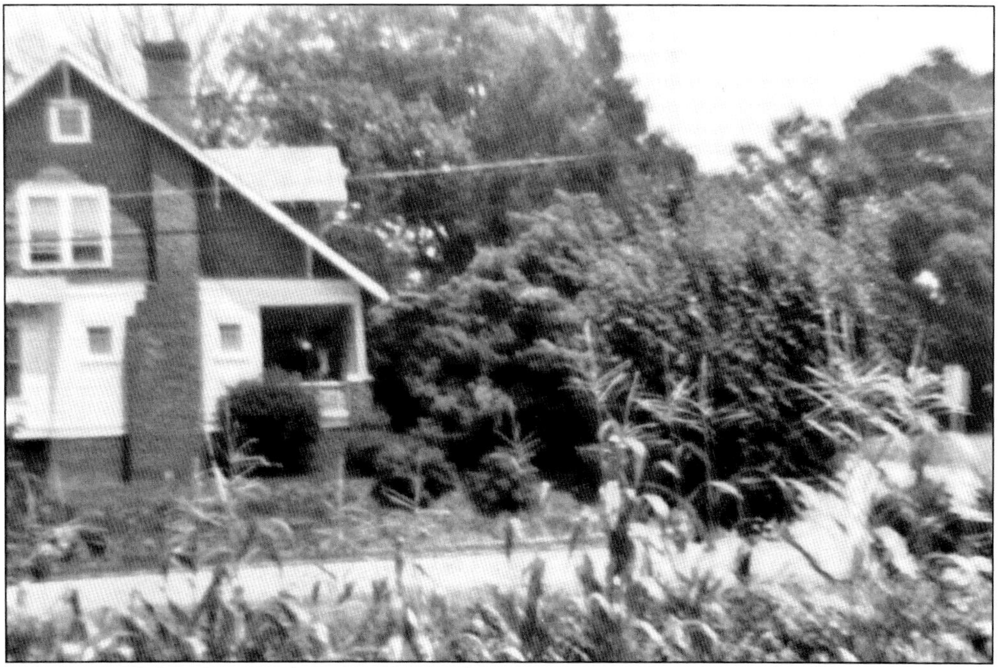

The Holcomb family arrived in Winston in the 1940s. Thomas Holcomb's garden was indicative of the many families and their neighborhood gardens. This garden from the 1970s is an example of earlier victory gardens, which were prevalent during the war years. The gardens were of top quality due to the land throughout the West Salem neighborhood being tilled for over 200 years.

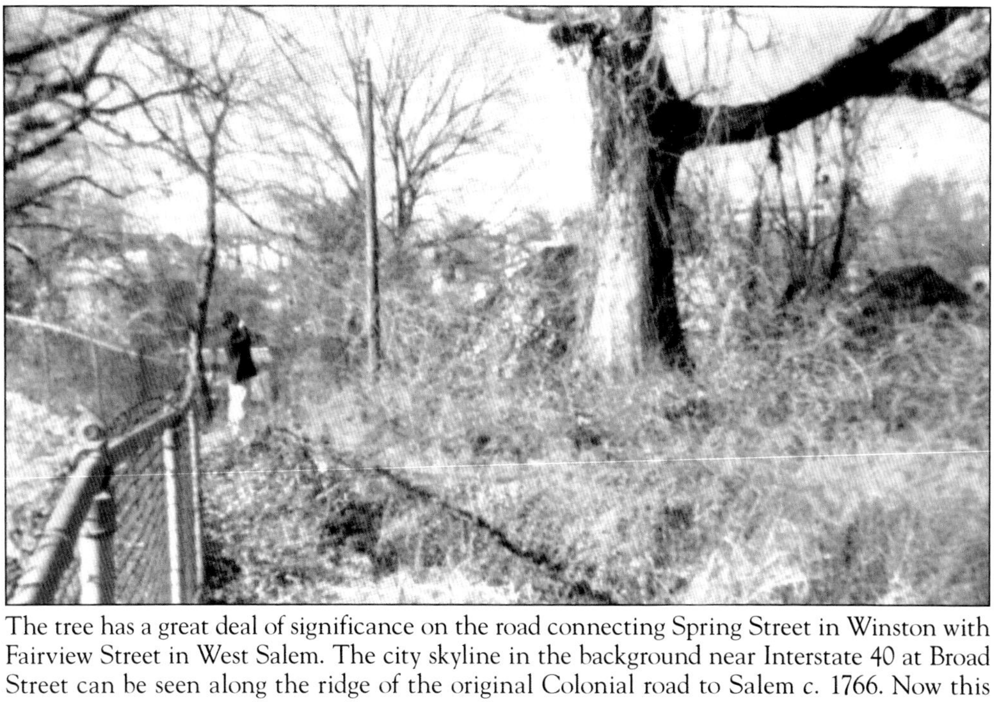

The tree has a great deal of significance on the road connecting Spring Street in Winston with Fairview Street in West Salem. The city skyline in the background near Interstate 40 at Broad Street can be seen along the ridge of the original Colonial road to Salem c. 1766. Now this Colonial road is known as Broad Street. Thomas Holcomb photographs another angle of the tree for posterity.

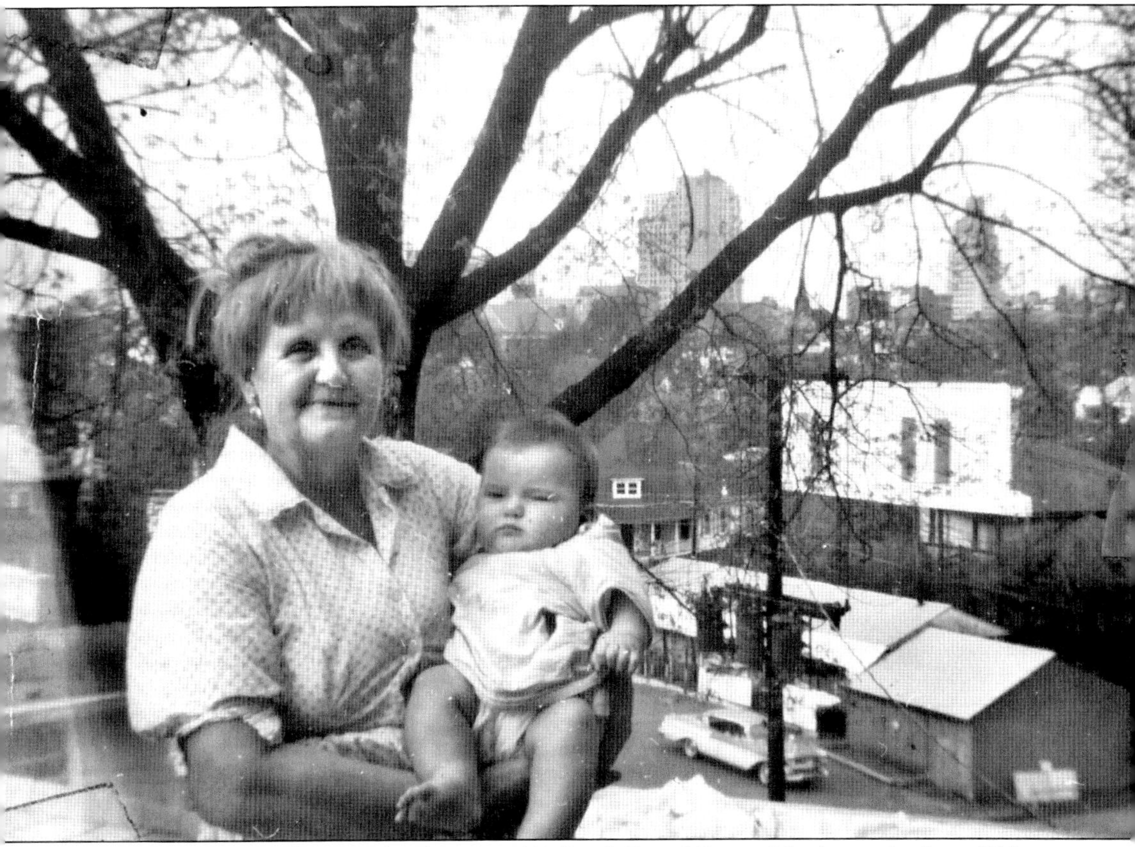

Mrs. Mary Bricker is shown at her home at 119 South Broad Street. The home, built in 1919, is an example of the architecture of the area of West End and West Salem. The three-story pebble-dash house was long and extended from Broad Street back nearly half of the block. The skyline in the background shows the height of the house as it overlooks First Street and Shallowford Street. The lay of the land in the Broad Street area was terraced in earlier years as farms.

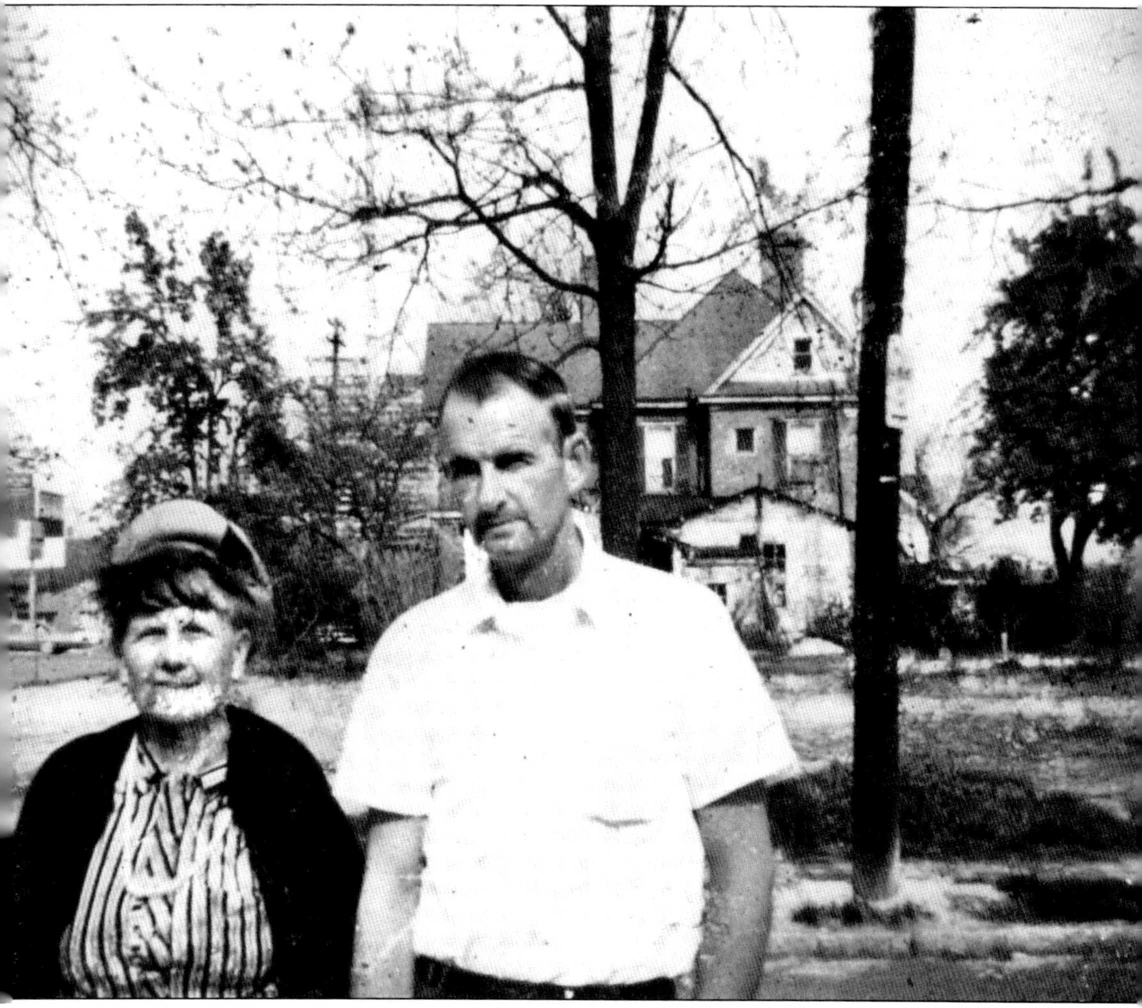

Mrs. Mary Bricker and son Donald are shown in front of 228 North Green Street, a 19th-century home. The home in the background is the Efird home. This was an 1880s brownstone home. The Efird family was an early tobacco family who expanded into grocery stores and department stores. The tree directly behind Mr. Bricker is a variety of pecan tree, which in today's landscape is the last remaining structure in the central part of the 1880s West End neighborhood. This will soon be home to the West End Village.

Four

ENTERTAINMENT

The Spice of Life

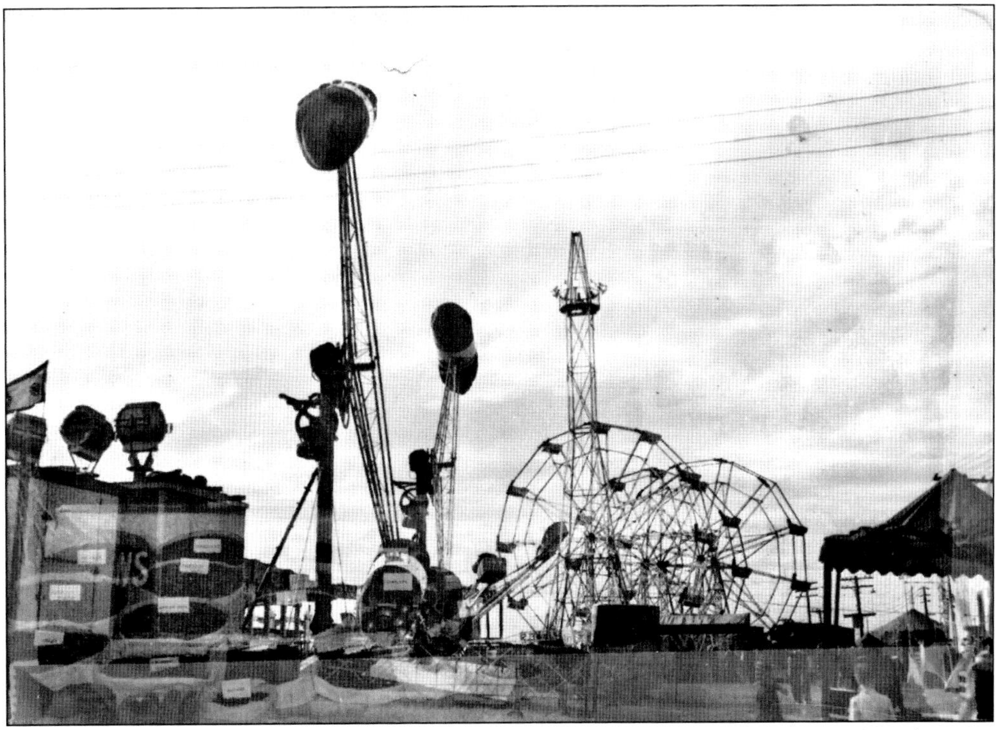

For Winston-Salem residents who have lived a year or more in town, an anticipated yearly event arrives in the fall, the Dixie Classic Fair. Before the Dixie Classic Fair, the fair was known as the Winston-Salem Agricultural Fair. Pictured above is a flash of this early fair around 1940 located on Liberty Street, north of downtown. West Salem residents experienced the enjoyment of fun and socialization. The fair paralleled the West Salem neighborhood in an evolutionary way. Both changed and progressed over a long period of time. The earliest incarnation of the Winston-Salem fair dated to the 19th century. In 1882, Salem held a "grain exhibition." Forsyth County held its first fair in 1896. The two fairs were consolidated in 1899 on Patterson Avenue near the present site and the entrance to Woodland Cemetery. In 1908, the fair moved to North Liberty Street and stayed until 1951. The above photograph shows one example of the rides that attracted the West Salem youngsters. The spinning cups and the round-up ride along with the Bullet and caterpillar coaster were their favorites.

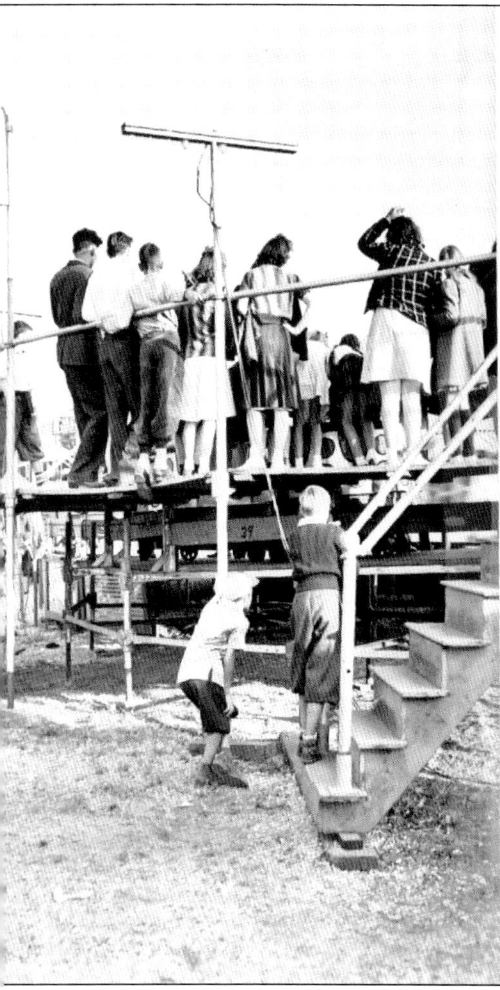

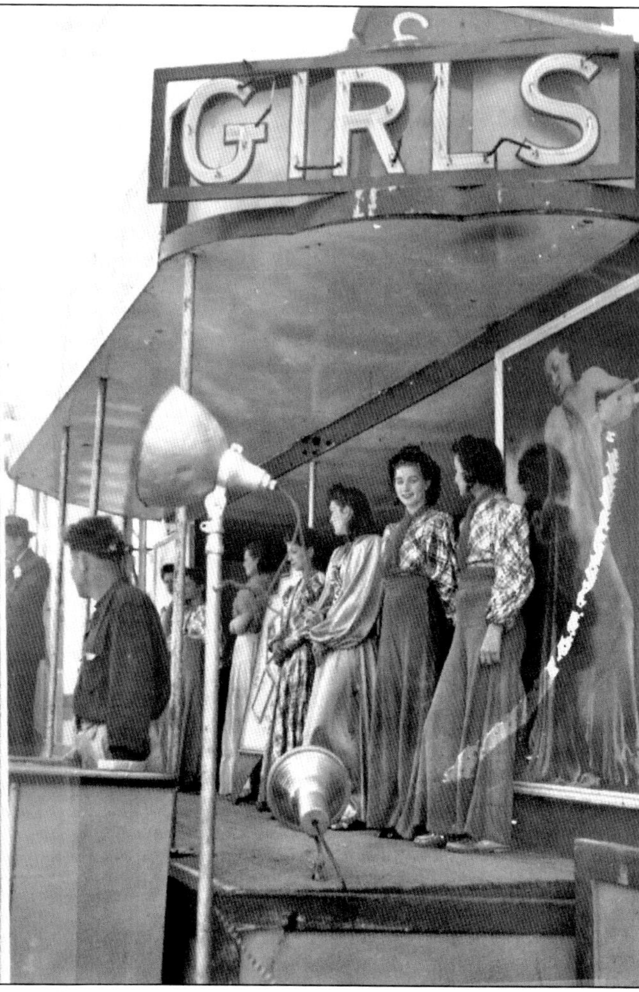

The fair had outgrown the North Liberty Street site in 1951 and moved to more spacious quarters on Cherry Street, now the University Parkway area. In 1956, the name was officially changed to the Dixie Classic Fair, so as to tap into the northwest North Carolina market. In earlier years, most fairs ran about four days. Today the fair runs 10 days and is the second largest fair in North Carolina. The photographs above show a simpler time in the 1940s when the fair was located on North Liberty Street.

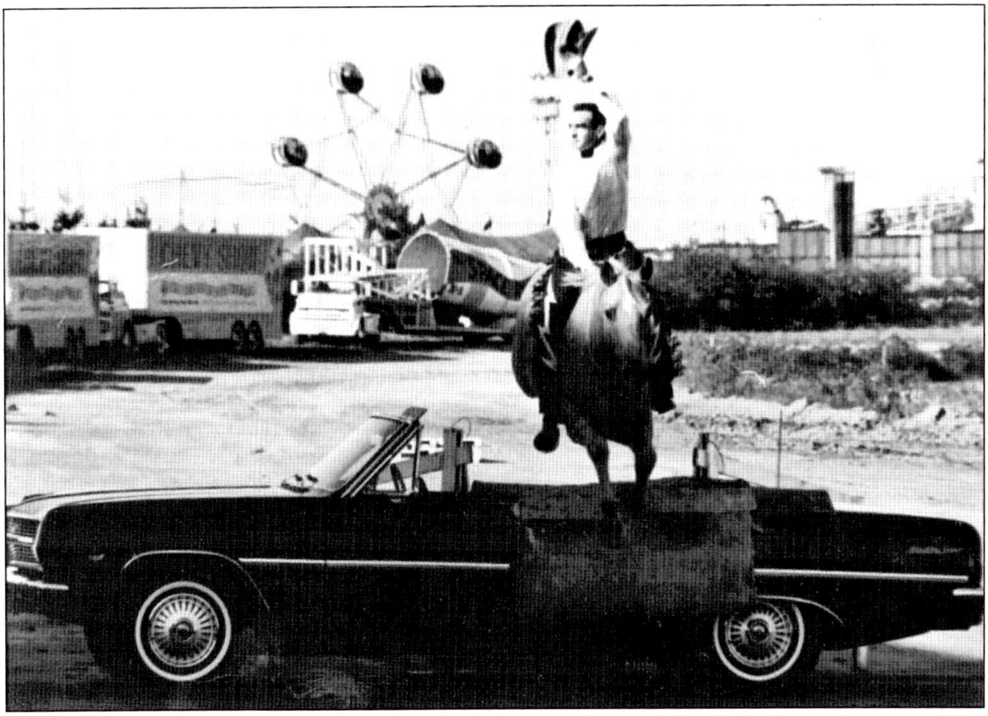

The cowboy shows off for the crowd with his horse's jumping abilities. In the early years of the fair, the rides were part of the carnival group called the "World of Mirth." The James E. Strates shows arrived in the late 1950s after the "World of Mirth" closed. The grandstand area had performances in racing, rodeos, and stunt acts. In the early years, the grandstand area was used for horse racing by the Reynolds family.

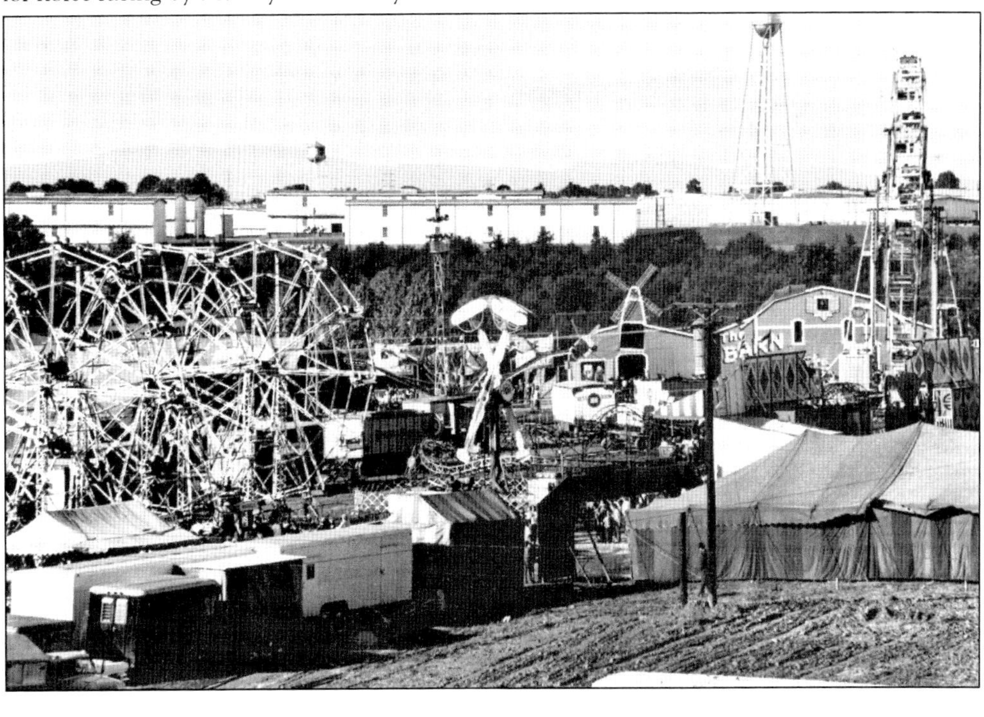

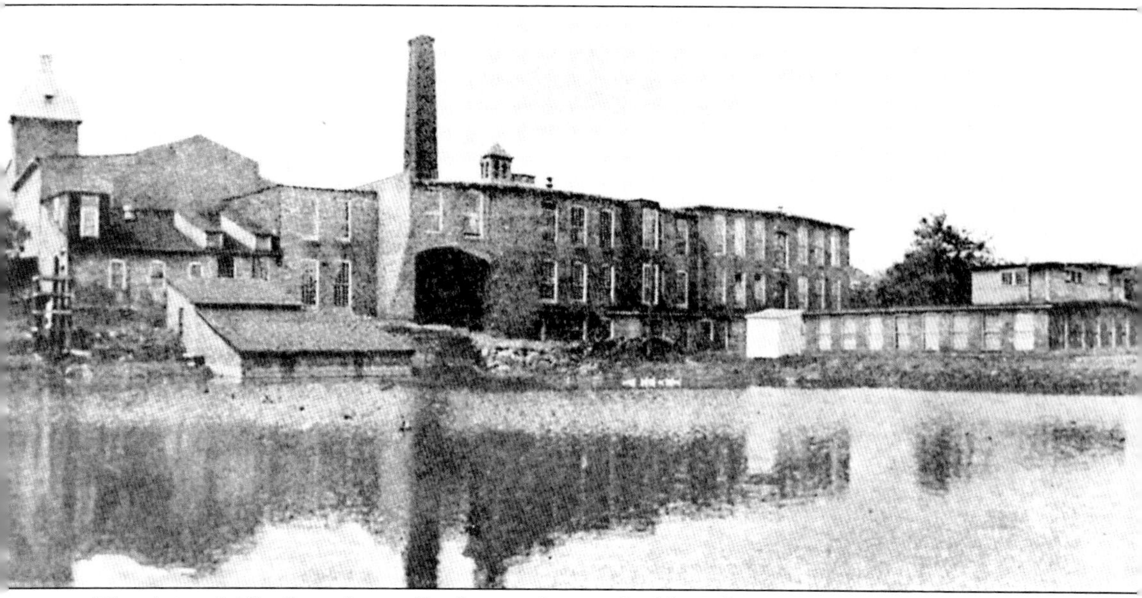

The Arista Mills Complex on Bradenton Avenue had been home to West Salem industrial businesses in the 1830s. The pond at the back of the establishment along Marshall Street is shown in this early-20th-century photograph. Pond Street in West Salem is a lost and forgotten street, which ran east to west between Trade Street and Marshall Street. However, this photograph shows where this name came from. This pond and Tanner's Pond to the south on Marshall Street were recreational areas for the local kids as related by Mrs. Marylin Ruff Clemmons.

Over the years, two holidays stand out in the hearts of West Salem adults and children, Easter and Christmas. The above photograph brings back memories to many older Salem and West Salem residents. With signs welcoming outsiders from all over America to neighborhood streets early on Easter morning, the thousands who visited Salem were treated with kindness, a cup of coffee, and the world-famous Moravian sugar cake. East Salem and West Salem participated in the baking of breads and treats served to the community on Easter morning. Christmas was no exception. One has not experienced Salem and its spice of life without tasting the world-renowned Moravian cookies.

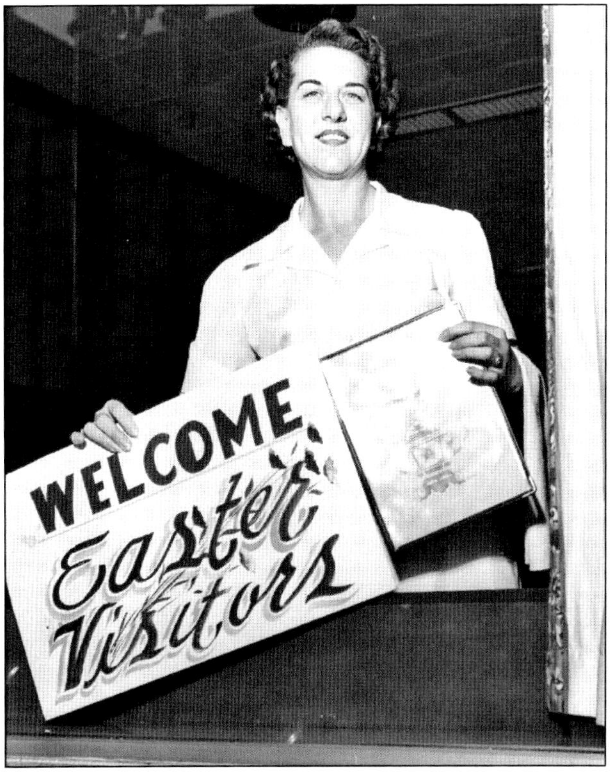

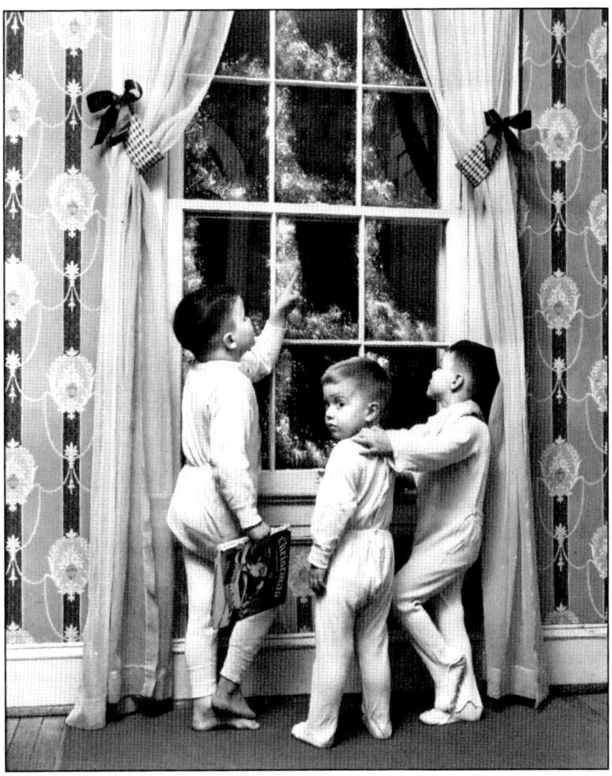

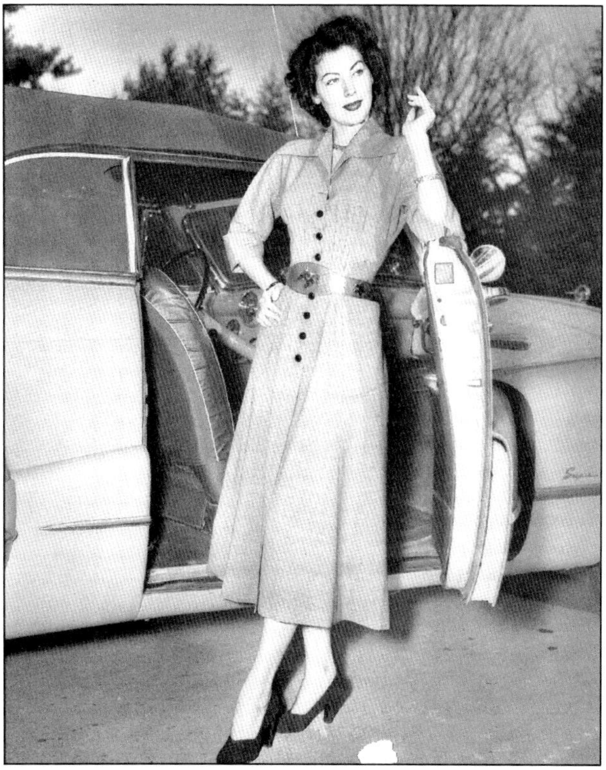

Celebrities and movie stars entertained residents on the large and small screen. The movie houses of the city numbered on the average of 10 movie palaces at any given time throughout the 20th century. Ava Gardner, in the photograph to the right, was a local North Carolinian. She was a major movie star in the 1940s and 1950s. Her visit to Reynolds High School in the 1950s was spoken of by West Salem children and other neighborhood children for years to come.

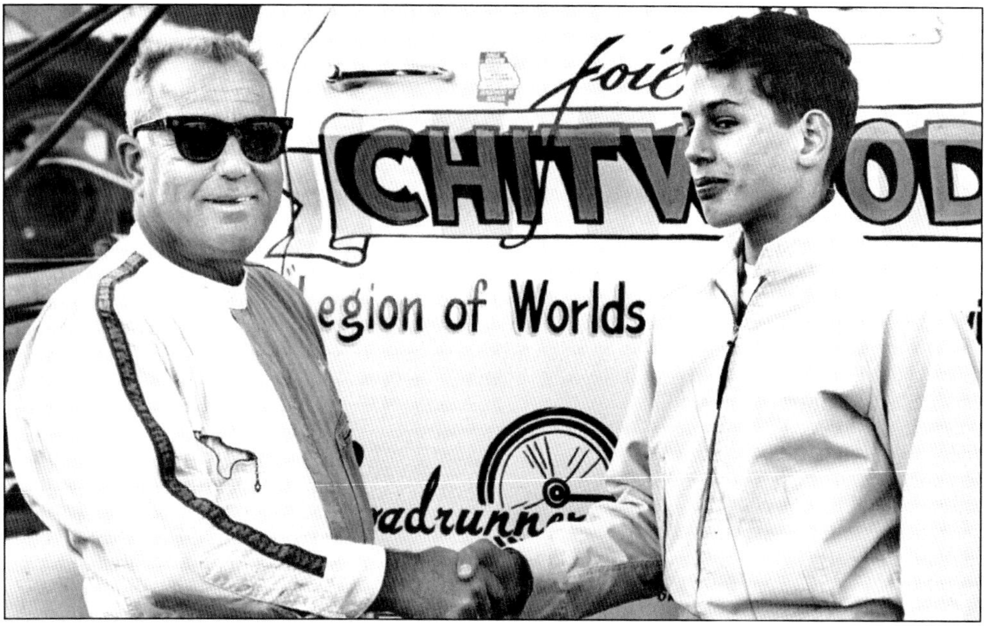

The Dixie Classic Fair brought many performers and their acts to Winston-Salem. One such act was the Joie Chitwood Thrill Shows. His automobile stunts and crashes rivaled the NASCAR racing circuit of the time. As the Dixie Classic Fair drew to a close, the taking down of the fair began. West Salem children and adults would often earn a little extra spending money by helping the carnival employees take down the rides.

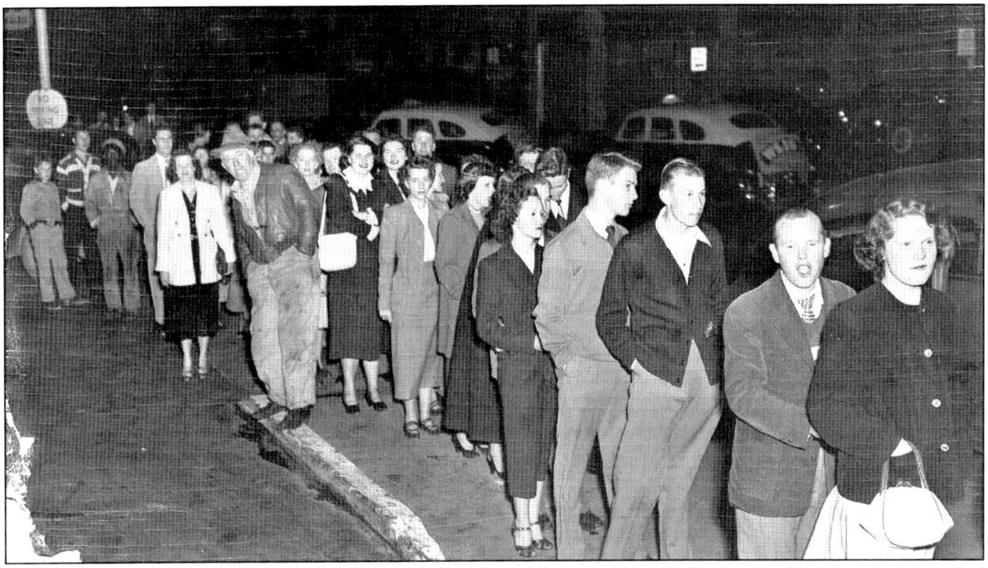

The downtown theaters were always a center of entertainment. The early-20th-century movie houses were the Amuza on Fourth Street, the Auditorium on Liberty Street, and many others. This photograph from the 1940s shows the usual long line of patrons waiting to enter the movie palaces of the era: the Winston Theatre, 1940s; Carolina Theatre, 1920s; and the State Theatre, 1930s. No one left disappointed during the golden years of Hollywood. Thomas Holcomb, a West Salem resident, reminisced about one visit to the Carolina Theatre in the 1950s, to see *The Outlaw* with Jane Russell. Many young boys came of age with this movie.

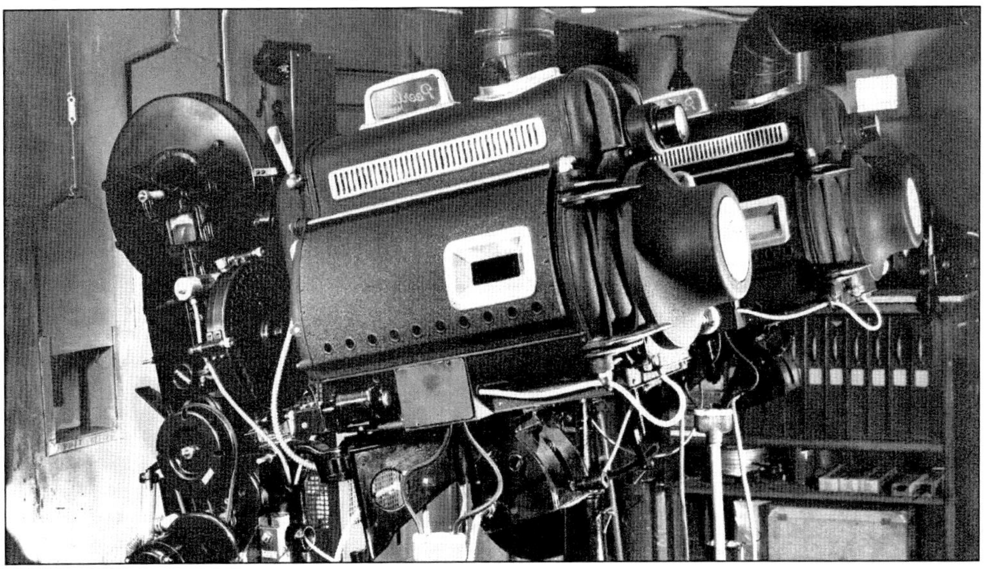

The indoors of the movie palaces were just as the grand as the outside. The ornate furniture and lightening mesmerized many a West Salem resident. One such resident was Bryant Lee of Green Street. As a young man in high school, he had the opportunity to be an usher at the Carolina Theatre in the late 1930s. One of the perks for the workers was to preview the movies before the general public. *Gone with the Wind* and *Wizard of Oz* were seen by Lee and his coworkers in 1939. The fondest memories for Lee were produced by these classic movies, which would forever be in his memory.

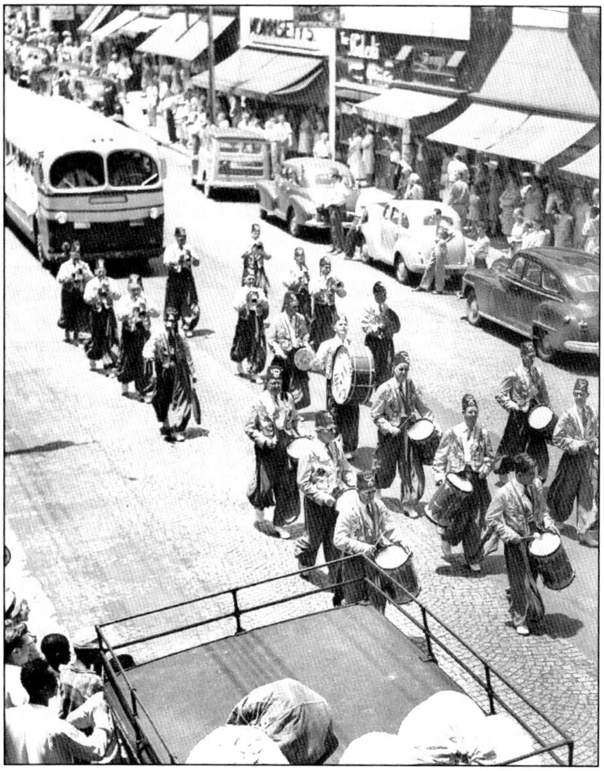

The Winston-Salem Retail Merchants Parade was another annual event in downtown Winston. Parades had arrived in Winston and Salem before the 20th century. The Ringling Brothers and Barnum and Bailey Circus traveled the North Carolina circuit, with Winston-Salem being a major stop. For many West Salem and city residents, this was their first glimpse of lions, tigers, bears, and elephants. The Retail Merchants Parade photograph shown gave residents a chance to have fun and at the same time perform for the rest of Winston.

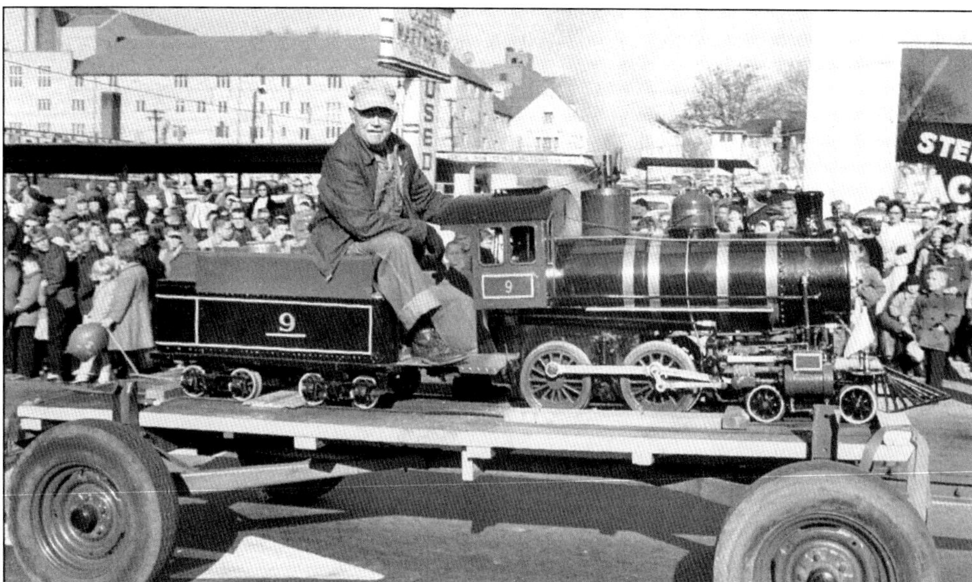

The uniqueness of a parade draws on the strange and unusual. The marching bands, performing cowboys and cowgirls, and floats presented by the retail businesses made up the typical performers. The photograph shows a more unusual participant, a miniature working train. The conductor with his train made up one of the few examples of miniature trains in Winston-Salem amusements. Several trains were found at Reynolds Park Amusements on Reynolds Park Road and at several drive-in theaters in the 1950s.

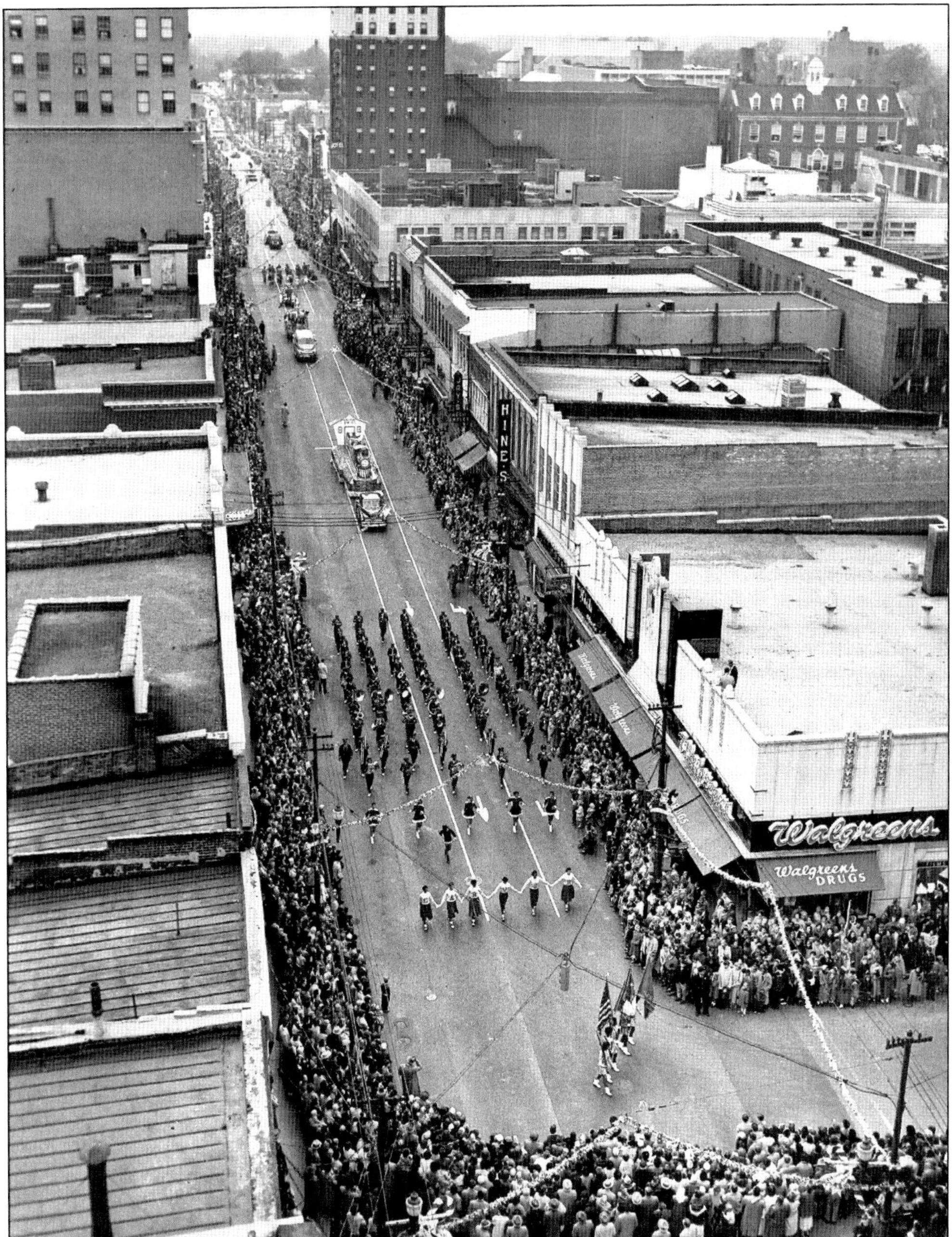

The parades of Winston-Salem expanded and grew to the point of stretching nearly throughout the town at their full expansion. This corner of Trade and Fourth Street was one of the largest concentrations of onlookers throughout the many years of the parade. With every year, the downtown parade grew larger. It became a rite of passage for children in the neighborhood schools to compete against their fellow students in the surrounding older neighborhoods. The bands played louder, the dancing boots kicked higher, and the majorettes twirled their batons faster. Bobbie and Marilyn Ruff of South Poplar Street remember these wonderful times and memories the parades brought as both performers and onlookers.

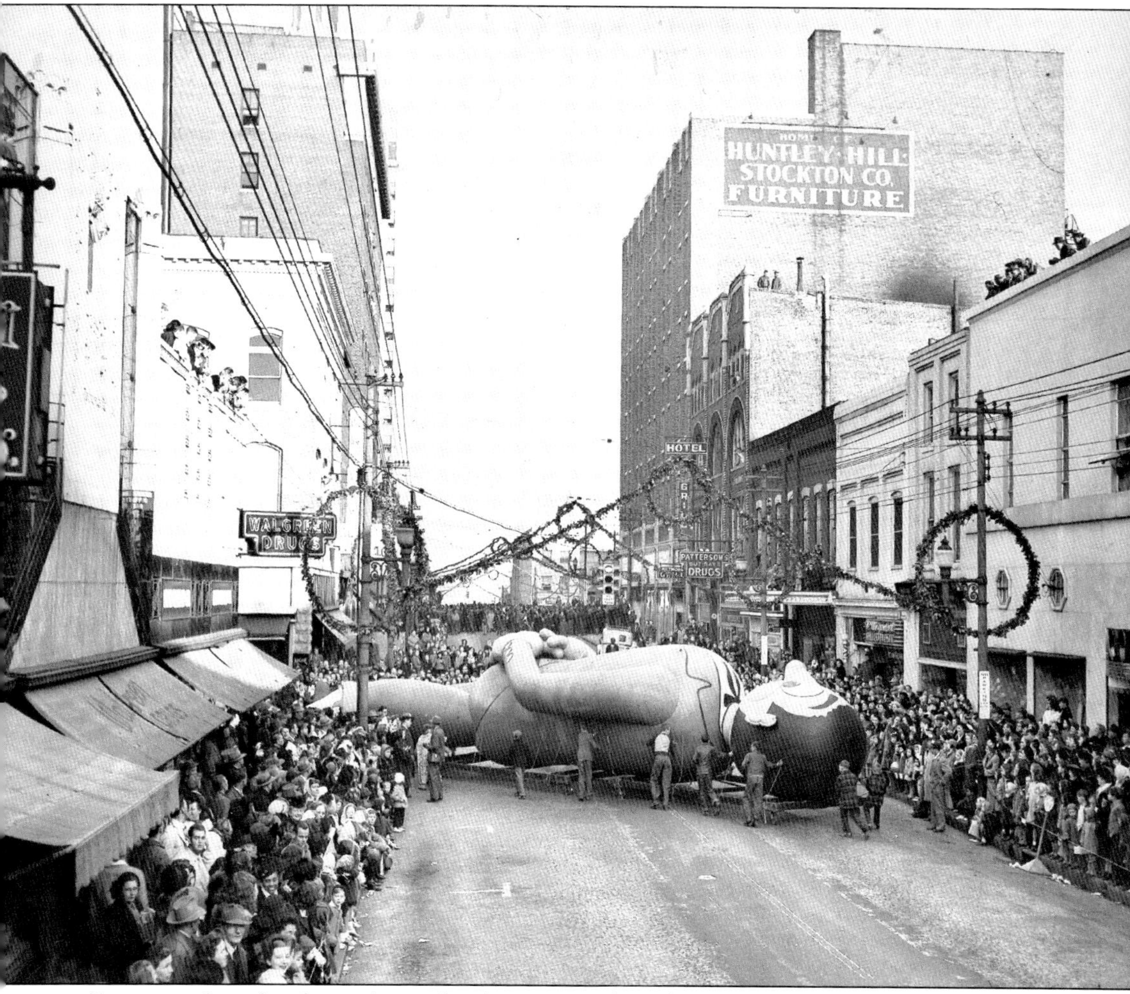

Everyone who is familiar with parades always remembers the granddaddy of all parades, the Macy's Parade on Thanksgiving Day. Not to be outdone, Winston-Salem decided on its own Macy's Parade including the large floating characters. Unfortunately there was one problem. The street poles and lighting decorations were much too low, but it would not stop a Christmas parade.

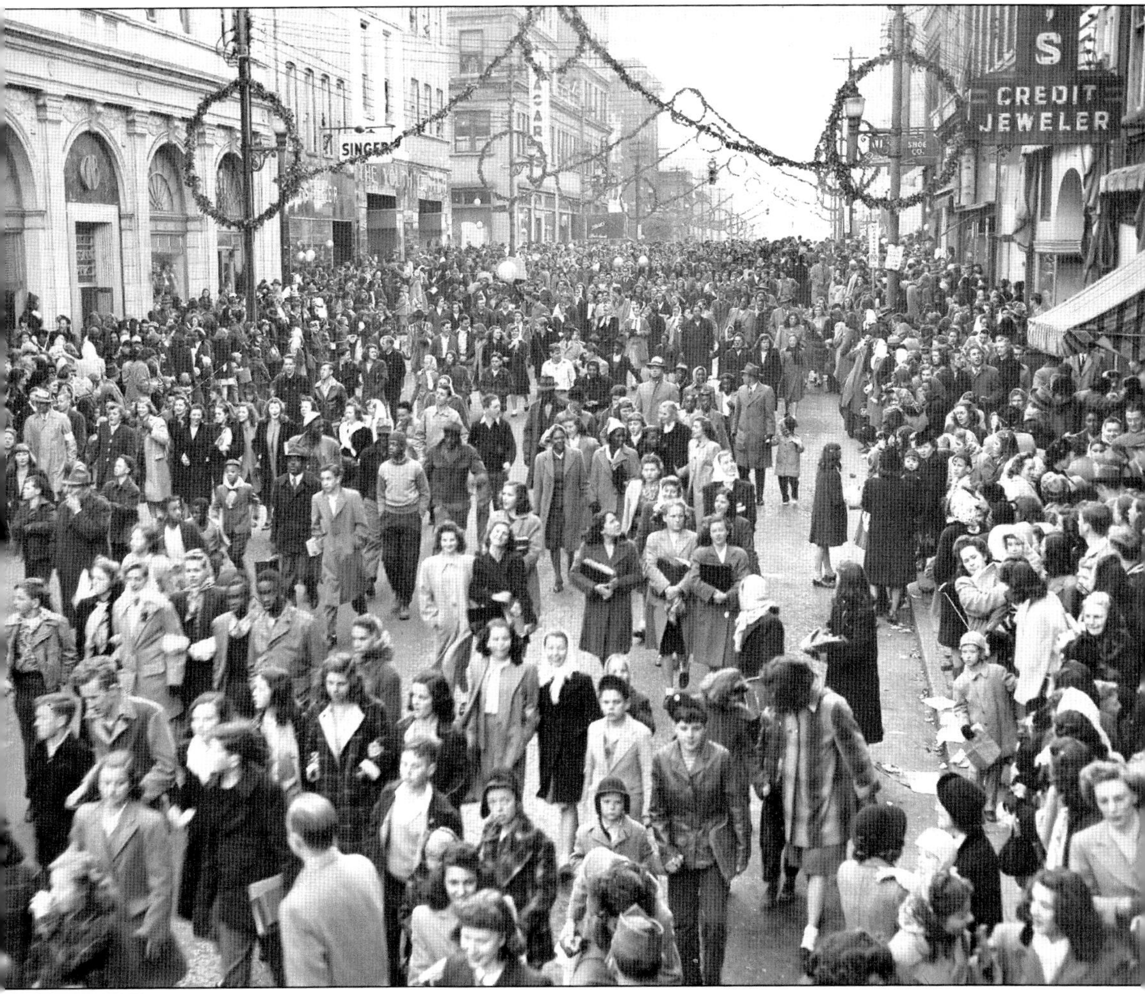

The end of the parade was at hand. The real part of the parade would begin. Masses of people after the Thanksgiving Day parade in Winston-Salem with gifts on their mind would venture to the stores for a purchasing frenzy.

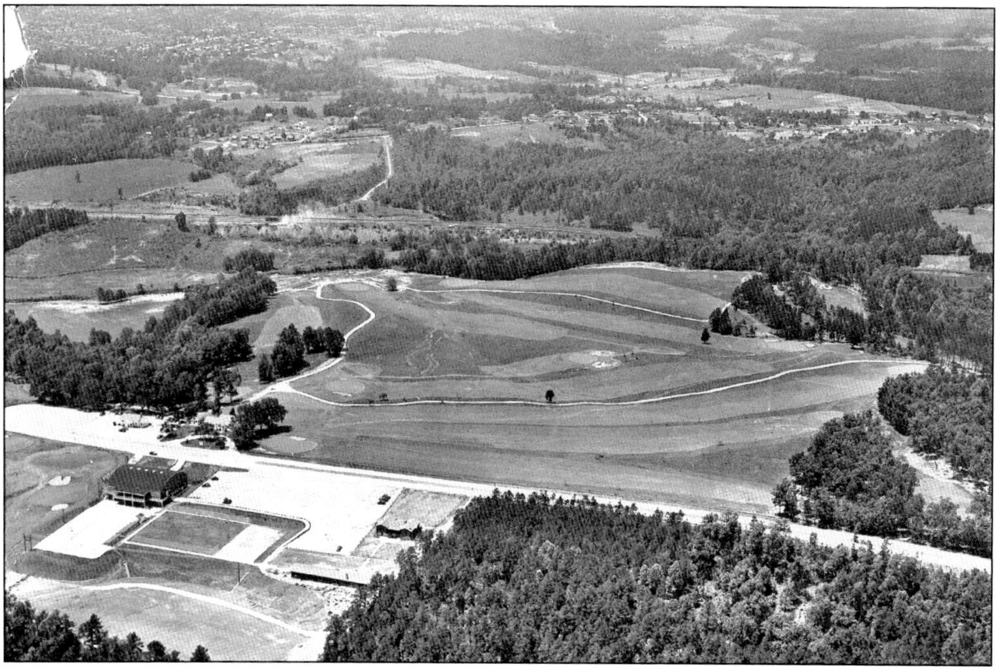

Parades, circuses, and moving pictures have entertained West Salem and city residents throughout its history. An amusement park joined the entertainment list in the early 1940s. Reynolds Park had a golf course, swimming pool, gymnasium, a miniature train, and carnival rides as depicted in this mid-1960s photograph. The swimming pool, gymnasium, and golf course still exist today; however, the amusement rides are history. A West Salem resident related her most enjoyable moment was had at Reynolds Park. It was 1945 and the loud speaker announced World War II had ended.

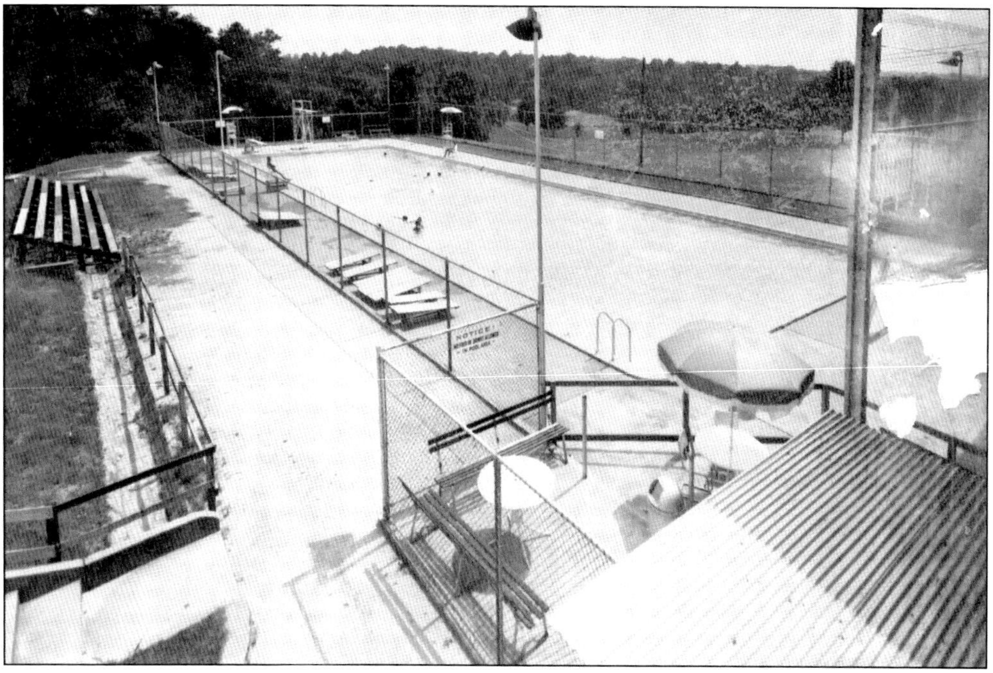

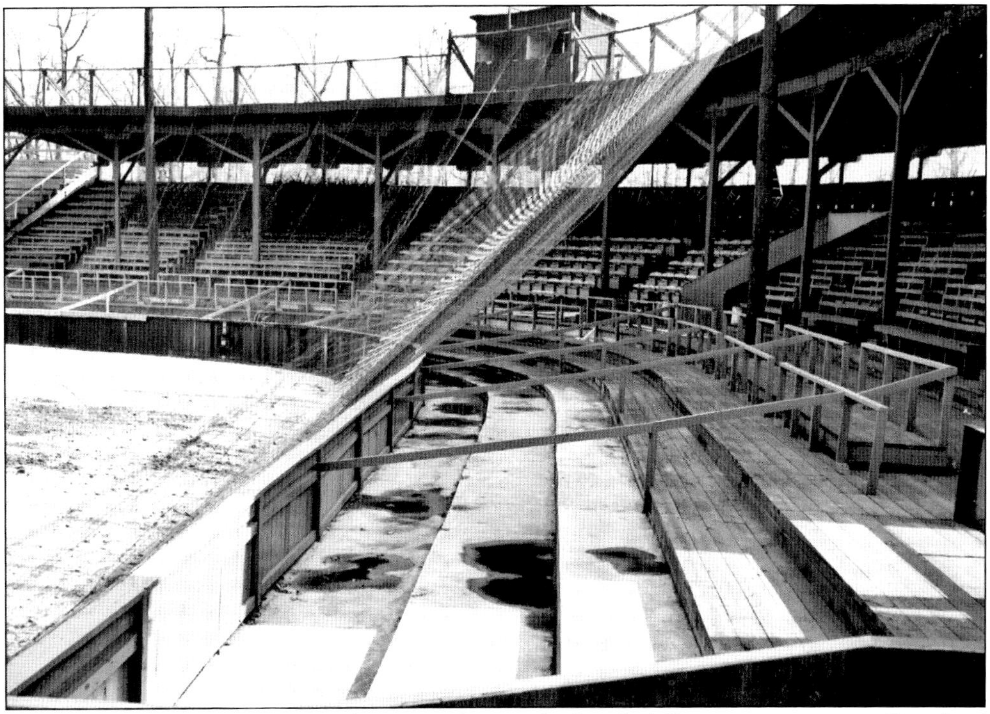

After Winston and Salem merged in 1913, fun was had with dollar train excursions, Fourth of July celebrations, summer band concerts on the Courthouse Square, and picnics in Nissen Park. Commercialized recreation began to develop with the expansion of the motion-picture theaters. In the late 1940s, the city had 6 motion-picture theaters, 11 swimming pools, bowling alleys, and stables and riding schools. Several golf courses were also made available to the residents. Southside Ball Field, pictured, was the premiere baseball park. It was home to many local celebrities and athletes. Even the first professional boxing match presented in the Twin City was fought with Jack Gross, who was billed in an article by Frank Spencer as a possible contender for the vacant heavyweight title. He scored a technical knockout over Billy Dugan in the third round.

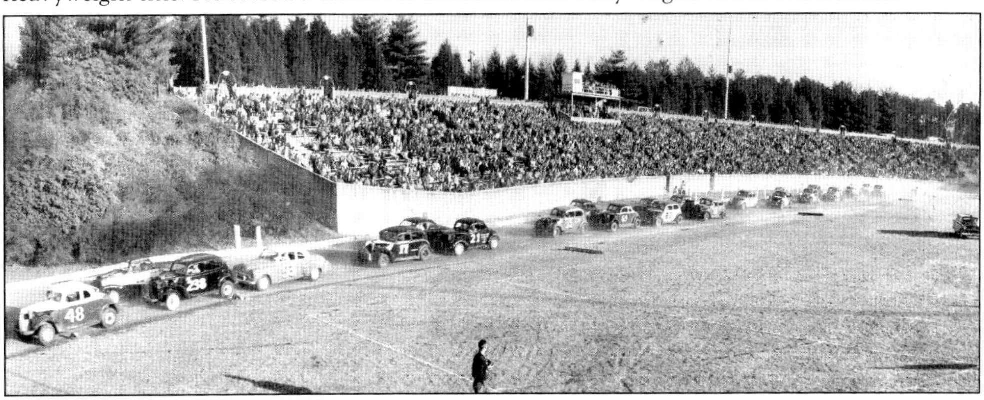

Bowman Gray Memorial Stadium was built as a Works Progress Administration (WPA) project aided by private funds from the Bowman Gray family. At a cost of $200,000 and with seating for 12,000, the facility was dedicated with the 1939 football game between Duke University and Wake Forest College. Soon a regular Saturday night program was established at Bowman Gray Memorial Stadium with the involvement of the National Association of Stock Car Racing. The track served as a proving ground for some of NASCAR's biggest names.

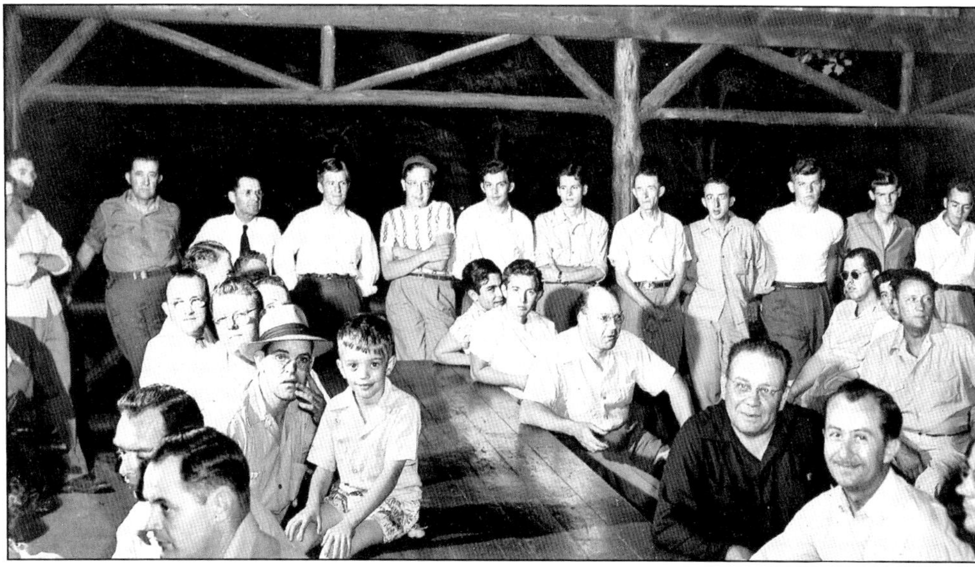

West Salem youth and adults were amazed and entertained by the newsreels and movie previews of the Saturday movie matinee playing at the State, Paramount, and Carolina theaters downtown. The newsreels ended, and the childhood fun began with the movie fantasies of cowboys and Indians, space explorers and G/men. Also the movie houses on Liberty and Fourth Streets would have live stag shows. The State Theatre, being the oldest at the time, began as vaudevillian performances and silent movies in the early 20th century. In the 1930s, 1940s, and even 1950s, movie stars and Hollywood cowboys would grace the stages of these local movie palaces to entertain their young audience. Hop-a-long Cassidy, Red Ryder, and others would join the list of earlier performers such as Hoot Gibson, Rudolph Valentino, and the greatest magician of all times, Harry Houdini, in playing the hallowed halls of the State and Paramount theaters.

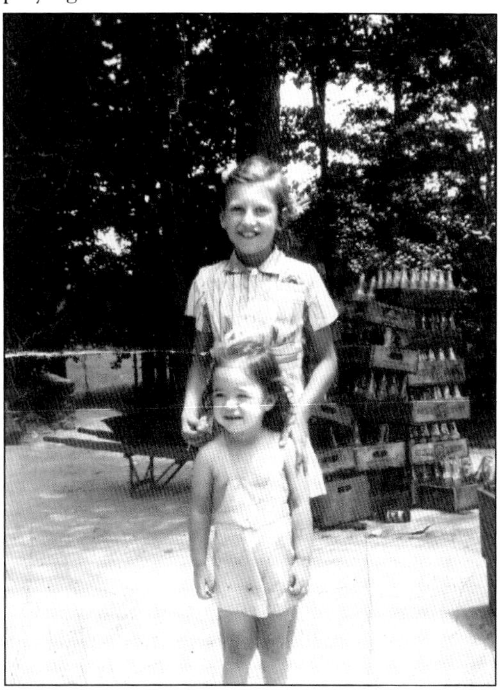

Picnics were some of the most enjoyable times for West Salem residents. It gave all a chance to relax and socialize. The relaxing at an afternoon movie at one of the movie houses, a church meeting, or discussing the past weeks always sounded better with good friends and good food.

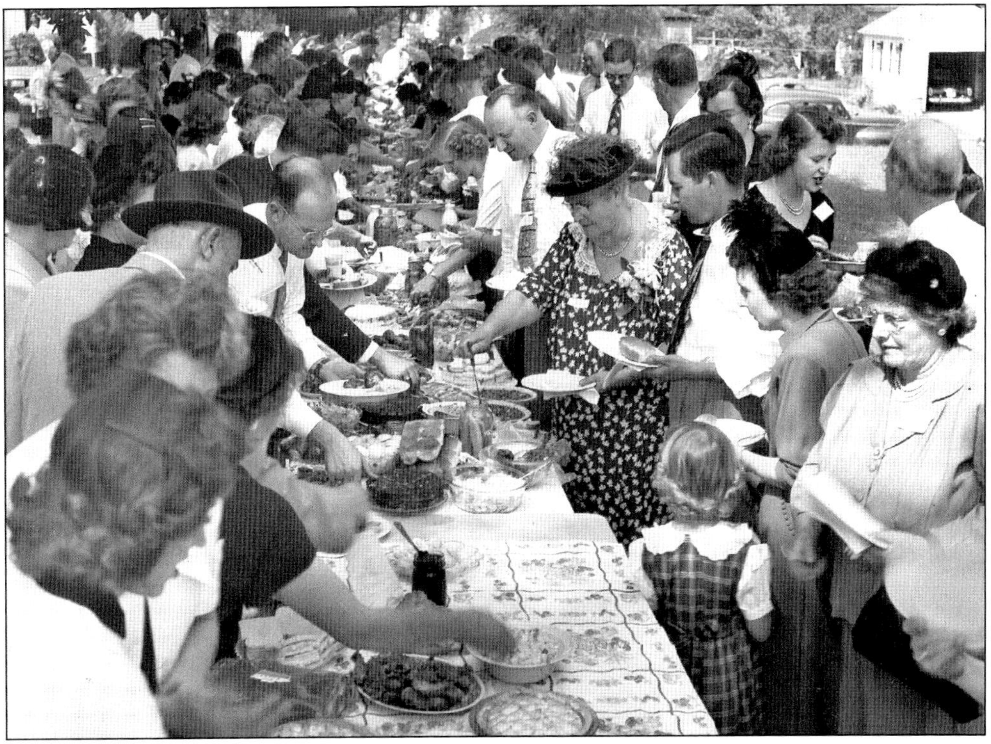

Bryant Lee of Holland Street relayed his involvement growing up in West Salem. One of his great memories is the many picnics and outings. The churches were the mainstay of most picnics, as shown here on the church grounds of Christ Moravian Church. Lee relays another place that was wonderful for a picnic was in the area of Peters Creek Parkway and Academy Street. This had originally been the home of the Salem Paper Mill and Industrial Complex. The complex had disappeared more than 60 years before, leaving a growth of beautiful flowers, a rolling creek, and quiet area for a picnic.

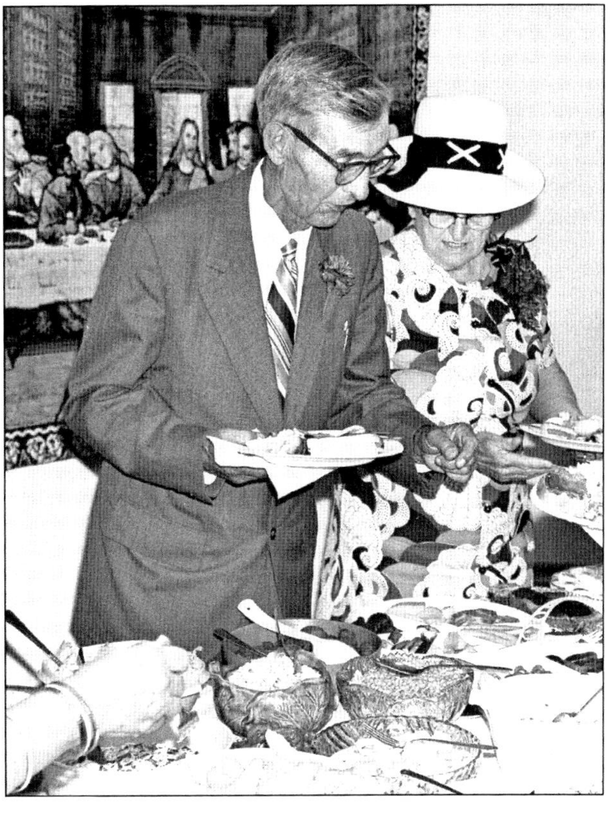

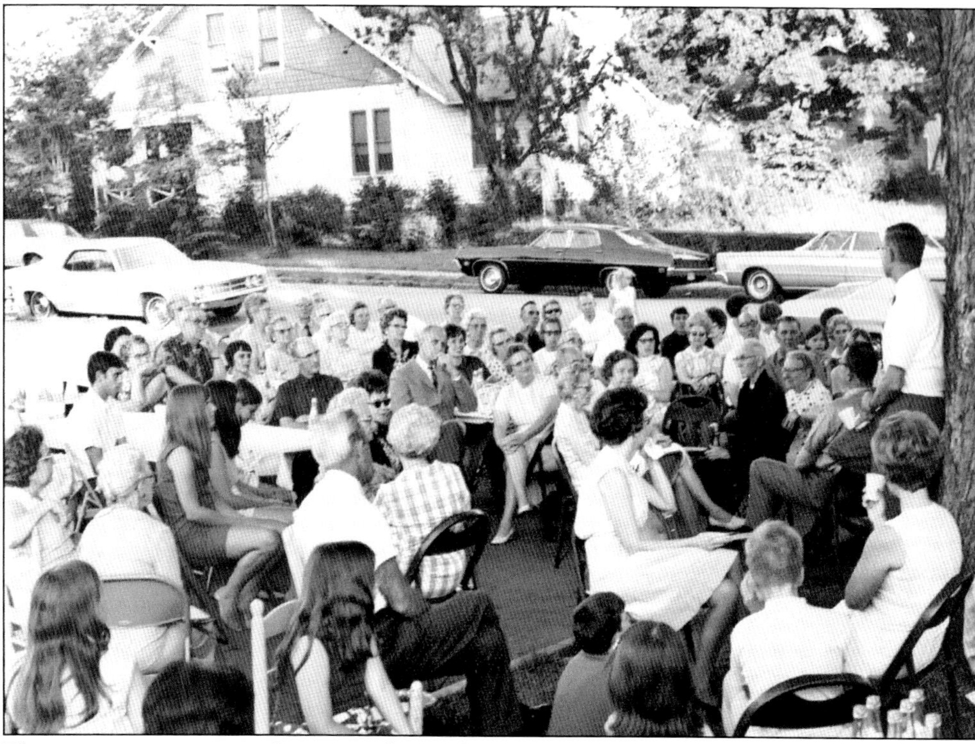

The picnics were a way to bring people together as shown above.

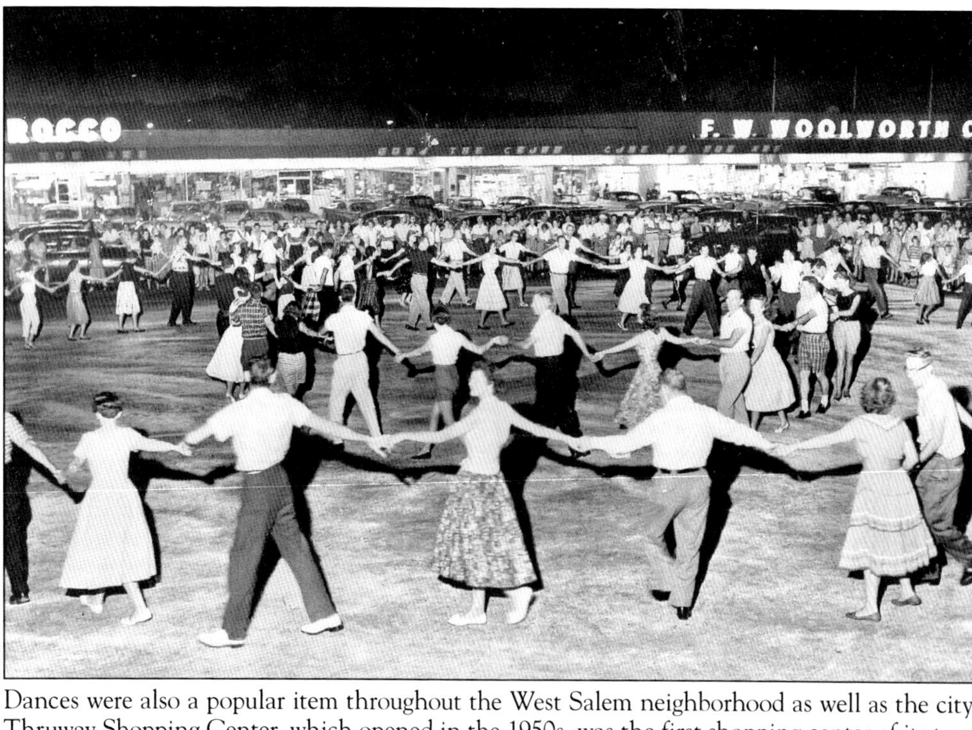

Dances were also a popular item throughout the West Salem neighborhood as well as the city. Thruway Shopping Center, which opened in the 1950s, was the first shopping center of its type in Winston-Salem.

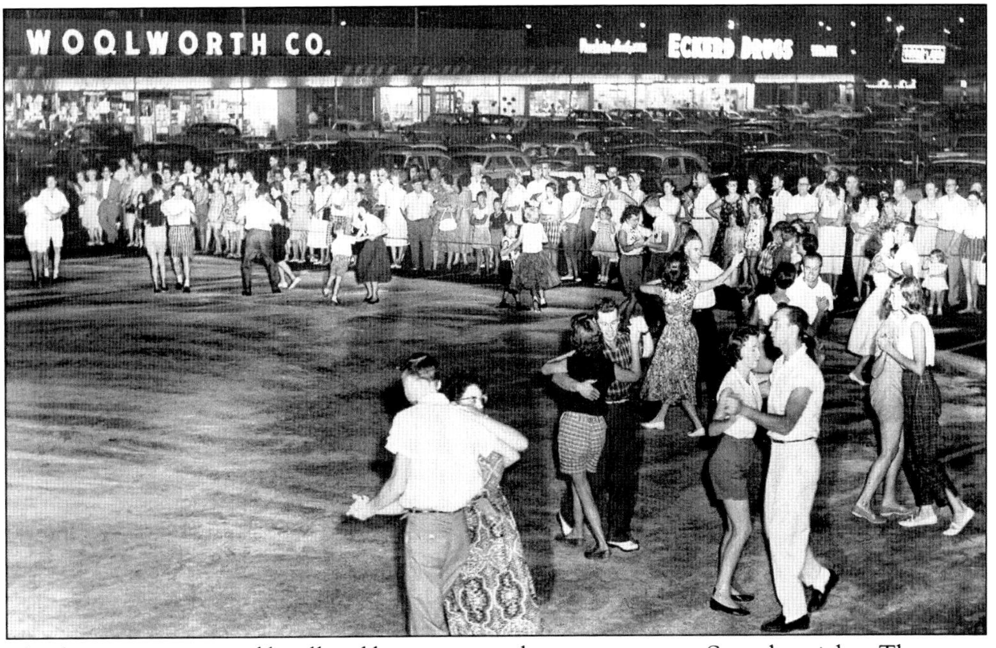

The dances were enjoyed by all and became a regular occurrence on Saturday nights. They were hosted by the Thruway Shopping Center and local radio channels.

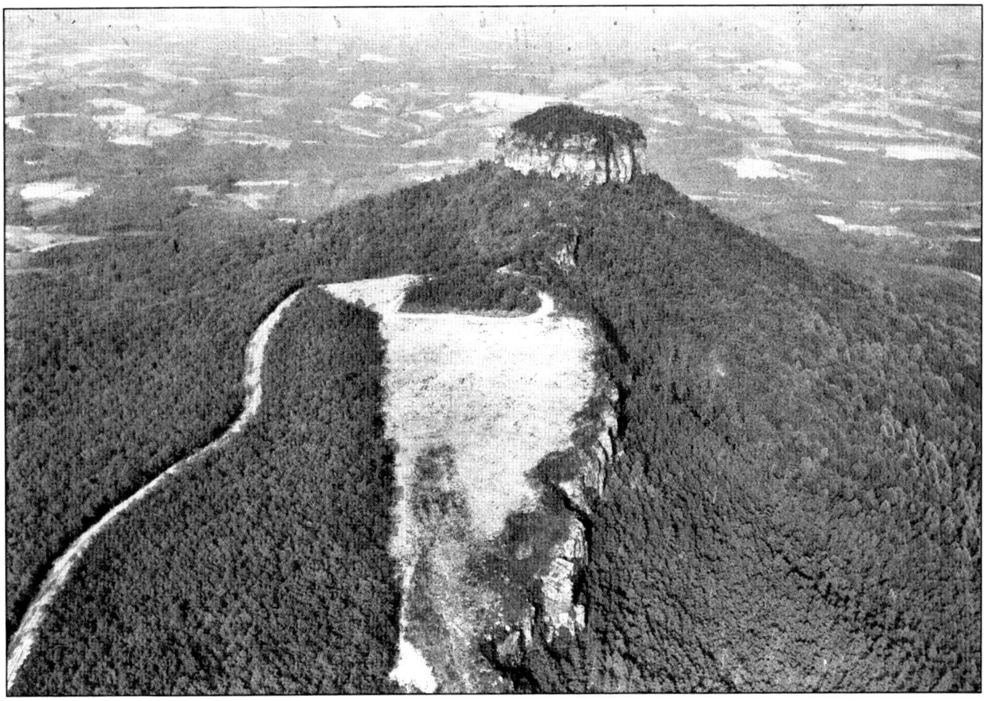
Excursion to Pilot Mountain had become more and more prevalent. Couples could hike, picnic, and enjoy the outdoors and their time together. One of the fascinations of the West Salem residents was in climbing the knob by way of the old steps, which had been constructed in the 1920s. The steps became unsafe by the 1960s and were torn down. The views of the knob are all that exist for couples today.

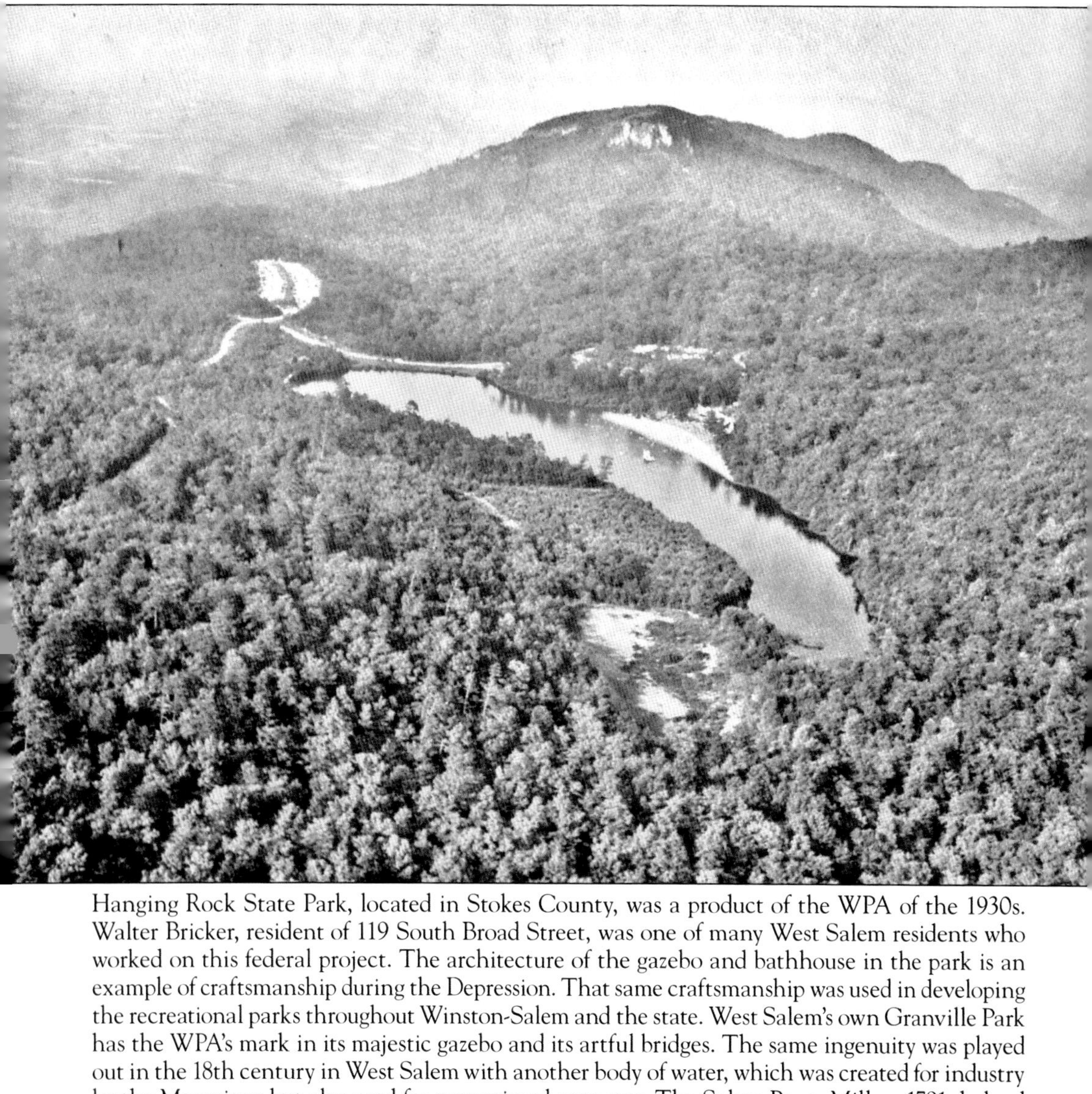

Hanging Rock State Park, located in Stokes County, was a product of the WPA of the 1930s. Walter Bricker, resident of 119 South Broad Street, was one of many West Salem residents who worked on this federal project. The architecture of the gazebo and bathhouse in the park is an example of craftsmanship during the Depression. That same craftsmanship was used in developing the recreational parks throughout Winston-Salem and the state. West Salem's own Granville Park has the WPA's mark in its majestic gazebo and its artful bridges. The same ingenuity was played out in the 18th century in West Salem with another body of water, which was created for industry by the Moravians but also used for recreational purposes. The Salem Paper Mill, c. 1791, helped to create the second industrial complex of the Moravians. The Paper Mill Settlement used the Paper Mill Pond for recreational purposes. During the summer, the Moravians swam and boated on it. The Single brothers built a boathouse on the pond. The winters in the 18th and early 19th centuries were much colder than today. The pond froze over every winter, and the water sport of ice-skating commenced. The industrial area closed in the 1870s after the paper mill burned. The area was almost forgotten except by neighborhood children in the 20th century looking for some summer fun from the heat. A dip in Peters Creek was always refreshing.

Five

West Salem Land Creates a City

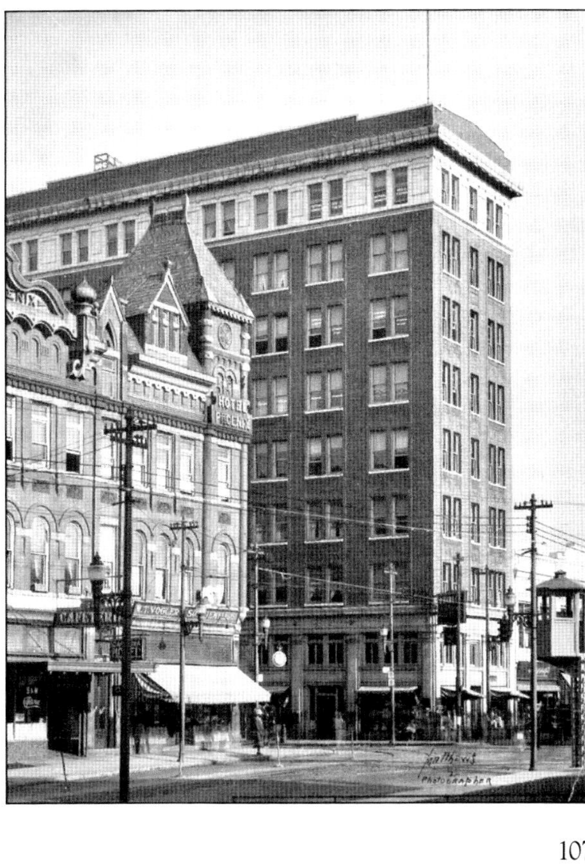

The beginning of the 20th century brought about huge growth in Winston, North Carolina. Winston had grown greatly from its 1847 beginnings from West Salem land owned by the Moravians. In 1915, E. W. O'Hanlon completed the construction of Winston-Salem's second "skyscraper" at the corner of Fourth and Liberty Streets. The building was eight stories with a mezzanine on the ground floor. For two years, it would reign as the city's tallest structure. The Phoenix Hotel was built in the 1890s. Each of its 72 rooms had steam heat and running water. It also had its own café, Phoenix Café. The Phoenix Hotel was torn down in 1928 to make way for the present Pepper Building.

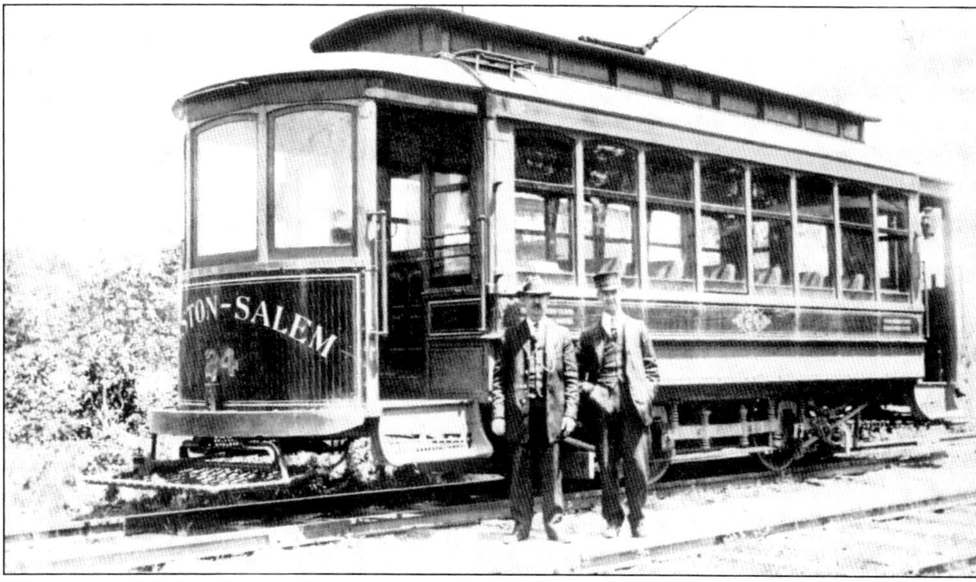

Winston and Salem began the movement for an electric street railway. In January 1891, the Electric Company and the Street Railway Company were consolidated under the name of Winston-Salem Railway and Electric Company. Several West Salem residents were employed by the Winston-Salem Street Railway Company. On March 11, 1899, the Winston-Salem Street Railway Company was incorporated.

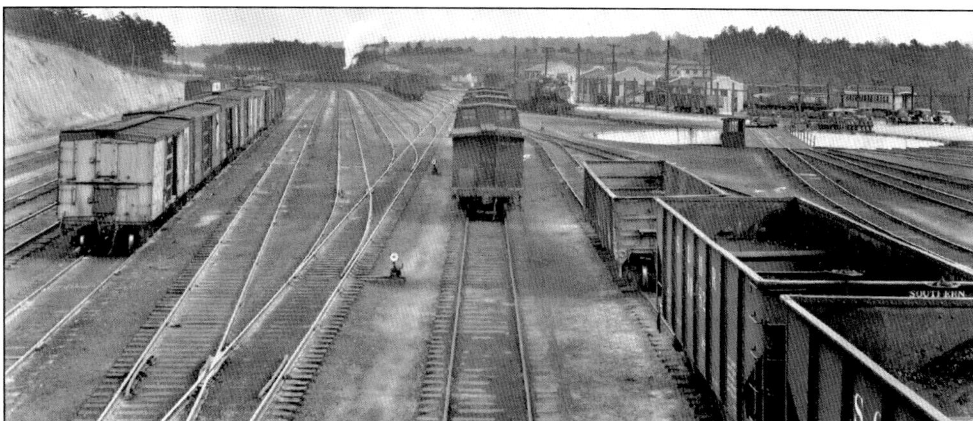

With the opening of the Southbound Railway, Winston's need for a central passenger terminal to service all lines increased. The passenger terminal opened in Winston at the corner of Third and Chesnut Streets in the early 1900s. The southbound freight terminal on South Liberty Street at Cemetery Street arrived in 1905 to the West Salem neighborhood. A West Salem resident who was also a Salem alderman, Mr. Chitty, related an occurrence from his youth that happened regularly along the lines of the southbound train in West Salem. The story goes that the train with its long line of cars loaded with beef cattle stopped at the freight terminal on Liberty. The cars of the full train stretched from the terminal south to West Street. The cattle were unloaded and literally driven through West Salem to the slaughterhouse. The slaughterhouse was located in today's landscape at Silas Creek Parkway near the present National Guard Armory and Forsyth Technical College. In the early 20th century, the land was swampy and very rural and also home to a garbage dump. The sound of the cattle drive was very loud and a unique experience for a young person growing up in West Salem.

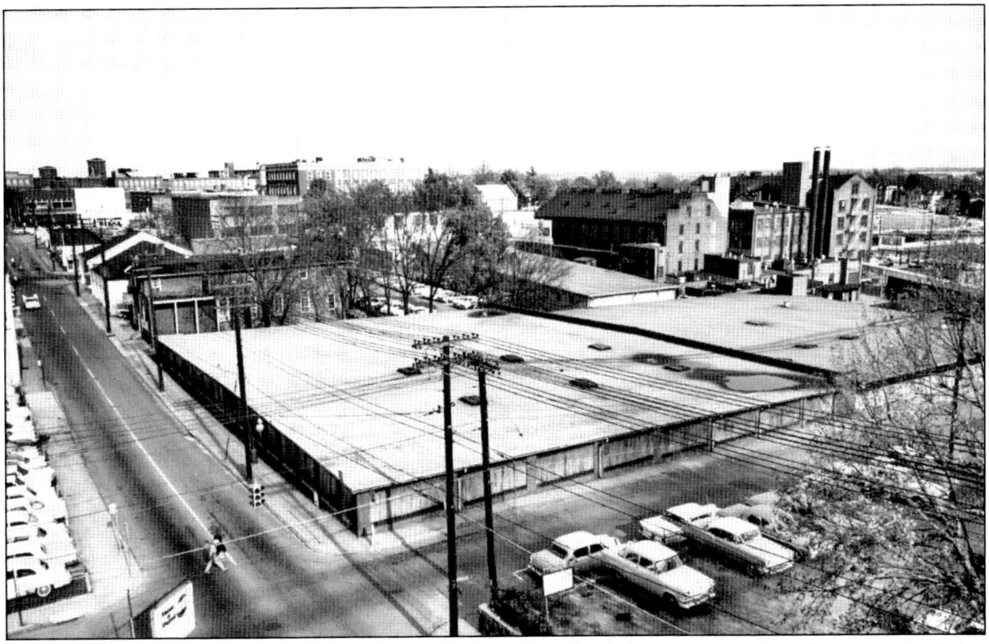

West End Resort Hotel was to be the prominent hotel of the city and the playground of the rich. That idea was destroyed with the burning of the hotel shortly after it was built in the 1890s. The neighborhood would grow up and connect with the West Salem streets of Broad and Green Streets.

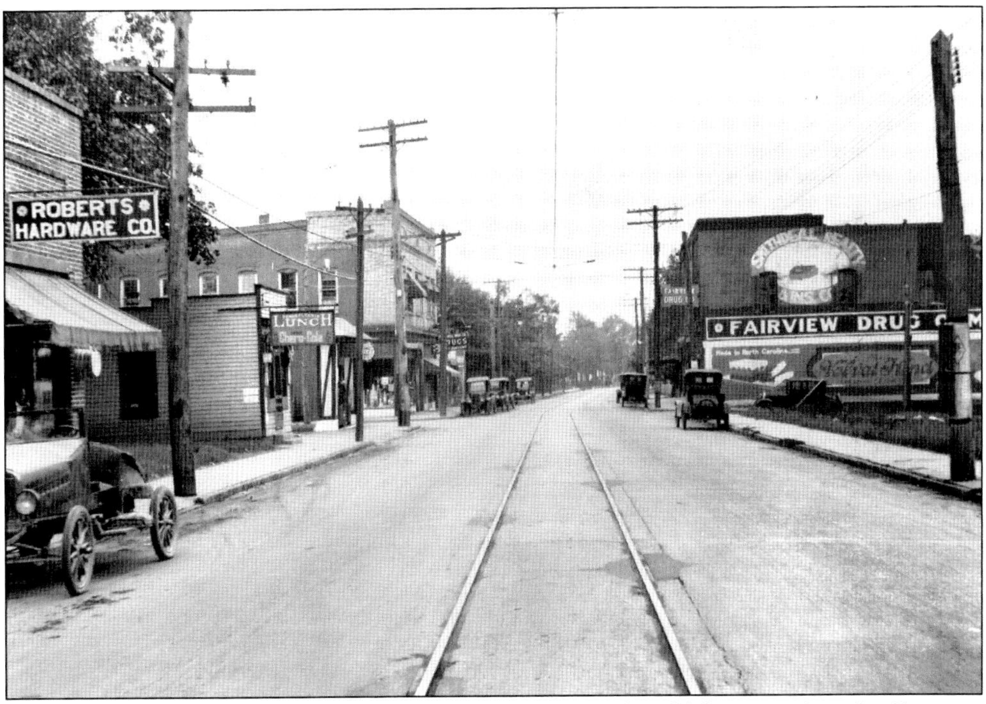

The trolley line extended out North Liberty Street past the old fairground to the Fairview community. The Fairview community had been anchored by the Moravian Church. This church was joined by several West Salem residents, including the Ruff family in the mid-20th century.

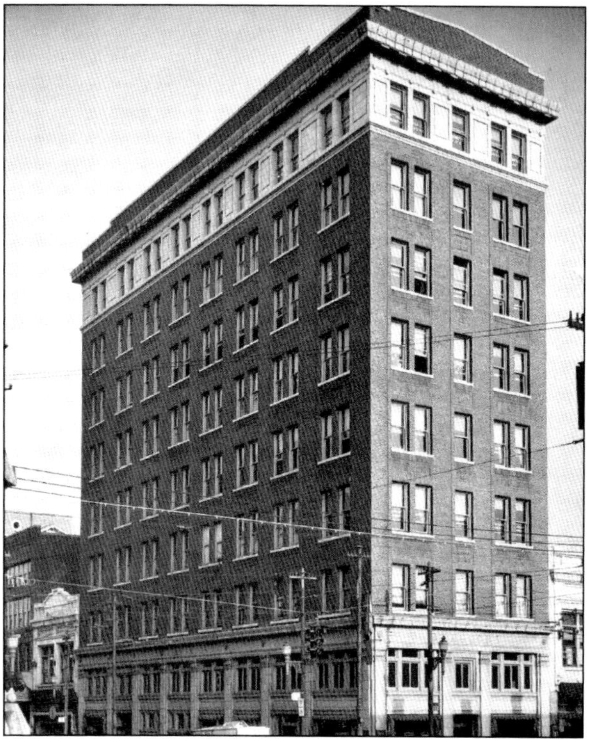

The O'Hanlon building was a hub of business and pleasure. The O'Hanlon Drug Store was a popular hangout and meeting place for West Salem teenagers throughout the 20th century. A downtown movie and a milk shake often topped off a wonderful Saturday night. The building is shown around the 1920s.

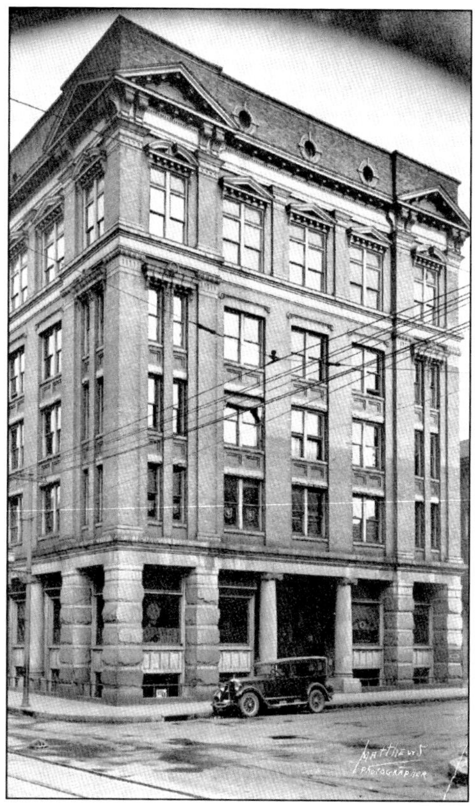

The Masonic Temple was erected in 1906 for the Masonic Order, a mainstay in Winston and Salem. On Fourth and Trade Streets, it was built with Masonic craftsmanship and Mount Airy granite. The building was built to last the test of time; however, for no apparent reason, it was torn down 20 years later. A one-story drugstore, Walgreens, took its place. Many West Salem residents remembered the temple, and for many years, it was a mystery story told at the Green Front Store by Frank Jones of the *Journal* and others. The story goes that the Masonic Temple was razed after it was discovered by the Masonic Order that war or some type of event of great importance was going to occur. This was such a negative occurrence that the Masonic Order decided that the power of the building could fall into the wrong hands. This razing of many of the Masonic temples throughout the United States occurred. Whether this is just an old wives' tale, some validity is had in the fact that a one-story business replaced it. In 1926, when the one-story building was built, the city's plans for Fourth Street was to have large skyscrapers from Fourth and Liberty Streets west to Broad Street. The temple is shown c. 1920 before it was destroyed.

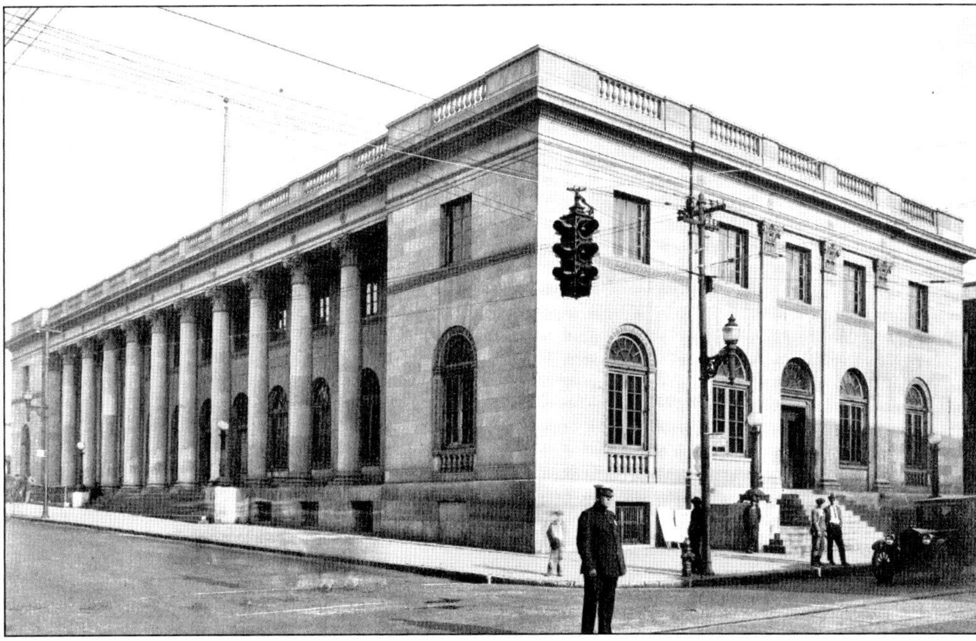

The post office, on its Fifth Street site, was then much smaller and had a working force of 40 at that time. There were 14 letter carriers and 4 substitute carriers; 10 railway mail clerks, who worked in and out of town, were paid through the local office. King Brown of 921 West Street was a postal employee for over 40 years. West Salem had a very large number of letter carriers who resided in the neighborhood over the years.

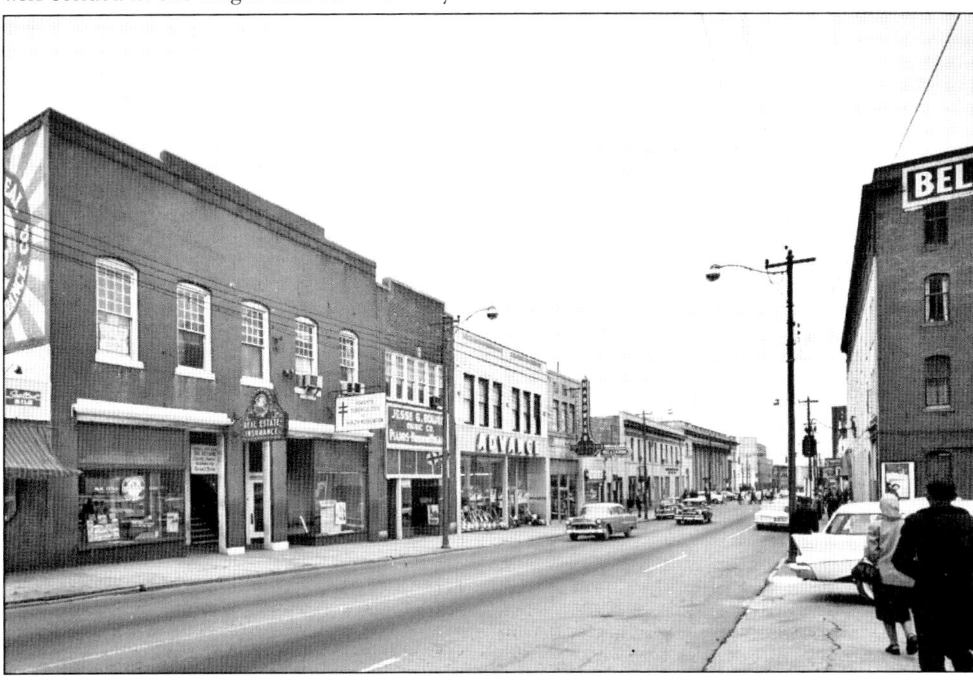

Fifth Street west of the post office saw many businesses grow and expand in this 1920s photograph. West Salem residents would be employed at the post office as well as the second Wachovia Bank and several of the clothing stores along Fifth Street.

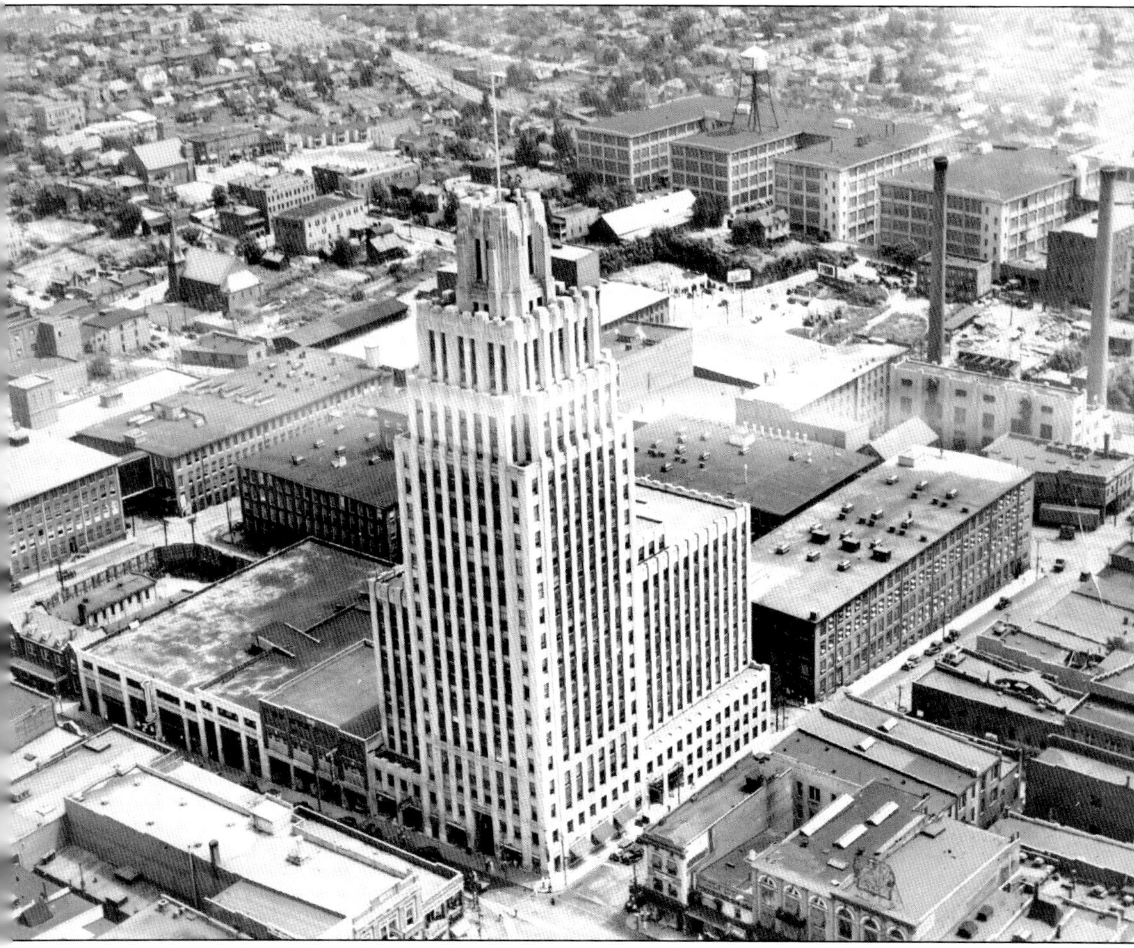

R. J. Reynolds Tobacco Company was chartered in 1890 by the State of North Carolina. Richard J. Reynolds was president of the company. He ran the company until his death in 1918. The Reynolds building, as it was known, was built in 1929 and was the prototype for the Empire State Building in New York City. Mrs. Mary Young Bricker relays that in the early 20th century, her first job was at 12 years old working on the Reynolds "baby line." This was an assembly line worked by young ladies who were brought in by the surrounding farms to learn the factory trade. In the 1950s, the West Salem neighborhood was employed by Reynolds nearly four-to-one over the other companies, and it was two-to-one over the P. H. Hanes Knitting and Hosiery Complex of the same time period.

The 1941 Union Bus Depot on Cherry Street between Fourth and Fifth Streets had an unlikely visitor one day in the 1960s. A Bluebird taxi decided to pick up a passenger a little too close to the bus terminal. The Greyhound Bus Terminal and Garage was another establishment used by West Salem residents. This was located on Marshall Street in the 1920s.

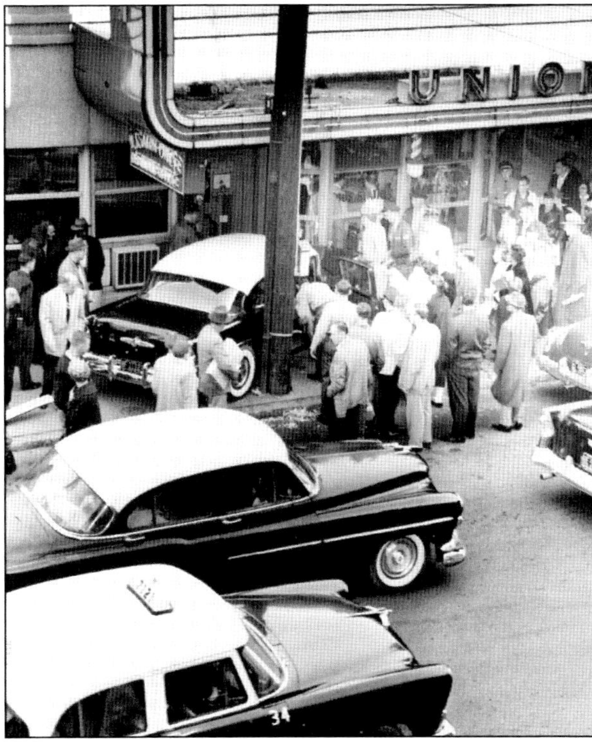

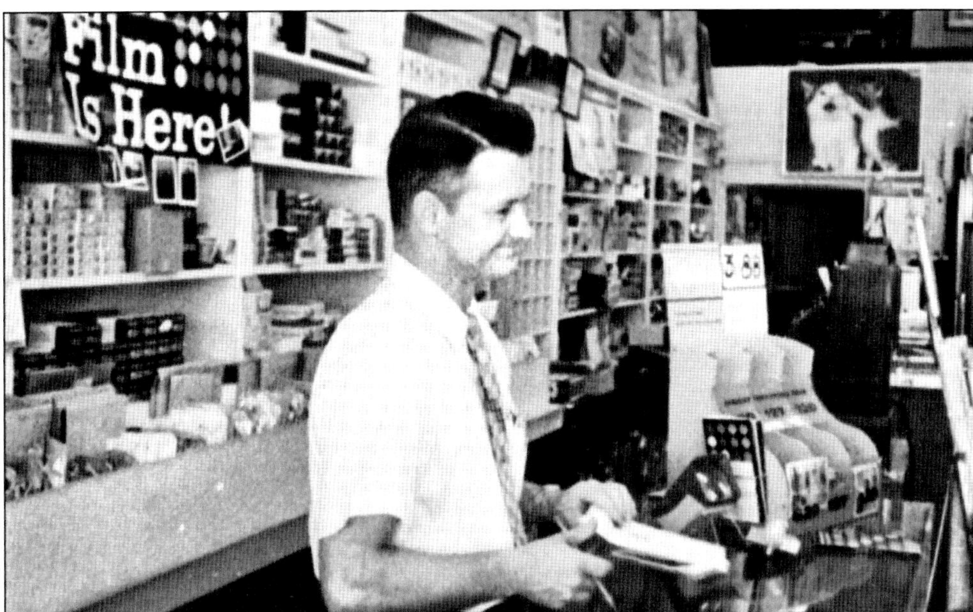

Lindley Photo Company on West Fifth Street was a photography store, which preceded photography shops of today. Mr. Lindley, pictured *c.* 1960s, could answer all questions related to photography. West Salem residents had their photography questions answered through much of the 20th century. Lindley often related stories of holding photographs taken in the 1930s and 1940s until after World War II and into the 1950s until the customers had enough money to pick them up. This is an understanding human trait, which is hard to find in today's world.

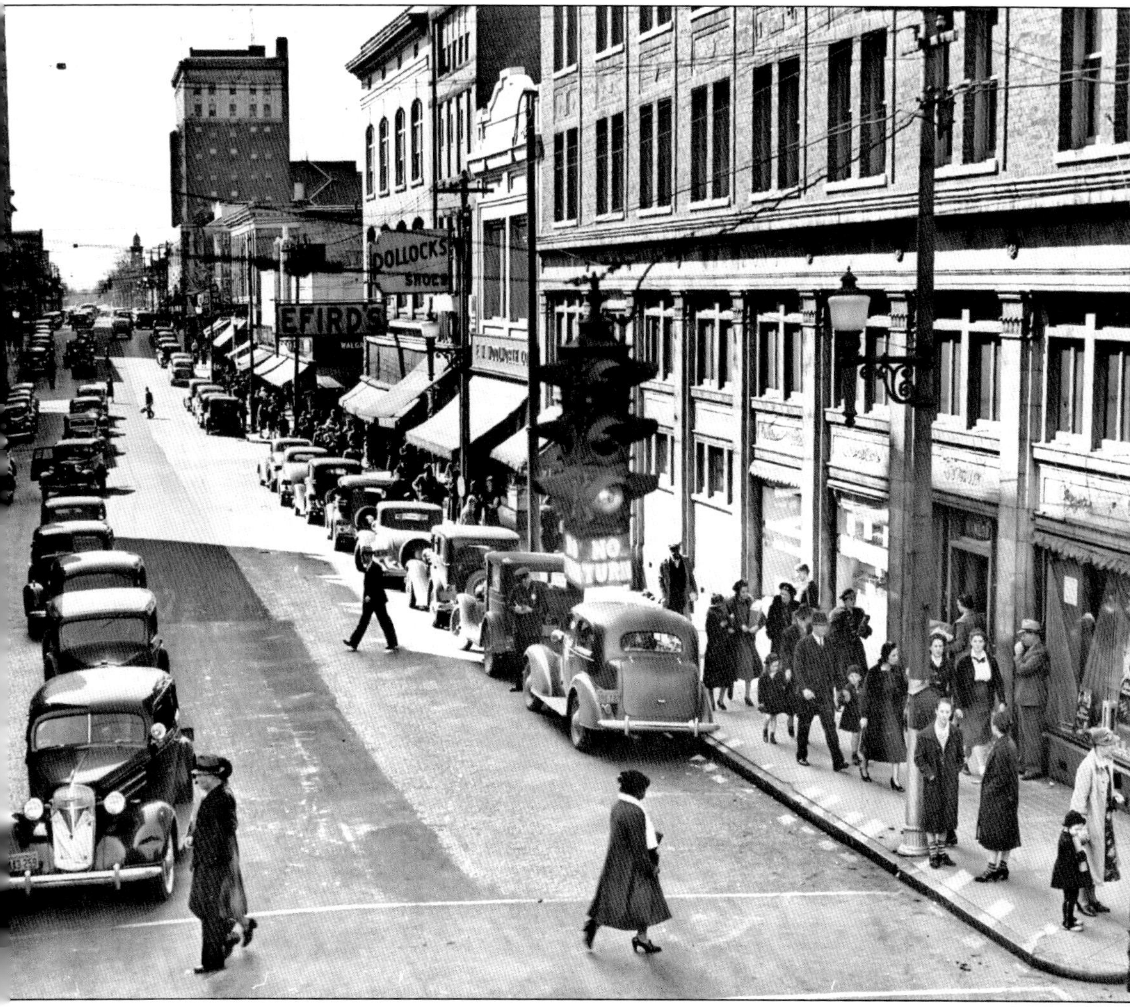

In the winter of 1939, a downtown intersection at Fourth and Liberty Streets gave a brighter depiction of West Salem's premium shopping and socializing experience. The Great Depression had passed, and the horrors of a great war loomed only in the future. The homegrown Efird's Department Store at the middle of the photograph was a benchmark clothing store. The Efird family, who had a tobacco business in the 19th century, called West Salem and West End home.

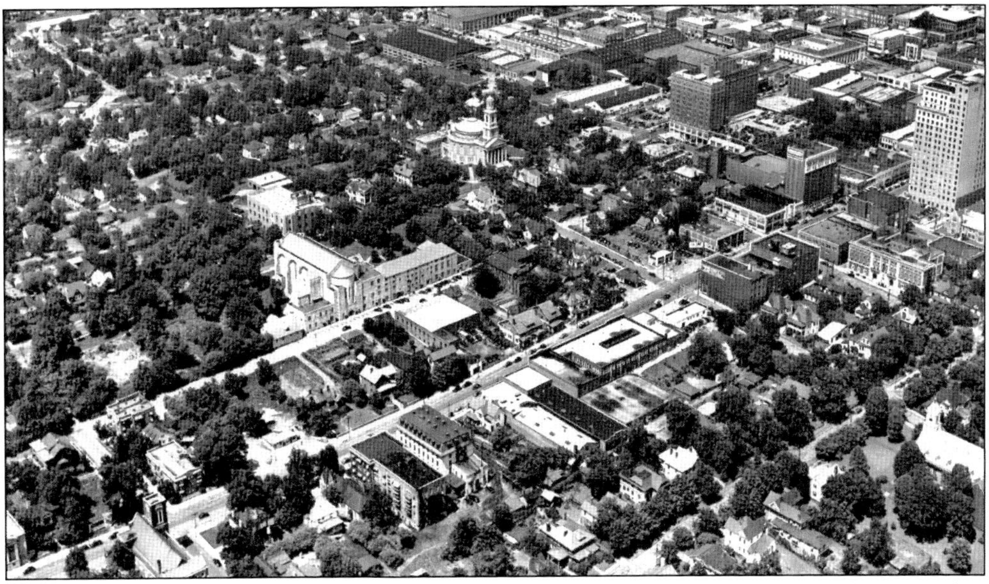

Next to E. W. O'Hanlon's drugstore and office building at left is the Woolworth building. Farther down the block, the Rominger Furniture Company was flanked by the Ideal and Colonial Theaters. East of it were D. G. Craven's department store and the Anchor Company. West Fourth Street looking west from Liberty Street. On the left, at the sign of the boot, is E. E. Hailey's Electric Shoe Shop and Shine Parlor. Between there and Patterson's Cut Rate Drugs are the Rialto Café and Nichol's Hat Shop. Beyond Patterson's are Bus Polite's Candy Kitchen, the Amuzu Theatre, and the Alpha Café. From the right are the Walk-Over Boot Shop, the Pilot Theatre, Efird's Department Store, and, across Trade Street, the Masonic Temple.

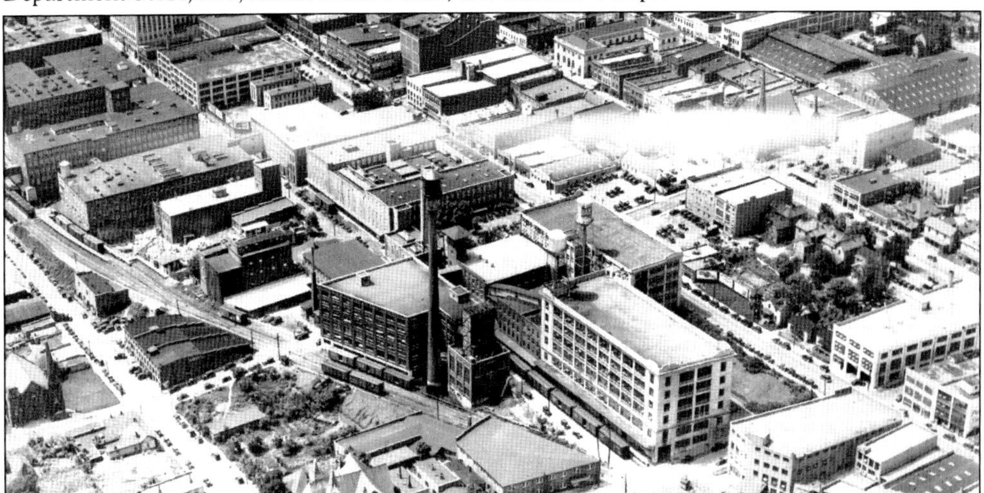

Behind the wagon at left on North Liberty looking south from Fifth Street is Mear's Jewelry Company. Farther down, near Rominger's Furniture Company, are the Broadway Theatre and the Wall-Huske Hardware Company. From the right are the Ideal Photo Company, Martin McNulty's florist shop, the Liberty Street store of the Frank A. Stith Company, Gilmer's Department Store, the Hawkins Company (dry goods), the Arcade Fashion Shop, Cohen's (ladies' clothing), and the Warner Millinery Company. In the distance can be seen the sign of Belk-Stevens' Department Store on the square.

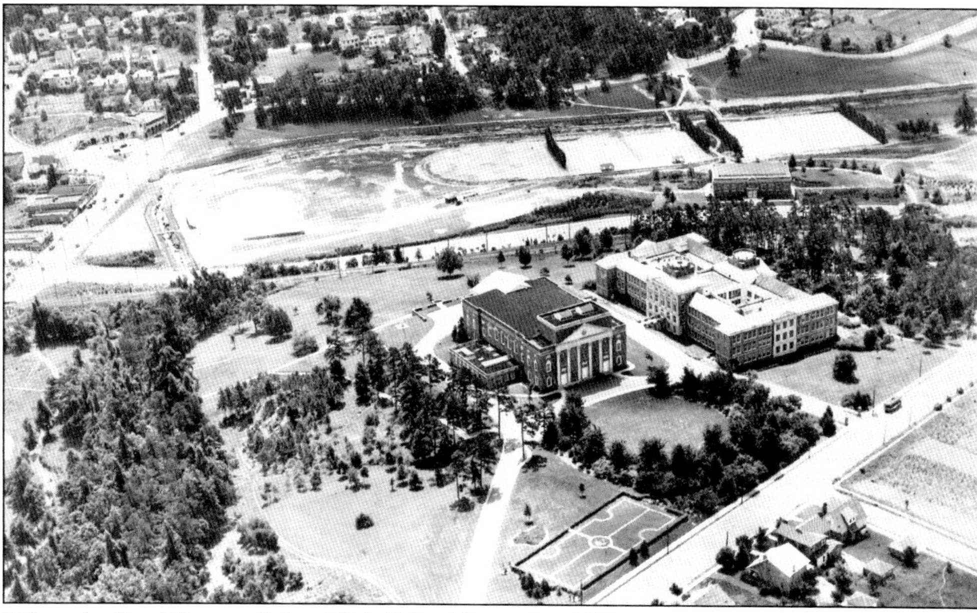

When the first Winston-Salem High School burned in 1923, a new structure was quickly put up on Silver Hill, overlooking Hanes Park and the West End. Catherine Smith Reynolds, widow of R. J. Reynolds, put up the money for a magnificent companion auditorium. It was the finest high school plant in the state, with a gilt-edged faculty to match, among them such mainstays in local education as Mary Wiley, Claude R. Joyner, John Watson Moore, and R. S. Haltiwanger. Seeds sown by Calvin Wiley in the 19th century came to fruition with erection of the James A. Gray (1930), John W. Hanes (1930), and Simon A. Atkins (1931) High Schools, giving Winston-Salem the best secondary education system in the South. West Salem land and the West Salem workforce helped to build this education complex. Travelers to Winston-Salem often remarked of the grandeur of Reynolds High, often mistaking it for a university instead of a high school.

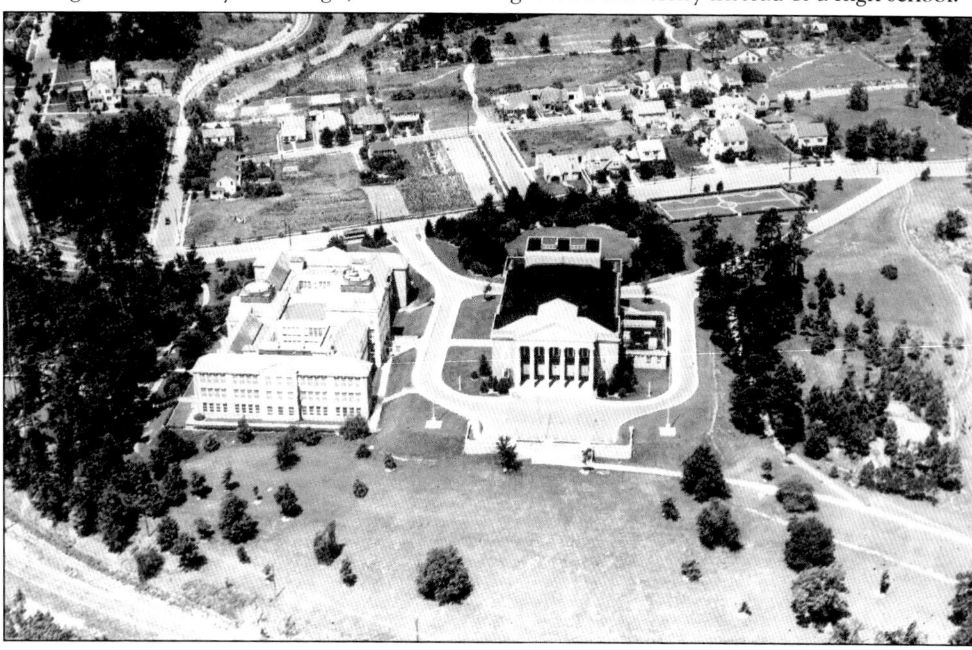

Six

The 19th Century Meets the 21st Century

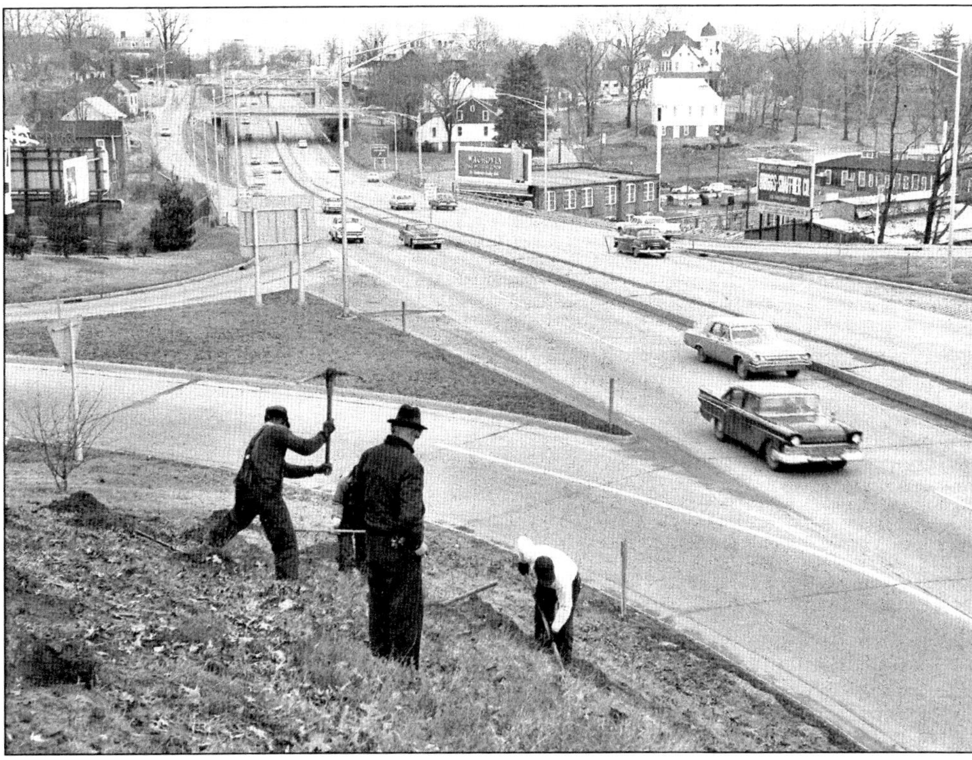

Interstate 40 cut a path of destruction through the West Salem and East Salem neighborhoods. This *c.* 1964 photograph, taken between Broad and Marshall Streets, shows the road's diversion of West Salem's northern part from its southern half. Twenty years after this photograph was taken, the decline of the eastern edge of West Salem was due to its isolation, which the highway brought to West Salem. The eastern edge of West Salem was cut off from its southern half. Older structures to the top and right of the highway visualize an earlier time. The Briggs and Shaffner Complex below the highway on Brookstown Avenue and the two white buildings at the top were examples of this earlier time. The complex of both white buildings dated to the 19th century. All are now history.

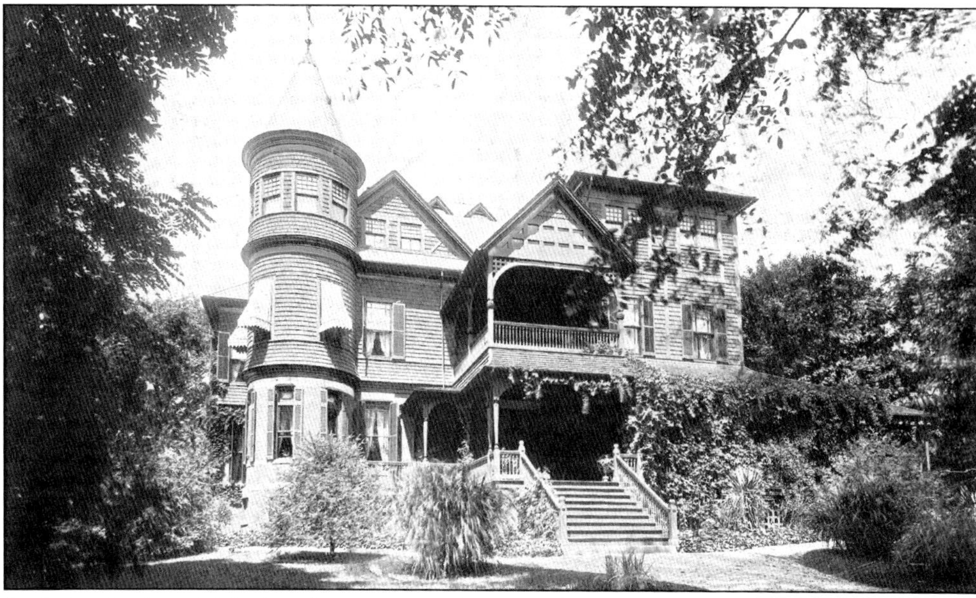

Evolution in the neighborhood compares to the many changes experienced by our county over its long history. North Carolina Moravians and fellow residents found them first in Anson County. The county changed to Rowan County and went through the Revolutionary War period as Surry County. The last descendants were in Stokes County during the War of 1812 and the Mexican War. Volunteers in the Civil War were Forsyth residents. Salem and later Winston found the city's geographical locations changing from county to county beginning in the 18th century. The Thomas Gray estate, shown c. 1880s, was contained in one complete city block. The estate resided at the dividing line between Salem and Winston on West First Street. Gray led the helm of Reynolds Tobacco Company for many years. The estate was razed for a larger living structure, the Downtown Motor Lodge.

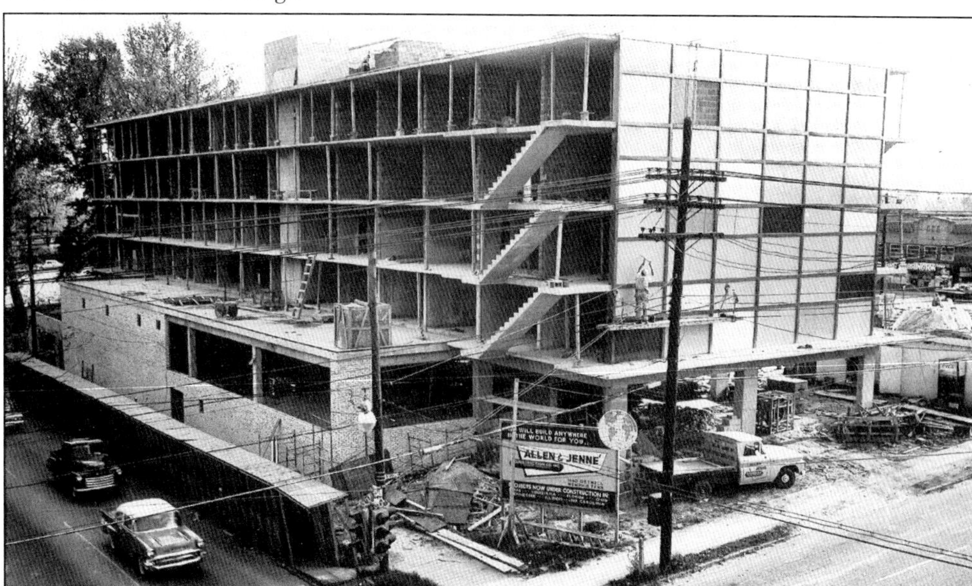

Downtowner Motor Lodge replaces the Thomas Gray estate with a larger structure. The hotel was state-of-the-art in the 1960s.

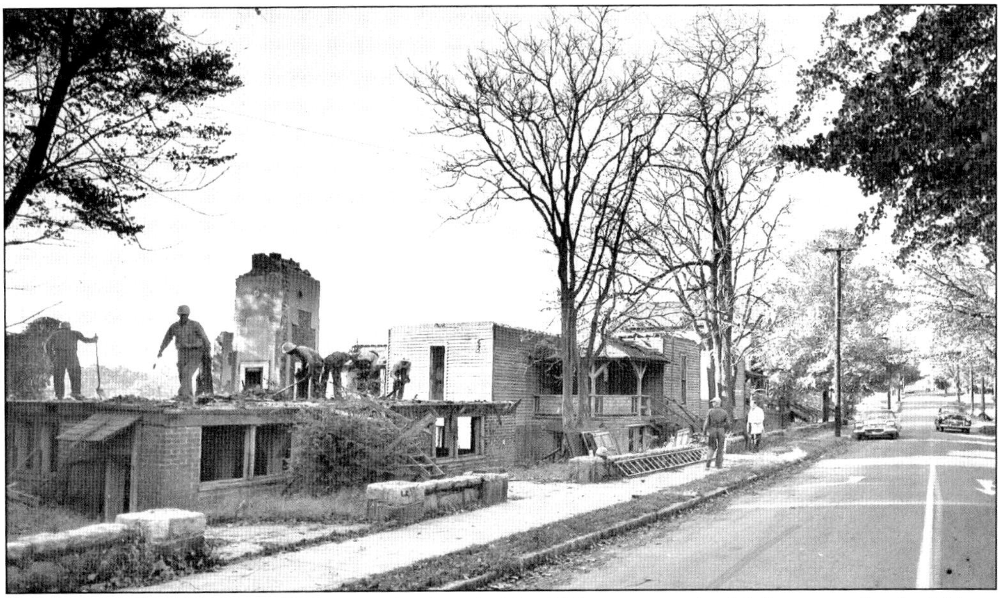

Urban renewal arrived in the city in the late 1960s. Old structures had fallen out of style. Urban renewal cleaned up many dilapidated and obsolete houses and buildings throughout the city. Unfortunately no foresight of historic preservation came with this renewal. The proverbial "throwing the baby out with the bath water" became the rule of the day. Many historical preservationists reworded urban renewal as "urban removal." The 1970s ushered in historical preservation, and older neighborhoods were saved from the wrecking ball. Sadly it was too late for these 1880s wood-frame Victorian-style homes on Green Street at First Street. These homes were part of the original West End and West Salem neighborhoods, which were anchored by the Winston/West End graded school, c. 1882, on Fourth Street.

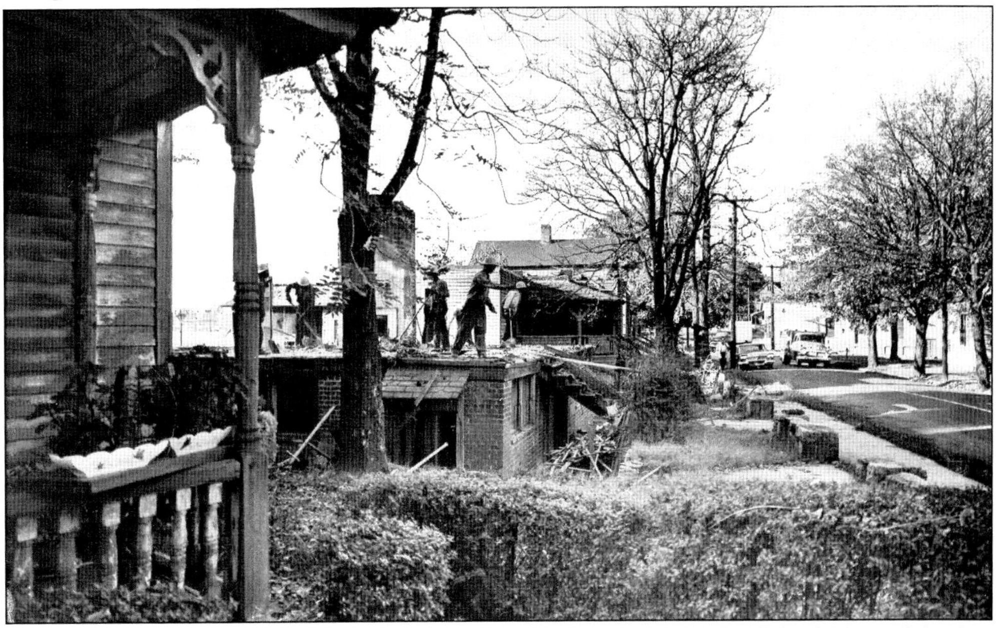

The Green Street removal of 19th-century homes was another example of the decline of the first West Salem and West End neighborhood.

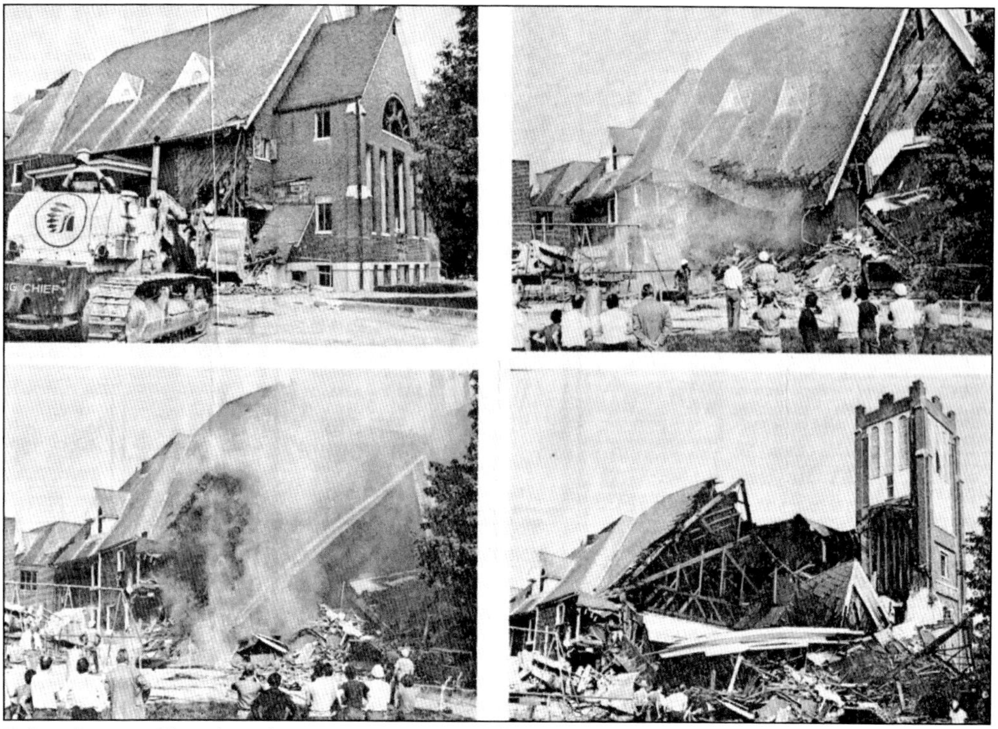

Salem Baptist Church is shown in stages as it falls to the demolition company. The church was razed at a time when the historical preservation movement in Winston-Salem was growing; however, Salem Baptist Church's foundation and supporting structure had irreversible rot damage. It could not be preserved.

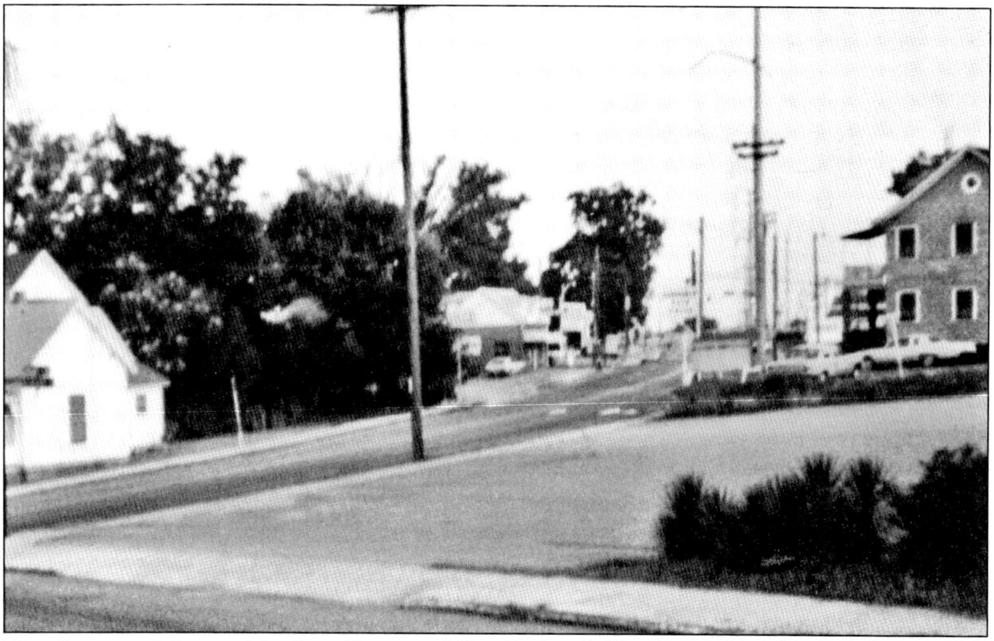

The changes of the neighborhood between West End and West Salem had declined to the point where only parking lots were to be found in this 1970s photograph.

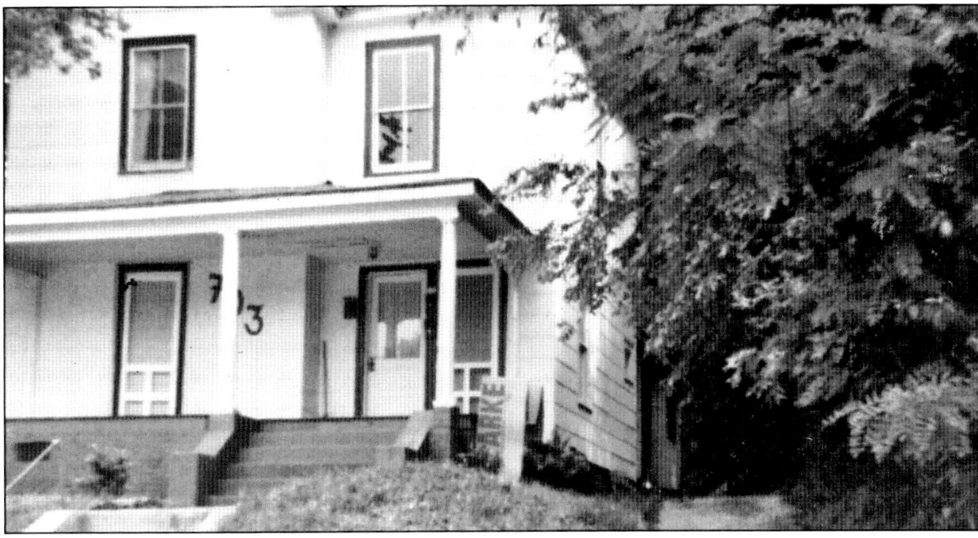

The home at 703 Shallowford is an example of the landscape of the West Salem neighborhood. The house is located on a hill overlooking New Shallowford Road. The driveway to the right of the home is shaded by an entrance located behind the bushes This entrance was the extension of Spring Street from Winston, south into West Salem center part of its neighborhood. Spring Street was divided and cutoff by the construction of Interstate 40 in the 1950s. Spring Street in West Salem was originally named Fairview Street. The last stretch of this 19th-century street exists as a forgotten dirt path on a ridge behind the new Kidney Dialysis Center of Wake Forest/Baptist Hospital Medical Center on Brookstown Avenue.

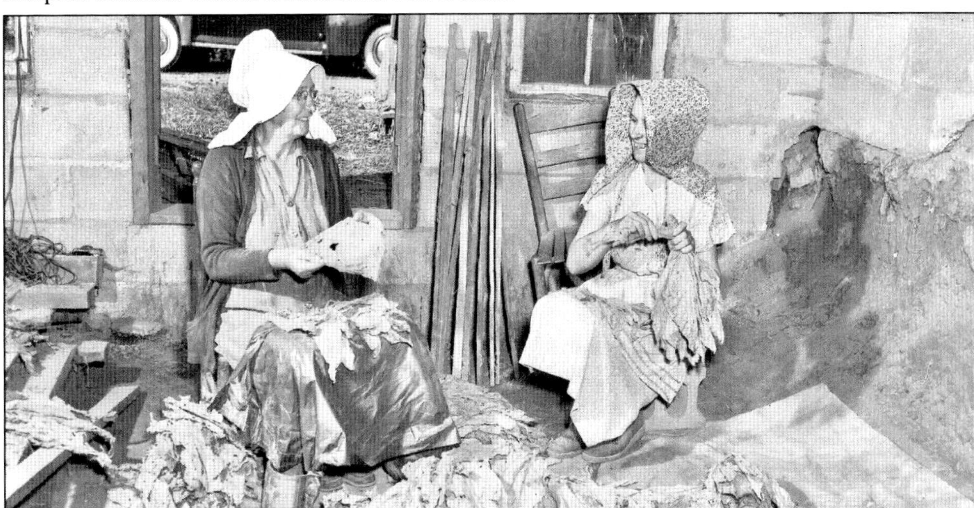

Sharp-eyed buyers follow the chant of the auctioneer. His song was so pleasant to the ear that the American Tobacco Company, archenemy of R. J. Reynolds, for years mounted a successful advertising campaign upon it., with the closing line "Sold American." A farmer unhappy with the price brought by his leaves might "turn the ticket," thereby refusing the bid, and put his goods up for sale another day. Sometimes a simple matter like cleaning the hands of tobacco, would bring on an increase in price. These ladies were not interested in the chants of the auction block of tobacco. This was a simpler time of priming tobacco by hand and cozy conversation. They wanted no part of the bickering and salesmanship of their male counterparts.

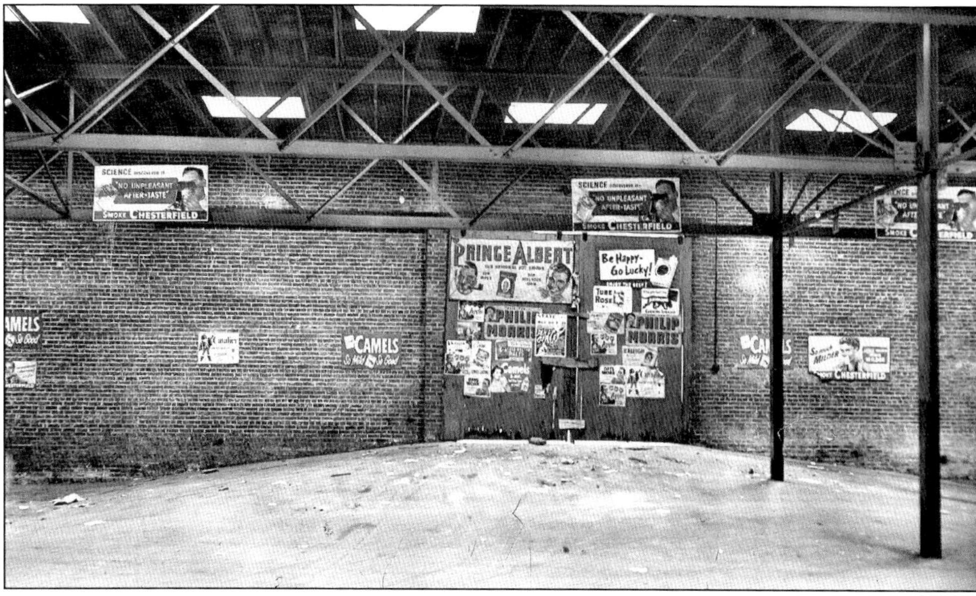

Hands of tobacco were stacked on circular baskets and dollied into the warehouse for weighing and grading. A "hand" consisted of the number of leaves the worker could hold in one hand while the tier knotted the stem ends with another leaf. The sights and sounds and the pungent aroma of cured tobacco are precious memories of childhood for those girls and boys lucky enough to have been there. Warehouses included Gorrell's, Pepper's, Piedmont, Planter's, George-Davis, and Carolina Central. On the streets, shoes, hats, crisp new overalls, and "Sunday suits" are offered for sale. After the sale, all that is left are old advertisements and an empty tobacco warehouse.

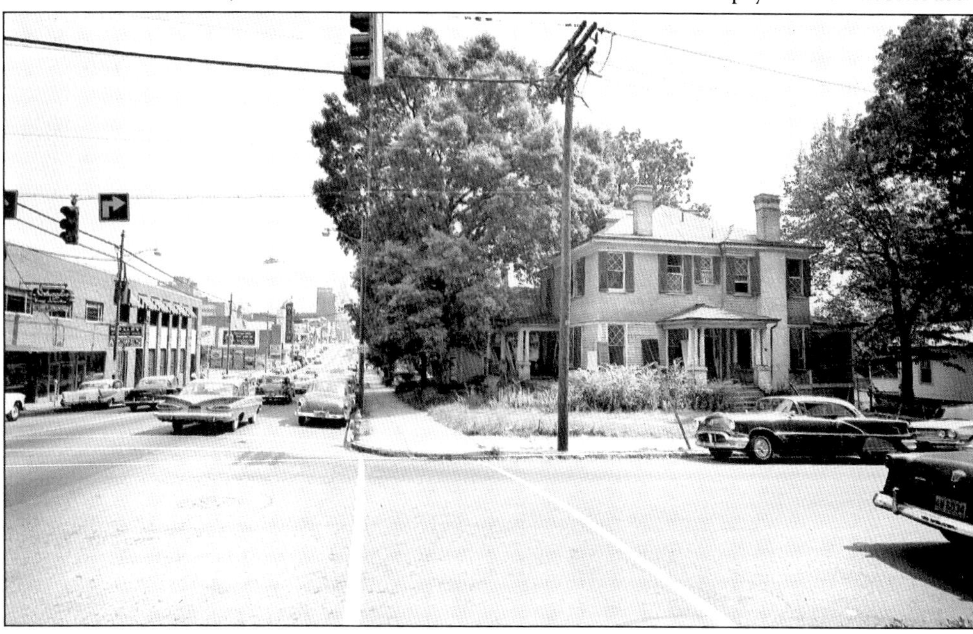

The intersection of Fourth Street and Spring Street in downtown Winston shows one such house that is being razed. Many West Salem residents not only tore down older homes, but also salvaged their remains. Before the historic preservation movement had found its way to Winston Salem, West Salem residents recycled and reused all forms of housing products.

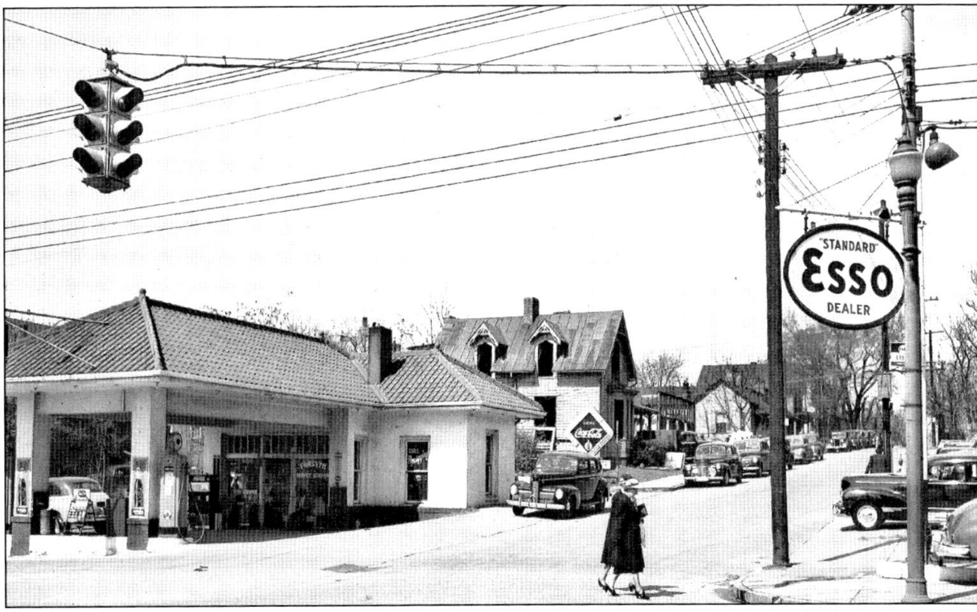

Fourth Street and Spruce Street was home to Woolworth's and Bocock-Stroud, which provided jobs for many West Salem residents. This section of downtown at Spruce Street and West Fourth Street is preparing for the expansion of business with soon-to-be-razed homes in the background.

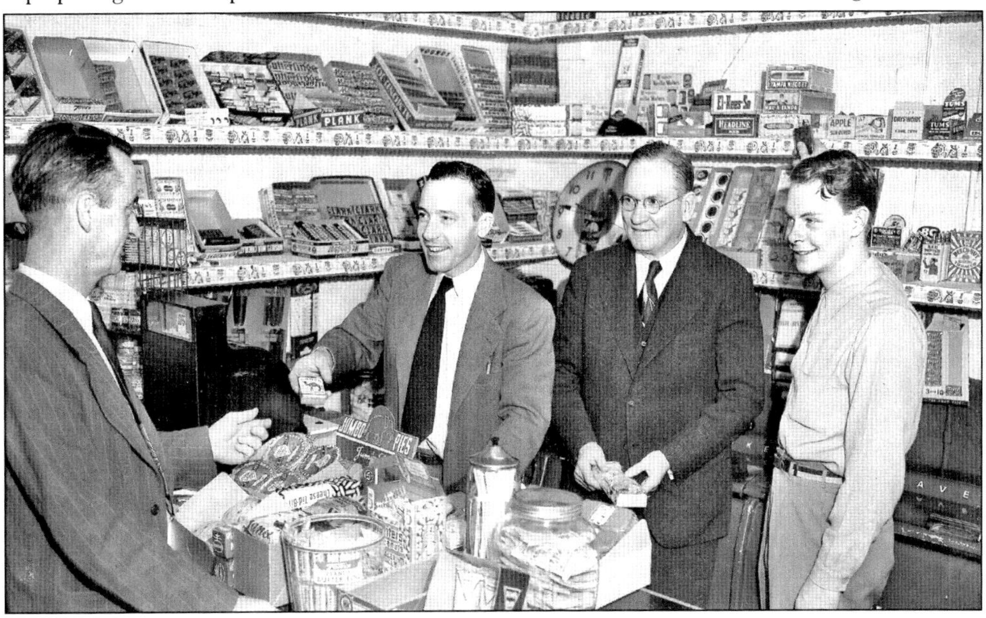

Neighborhood grocery stores were found throughout the older neighborhoods of Winston and Salem. Beginning around 1910 to the 1960s, family-run stores, some as small as 10-by-10-feet, were found on nearly every block. The city directory of 1918 recorded a total of 135 white and black grocery establishments in the city limits, which measured only a couple of miles in circumference. Eighteen stores alone were found in West Salem. An example of one of these smaller stores is shown in the photograph from the late 1940s. Frank Jones, photographer for the *Winston-Salem Journal and Sentinel* for over 40 years, is shown second from left buying one of the city's trademarks, a pack of Camel cigarettes. The other gentleman may have other purchases in mind—snacks.

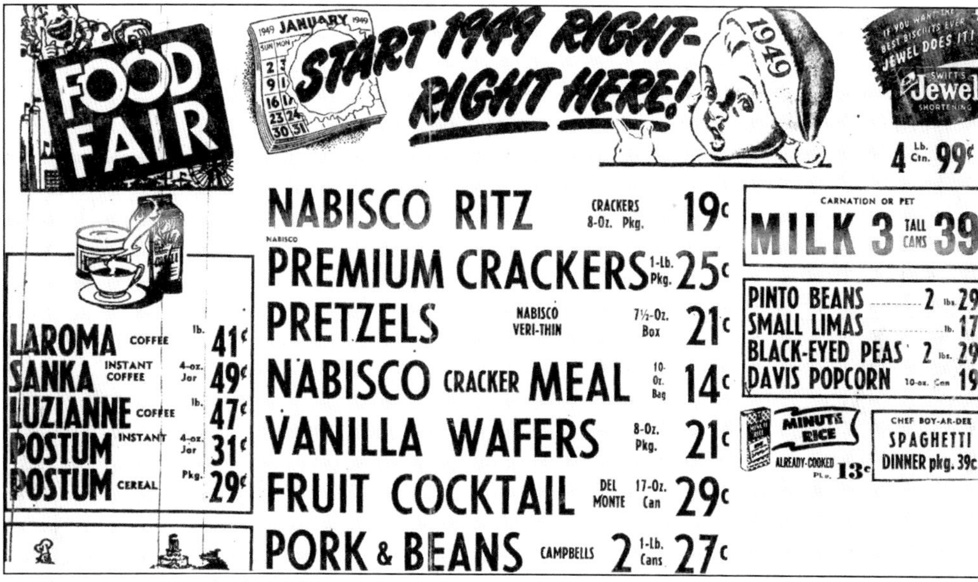

Food Fair was an early chain founded by the local Messick family after World War II. These chain stores were the demise of the "ma and pa" grocery stores of yesteryear. Many residents worked and retired from this establishment.

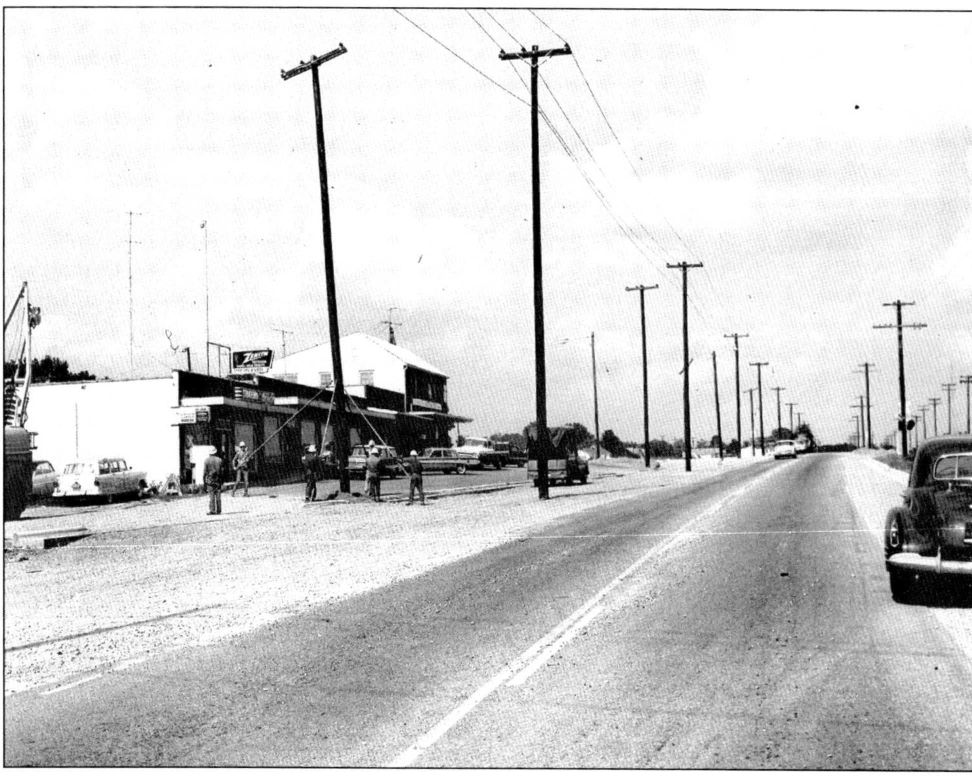

Stratford Road is shown in the 1950s. Notice there are no buildings or any structures. This became the center of commerce after the decline of the downtown area.

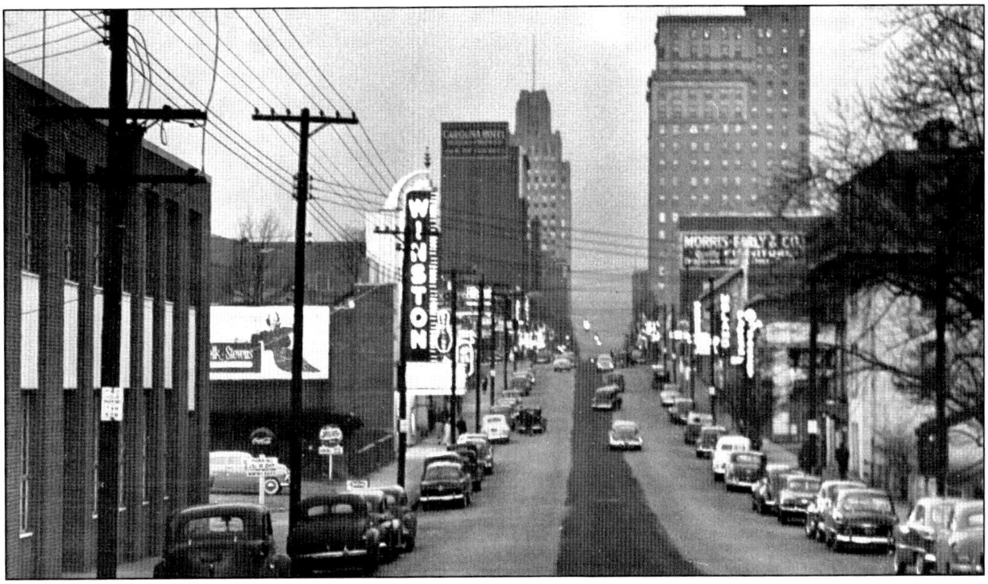

This 1952 photograph shows that evening has fallen, and Frank Jones, photographer for the *Journal* newspaper, gives a presentation of neighborhood businesses and entertainment along West Fourth Street. At the street are the Alexander Apartments. Next door is Doby's Bakery and farther is the Noland Company, a heating supply company. Across the street to the left is the newest Winston-Salem theater, the Winston, with air conditioning. The Winstonette Restaurant and the Twentieth Century Bowling Alley, featuring duckpins, followed. West Salem residents were employed and shared ownership with these business establishments.

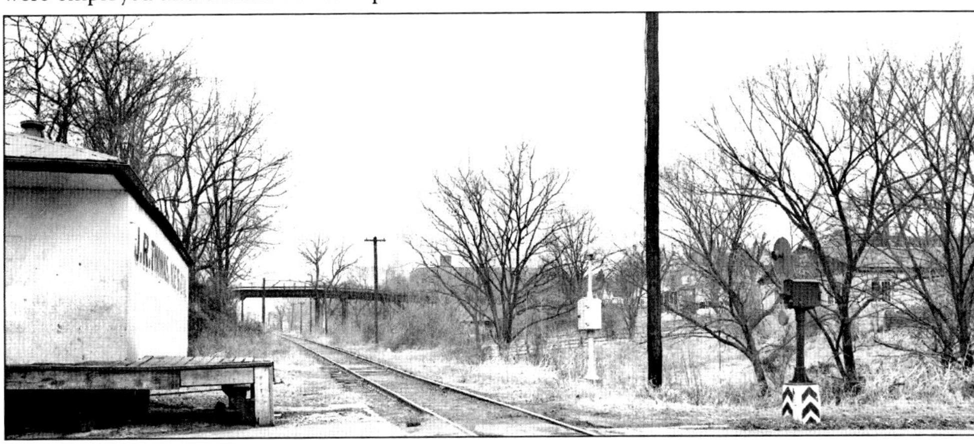

West Salem is home to many 19th-century bridges, which helped the neighborhood connect to the other younger neighborhoods developed in the late 19th and early 20th centuries. In 1905, a connection was made between West Salem and East Salem. The Southbound Railroad had arrived in Salem. Its terminal was located on Liberty Street at Cemetery Street. The train's path running north to south followed the original dividing line between Salem and West Salem, which Brother Gottlieb Rueter had surveyed in the 1760s. Two iron and wood bridges extended from Bank Street and Washington Avenue extending over the railway's path to Liberty Street and East Salem. Even though the connection was made out of convenience for the railway, the connector bridge allowed West Salem and East Salem residents to glimpse one Salem united. The bridges were demolished in the 1950s. Hopefully with the 21st century, these bonds will be reunited, and the complete story of Salem can be presented.

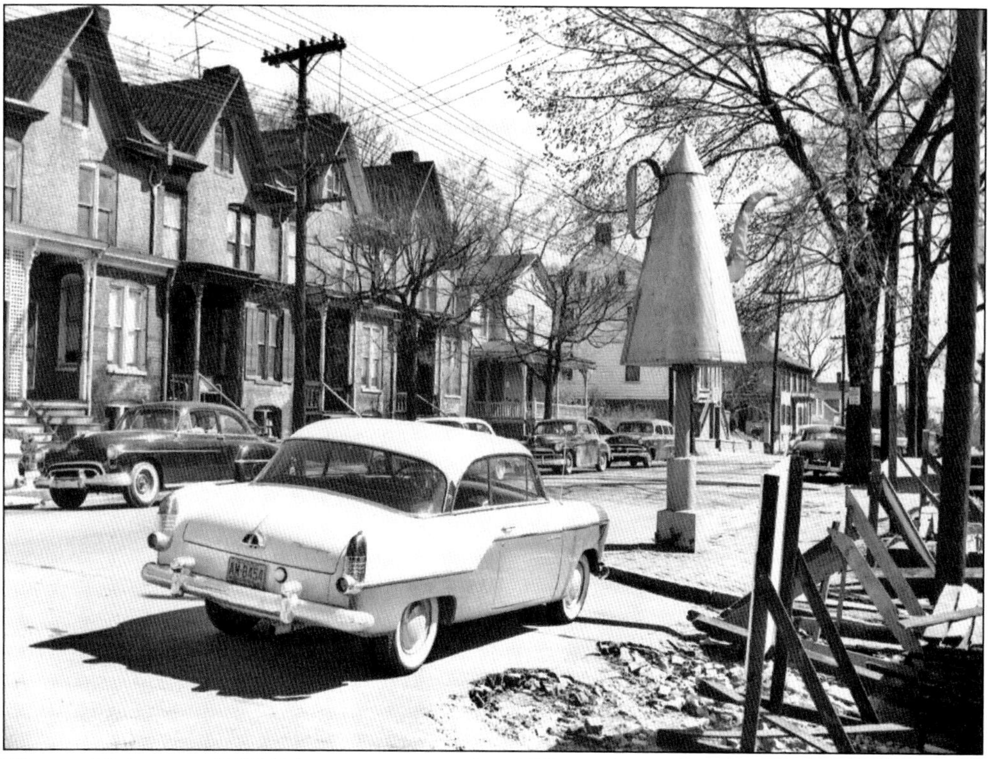

The establishment of Old Salem, incorporated in 1950, set the motion for change in East Salem. The centerpiece and symbol of Salem, the Coffee Pot, was in jeopardy of being razed. The landscape in this photograph along Main Street was destroyed, not by Old Salem restoration but by West Salem's old foe, Interstate 40. This photograph is especially important to the author of this publication since, as a child, he lived in the row houses opposite the Coffee Pot.

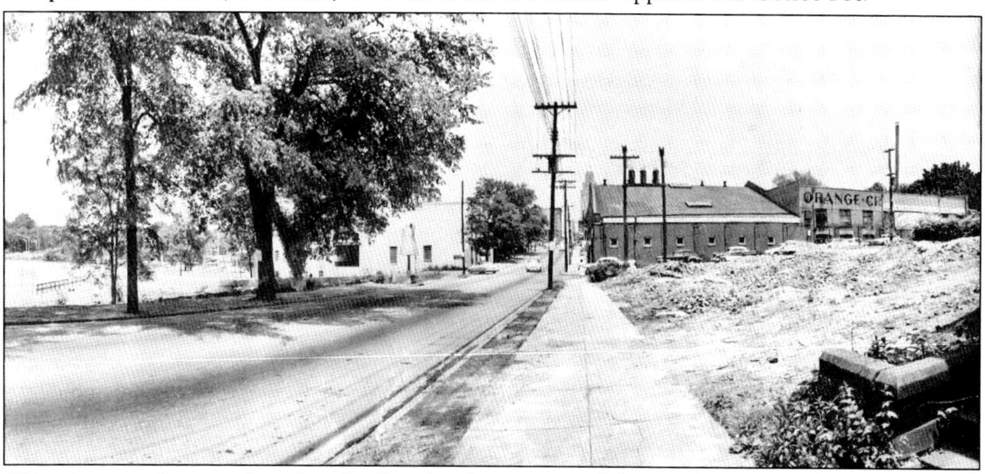

This photograph was taken shortly after the destruction of the residences and businesses in the above photograph. The Coffee Pot is still visible. It was moved to its present location farther south on Main Street within a couple of weeks after the photograph was taken. Belews Street is the location of the Orange Crush Bottling Company across from the Coffee Pot. Both buildings are long gone. The only business and building existing today is beside the Coffee Pot. The Vogler Funeral Home from the 1850s is the only structure remaining today.

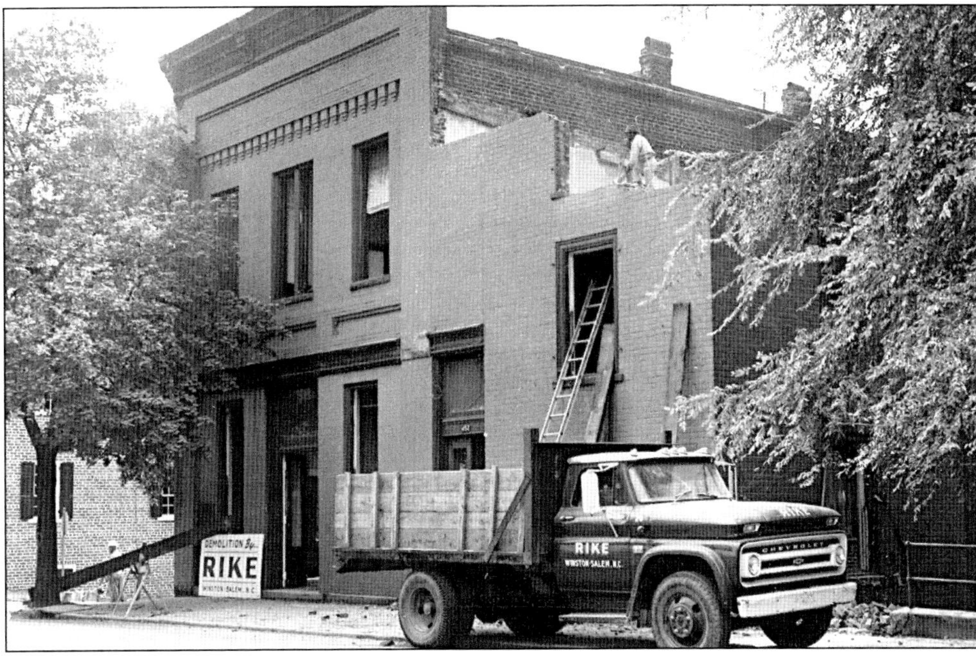

The reconstructed village of Old Salem, c. 1950, came with a price. Many structures within the borders of the 18th- and early-19th-century museum village were razed. The Pike Company demolished countless houses and buildings in the 1950s and 1960s. Mr. Pike resided in West Salem. This 1960s picture shows one of his demolition projects at the corner of Main and Bank Streets.

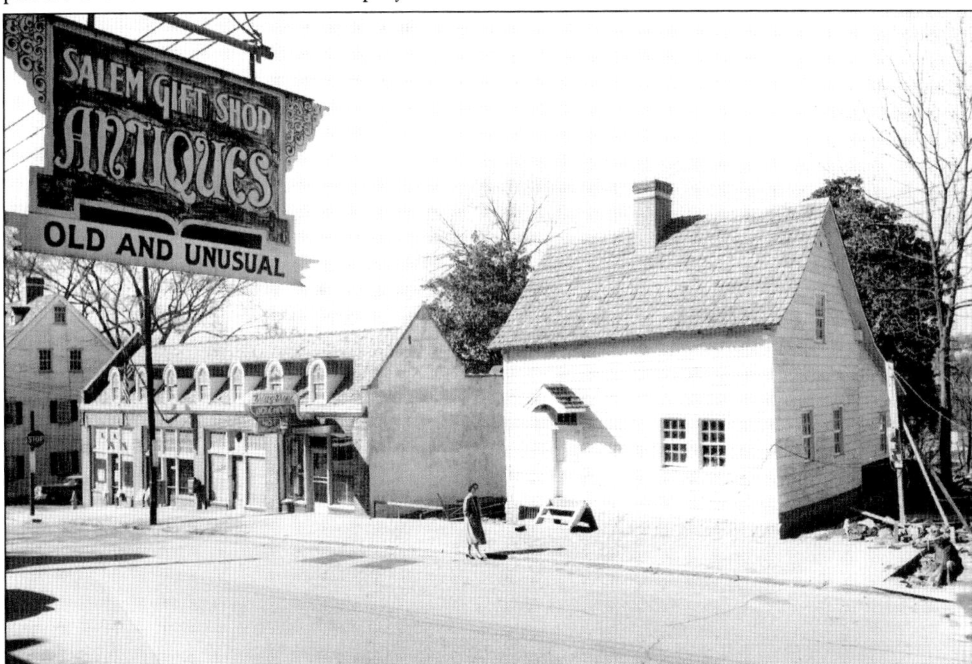

The 18th century is reborn. The restoration of Salem is shown with the tobacco house being reclaimed from the neighborhood of the early 20th century. West Salem is beginning the process of reclaiming its history as well.

Consistent with our mission to preserve history on a local level, this book was printed in South Carolina on American-made paper and manufactured entirely in the United States. Products carrying the accredited Forest Stewardship Council (FSC) label are printed on 100 percent FSC-certified paper.

MADE IN THE USA